D1256295

Dynamic Data Structures

Dynamic Data Structures

Theory and Application

Todd King

Academic Press, Inc.
Harcourt Brace Jovanovich, Publishers
San Diego   New York   Boston   London   Sydney   Tokyo   Toronto

This book is printed on acid-free paper. ∞

Academic Press, Inc.
1250 Sixth Avenue, San Diego, California 92101-4311

United Kingdom Edition published by
Academic Press Limited
24–28 Oval Road, London NW1 7DX

Library of Congress Cataloging-in-Publication Data

King, Todd
    Dynamic data structures : theory and application / Todd King.
      p.   cm.
    Includes bibliographical references and index.
    ISBN 0-12-407530-4
    1. Data structures (Computer science)   I. Title.
    QA76.9.D35K52   1992
    005.7'3–dc20   92-3805
                                           CIP

PRINTED IN THE UNITED STATES OF AMERICA
92 93 94 95 96 97   HA   9 8 7 6 5 4 3 2 1

For my wife, Patricia,
whose tolerance of a computer in the family made this book possible,
and to my sons, Garreth Merlin and Brendon Galen,
two great kids.

Contents

11. *Nth-Generation Languages*

12. *Database Applications*

13. *Information Transfer*

14. *Distributed Information*

15. *Object-Oriented Systems*

List of Figures

List of Tables

Source Listings

Preface

The subject of dynamic data structures has a history that dates back nearly 20 years, with the bulk of the research and innovations occurring in the 1980s. This book is the result of the merging together of the theories, concepts, and approaches developed independently by several people and groups. Some of the people whose work has influenced the content of this book are Jonathon Louis Bentley, P. Flajolet, J. Francon, D. E. Knuth, Mark H. Overmars, and James B. Saxe. Standardization efforts by ANSI, Consultive Committee on Space Data Systems (CCSDS), and NASA's Planetary Data Systems (PDS) have also been influential.

This book should not be considered a definitive reference for all research on dynamic data structures. It is quite possible that some research in the field has been overlooked simply because people have referred to dynamic data structures by many different names. Any omissions are not intentional.

Naturally I have many people to thank for making this book possible, either because of the personal influence they have had in my life or because of the intellectual and technical challenges they have presented me. First is my wife Patty, whose patience and support are deeply appreciated. Next are my father John F. King III and my mother Audrey, my brothers John and Craig, and my sister Shannon. I'd like to thank Neal Cline, Dr. Paul Coleman Jr., Dr. Margaret Kivelson, Dr. Robert McPherron, and Dr. Raymond J. Walker for the opportunities they have provided. I'd also like to thank Jonathon Erickson of *Dr. Dobb's*, and Harry Helms (formerly of Academic Press) and all the talented people at Academic Press who took this book from its inception to print. Finally, I'd like to thank all my English teachers (honest), especially Ms. Thompson and Ms. Thurber, for their guidance in my early years.

Todd King

Introduction | **1**

There are numerous books on the subject of data structures. In general, all these books discuss the classification and usefulness of data structures. One thing that most books do not discuss is how to create, manage, and use data structures that are instantiated by an application for its own purposes. Collectively, such data structures are called "dynamic data structures," and in this book we will explore the theory, nuances, and techniques of working with dynamic data structures.

Before we begin this journey, let's take a moment to explore the reasons for dynamic data structures. Since the inception of computers, whether you consider that to be the abacus[1] or the ENIAC,[2] data and computers have been inseparable. This association arose because the purpose of the computer is to work with data. The kinds of data computers work with is diverse and can be anything from machine-level instructions, demographic information, engineering information, or . . . (you get the idea).

To make working with data easier, programming languages were conceived. In the earliest languages a data item represented a single value. At the time this was reasonable; but as programming tasks became more complex, so did the structure and interrelation of the data items.

Developers addressed this complexity with techniques such as parallel arrays and incremental naming conventions. To a point these techniques are adequate, but they become unmanageable and prone to errors as the complexity of the data increases. There have been various attempts to address the problem. In general, these data management solutions are a combination of semantics and physical storage techniques.

Some example solutions are records in Pascal, common blocks in FORTRAN, structures in C, and classes in C++. These techniques make managing data easier, but they all share one common attribute: they're rigid. That is, once they are declared and compiled, they remain in the same form forever. In many cases this is desirable, but we are now at a level of application complexity where rigidity of data form is an unacceptable constraint.

Making a data structure pliable (removing the rigidity) gives rise to dynamic data structures. A dynamic data structure can be shaped, used, and reshaped at run-time.

---

[1] In existence since Babylonian times.
[2] The Electronic Numerical Integrator and Calculator (ENIAC), demonstrated in 1946.

Dynamic data structures take us the next step in the evolution of data management techniques. With dynamic data structures, applications can adapt at run-time to the task they are addressing; thus, a single application can be more versatile. In addition, dynamic data structures open the door to a higher level of application development. They shift the burden of determining all permutations of data configuration from the developer to the application.

1.1 WHAT YOU SHOULD KNOW

To get the full benefit from this book, you should have a general understanding of data structures. You won't find definitions of a bit or byte in this book. You also won't find bit-level definitions of atomic data types like **int** and **float**. It would also be useful to have some understanding of set theory since some techniques for designing dynamic data structures rely on some principles found in set theory. Finally, a familiarity with how algorithms are designed and analyzed will help in understanding some discussions.

It would also be advantageous to have a working knowledge of C [KBR78]. The primary reason is that almost all the discussions in this book are presented from the perspective of how they would be implemented in C. You might wonder why I choose C. Well, I feel that pseudolanguages or pseudocode do not present how to implement an algorithm in sufficiently clear detail. Pseudocode can help in the analysis of algorithms, but the main focus of this book is how to apply the dynamic data structures. Presenting concepts in a real programming language makes this easier. Another reason is that C is a widely used language and so should be familiar to many of you (pseudolanguages are probably not). Finally, C is a rich and flexible language[3] in which dynamic data structures can be readily implemented.

1.2 ORGANIZATION OF THE BOOK

The following is a synopsis of each chapter in this book (except this one), and it details what you can expect to find in each chapter. Part I of this book is dedicated to the theory of dynamic data structures, whereas Part II concentrates on the application of dynamic data structures in real-world situations.

Part I: Theory

In Part I the theory of dynamic data structures is discussed. This includes discussions of the building blocks of dynamic data structures (atomic data), the concepts of pliable data, expandable (dynamic) data structures, dynamic adaptation, and data description standards.

[3]Some might say too flexible.

Chapter 2: Dynamic Data Structures

In this chapter a dynamic data structure is defined. Once defined the formal ways to classify and qualify a dynamic data structure and the evolution it undergoes is discussed. This includes discussions of operations, schema, level sequences, rank, histories, states, possibilities, and standard probabilities.

Chapter 3: Designing Dynamic Data Structures

This chapter discusses in detail how a dynamic data structure is designed. Definitions of local rebuilding, partial rebuilding, and global rebuilding are introduced. Then the subject of decomposable data structures is introduced. Particular classes of decomposable problems are discussed. Finally, the concept of transforms is introduced and discussed in detail. Specific transforms are described.

Chapter 4: Dynamic Data Structure Analysis

In this chapter the subject of dynamic data structure analysis is discussed. The topics of performance factors and performance trade-offs are discussed. What makes a transform admissible is defined and specific transforms are analyzed in detail.

Chapter 5: Configuration Control

The subject of configuration control is concerned with how a dynamic data structure is physically constructed and maintained. In this chapter various methods of configuration control are discussed. This includes the discussions of the freedom of access to elements in a dynamic data structure. Also discussed are the basic methods for maintaining information about the organization and structure of a dynamic data structure. The chapter concludes with a discussion of the various ways in which physical media are used by dynamic data structures.

Chapter 6: Dynamic Adaptation

After you've defined a dynamic data structure, you must be able to use the information it contains. This is accomplished with dynamic adaptation. In this chapter various methods of dynamic adaptation are discussed. These include context switching, set expansion, and value realization.

Chapter 7: Data Description Standards

Because of the run-time nature of dynamic data structures there is a need to maintain descriptions of the exact form of and interrelationship between elements in a dynamic data structure. There are various data description standards. In this chapter the C structure syntax, flattened-format descriptors, Object Definition Language, Standard Formatted Data Unit, and the ANSI X12 standard are looked at in detail.

Chapter 8: A Software Engineering Perspective

In the previous chapters data structures and, more importantly, dynamic data structures were discussed in an abstract, theoretical sense. In this chapter we take a look at how dynamic data structures fit into the realm of design and software engineering. We'll explore under which conditions using dynamic data structures can be useful and time-saving. We'll also take a look at the situations in which using dynamic data structures can improve system reliability and application management.

Part II: Application

In Part II the usefulness and viability of dynamic data structures are put to the test. Explored are the various environments in which dynamic data structures can be used. This includes dynamically linked applications, Nth-generation languages (like C++, LISP, and ADA), systems for information transfer and data management, and object-oriented applications.

Chapter 9: Basic Toolkit

Presented in this chapter is a basic toolkit of functions that can be used to build, maintain, and manage dynamic data structures. Among the many functions are ones to create, destroy, and add elements and extract values from dynamic data structures.

Chapter 10: Dynamically Linked Applications

In this chapter we take an in-depth look at how applications that are dynamically linked can be implemented using dynamic data structures. To exemplify this, a function-based interpreter is implemented. The interpreter allows for registering application functions that can be called at run-time by the interpreter.

Chapter 11: Nth-Generation Languages

This chapter discusses how portions of some high-level programming languages can be implemented using dynamic data structures. Examples include signature-based function calling of C++ and a LISP interpreter. A discussion of how Ada's generic facility can be implemented using dynamic data structures is included.

Chapter 12: Database Applications

This chapter discusses database-oriented applications of dynamic data structures. It shows by example how the concepts and methods presented in the previous chapters can be applied to database systems. The examples will show how database applications can be written in a very simple and generic manner with the application adapting at run-time to virtually any record configuration. The examples are based on the relational database model.

Chapter 13: Information-Transfer Systems

Information-transfer systems are similar to database systems. Where they differ is that the information that is being used by the system is not required to have a static source. This distinction makes information-transfer systems unique. Specific examples will demonstrate how dynamic data structures can be used by communicating processes. The examples are based on the remote procedure call (RPC) methods of interprocess function calling.

Chapter 14: Distributed Information

Bringing together information stored in more than one location is a real-world application of the concepts of decomposable problems. In this chapter we look at how dynamic data structures can be used to solve the problem of collecting data from a variety of sources and presenting a unified answer.

Chapter 15: Object-Oriented Systems

This chapter provides examples of using dynamic data structures in object-oriented systems. In this chapter a large portion of the basic toolkit presented in Chapter 7 is reimplemented in C++. To demonstrate the effectiveness of this reimplementation, an example that will provide access to an object-oriented database is implemented. Some of the object-oriented topics that are touched on are virtual functions and methods of creating records consisting of heterogeneous objects.

Appendix A: Answers to Points to Ponder

In this appendix you'll find answers to all the points to ponder presented at the end of each chapter.

Appendix B: Makefile

This appendix contains the source for a makefile that can be used to compile all the code presented in Part II of the book and to build the example applications.

Selected Bibliography

This section contains a bibliography of selected readings that contributed significantly to the formulation of the concept of dynamic data structures and the methods of implementation. The bibliography has three headings under which all references are categorized: books, academic papers, and other publications.

1.3 SOURCE CODE

As you read this book you'll find many application snippets and some example applications, especially in the later chapters. Most of these are written in C; those that aren't are written in C++.

In the past, technical books such as this wrote examples in either Pascal or a pseudolanguage. This usually resulted in a minimal amount of elucidation, especially since Pascal has fallen from favor.[4] Since C is the most widely used production language, it's a good chance you know C and will readily understand the examples. Even if you don't know C, the examples should still provide insight since the variable and function names were chosen to reflect their purpose. For example:

```
main( )
{
    read_chapter_2( );
}
```

[4]Some schools don't even teach it any more.

Part I
Theory

Dynamic Data Structures | **2**

In this chapter the definitions and terminology that are used to describe dynamic data structures are introduced. This chapter begins with a formal definition of a dynamic data structure. Then detail is added to this definition by looking at the operations that may be performed on a dynamic data structure, how elements are distinguished from one another, and how to record the evolution of a dynamic data structure. In addition, some notational methods for describing operations that are performed on dynamic data structures are introduced. The chapter ends with a look at some of the most common data structures and how they may be described using the terms defined in this chapter.

2.1 DEFINITIONS

The first definitions we need are those for data structure, method, and data class. A data structure is a specification of how a collection of data is to be organized. A collection of data may consist of any combination of elemental and derived data types. An elemental data type is any data type which is inherit to the programming language in which the data structure is implemented. For example, **int** and **float** are elemental data types in C. A derived data type is a self-contained unit of data. A derived data type can contain elemental or derived data types as well. An example of a derived data type is structures in C. The definition of a data structure is circular in cases where a derived data type is also a data structure. This is a very general definition of a data structure and allows for a data structure to contain other data structures. A "method" is the implementation of an algorithm that performs a specific operation on a data structure, and a "data class" is a combination of a data structure and the methods pertaining to that data structure.

These terms are consistent with those used in object-oriented circles, especially those that use C++. Earlier works on dynamic data structures ([Knu77], [FFV80], [FRS88]) use the term "data organization" to describe what has just been defined as a "data class" and the term "algorithm" to describe what has been defined as a "method." Because of the growing prominence of object-oriented paradigms and the close relationship that dynamic data structures have with data objects, we will use the object-oriented terms.

9

Given the preceding definitions, we can now define what a dynamic data structure is. A dynamic data structure is a special instance of a data class that is required to have methods that perform certain operations on the data structure. The specific operations are insertion, deletion, and query. To be a dynamic data structure, a data class must have either an insertion or a deletion method. Typically both insertions and deletions are allowed. A query method is optional. An important observation is that a dynamic data structure is a data class, but not every data class is a dynamic data structure.

2.1.1 Operations

Collectively, insertions, deletions, and queries are referred to as "operations." We'll define each of them now. An insertion, denoted by I (there will be more about notations in Section 2.2), is the addition of a new element to the data structure. A deletion, denoted by D, is the removal of an element from the data structure. A query, denoted by Q, is the searching of a data structure for an element. All these operations use a key to determine relative position or location of each element in the data structure. A key may be a numeric value, position, or some other distinguishing characteristic of an element.

Given any dynamic data structure a "sequence of operations" [Knu77] (sometimes referred to simply as "a sequence") is denoted as: $O_1(x_1)O_2(x_2)O_3(x_3) \ldots O_n(x_n)$, where O_i is any allowed operation and $1 \le i \le n$. The quantity x_i is the key the operation is performed on. The set of operations with the maximum number of members is $\{I, D, Q\}$. An example sequence of operations is $I(1)I(2)D(1)D(2)$. This could be a sequence of operations for a first-in–first-out (FIFO) queue in which two entries are placed in the queue and then both are removed.

A final observation about sequences is that two sequences are equivalent if and only if they are order-isomorphic. In other words, one sequence is equivalent to another if, when both sequences are applied to the same initial data structure, the resulting data structures are identical. An example of two equivalent sequences is $I(1)I(2)I(3)D(2)D(3)$ and $I(1)I(2)D(2)I(3)D(3)$. The end result of both sequences is the insertion of key 1.

2.1.2 Schema

Every sequence of operations has a schema. A schema [FFV80] is defined as the ordered set of operators used in a sequence of operations. For the previous FIFO queue example the schema would be $<IIDD>$. In general, the schema for the sequence of operations $O_1(x_1)O_2(x_2)O_3(x_3) \ldots O_n(x_n)$ is $<O_1O_2O_3 \ldots O_n>$. A schema is denoted by Ω. Ordinarily the numeric subscripts are dropped from the operations unless they are significant to understanding the schema.[1]

The schema of a sequence is also used to determine the size of a dynamic data structure. The size [FFV80] of a dynamic data structure is the measure of the number

---

[1]What is the schema for the first four notes of Beethoven's Fifth Symphony? $<DDDD>$ (pronounced with a slightly different emphasis on each D).

of elements in the dynamic data structure. At any given instant i, the size of a dynamic data structure, denoted by $\alpha_i(\Omega)$, can be determined by taking the difference between the number of insertions and the number of deletions. That is, if a schema is divided into two sets, one set consisting only of insertions and one of only deletions, then the size at i is $\alpha_i(\Omega) = |O_1 \ldots O_i|_I - |O_1 \ldots O_i|_D$. The size of a sequence is always nonnegative.

2.1.3 Level Sequence

If the size of a dynamic data structure is determined before each operation is performed and collected into a set, this set would be called the "level sequence" [FRS88] of the sequence of operations. Actually, the terms "level" and "size" refer to very similar things. The level [FRS88] is the instantaneous size of a dynamic data structure prior to the assertion of an operation on the dynamic data structure. An example of a level sequence is the following. Given the schema $\Omega = <IIQIQDQI>$, and starting with an empty dynamic data structure, the level sequence is (0, 1, 2, 2, 3, 3, 2, 2).

2.1.4 Rank

Every operation in a sequence of operations has a rank associated with it. The rank [FFV80] of an operation is defined to be the relative position of the element associated with a key in the dynamic data structure. In mathematical terms a rank is defined as $\text{rank}(k, F) = i - 1$ for any arbitrary key k that is in the set of valid keys $F = \{k_1, \ldots, k_i\}$, for the data structure. Specific data structures may impose some conditions on the order of keys. For example, a dictionary would require that $k_1 \leq k_2 \leq k_3 \ldots \leq k_i$. The rank of a key can be thought of as the count of the number of elements, beginning at the first element in the dynamic data structure, which must be searched in order to locate the key.

2.1.5 Histories

Both the schema and the set of ranks for all keys for a data structure are combinatorial objects. A history [FFV80] is defined to be the pair (S, V), where S is the schema and V is $<\text{rank}(k_1, F_1), \ldots \text{rank}(k_i, F_i)>$ and is called the "valuation of L." The value of i is called the "length of the history." Because histories are combinatorial objects, their number for a given length is finite. Two sequences of operations with the same underlying histories are said to be equivalent. The set of histories H of a given length is said to be complete if it contains all equivalent histories for a given state.

2.1.6 States

As a sequence of operations is applied to a dynamic data structure, the structure may change in some fashion. Operations like insertions and deletions certainly change a dynamic data structure since they alter the number of elements in the structure. Operations such as queries are typically passive and do not alter the data structure.

In the course of analyzing dynamic data structures it is often useful to look at instantaneous moments in the evolution of the data structure. At any moment a dynamic data structure has a specific arrangement of elements, and those elements have specific content. This is called a "state."

The state of a dynamic data structure may be described by removing all operations from a history that do not alter the dynamic data structure and by removing all operations that cancel one another. For example, queries usually do not alter the dynamic data structure, and so they are removed. In addition, deletions typically cancel a previous insertion. In this case both the deletion and the correspnding insertion are removed from the history. For example, given the sequence of operations $\{I(1)I(2)I(3)D(2)QI(4)D(1)I(5)\}$, the state of the dynamic data structure after applying the operations is described with the following sequence of operations: $\{I(3)I(4)I(5)\}$. The schema of this set is $<III>$, and it has a size of 3.

A state is actually a minimal description of a dynamic data structure and can be described by a history that consists solely of insertions. A state is a history that contains the minimum number of operations required to construct a particular dynamic data structure. The complete set of histories for a given state is denoted by E_k, where k is the size of the state.

2.1.7 Possibilities

In order to determine the number of histories in a complete set of histories, we must determine every equivalent permutation of a given history. In general, the number of permutations is determined by the formula

$$p(n) = \pi_{1 \leq i \leq n} \text{pos}(O_i, h_{i-1}) \tag{2.1}$$

where $\text{pos}(O_i, h_{i-1})$ is the possibility that operation O_i will occur at length h_i. The possibility function is dependent on the characteristic of the data class. So, to determine the precise number of permutations, we need to know some details about the particular data structure we are using. Take, for example, a dictionary in which the keys are to be sorted in either ascending or descending order. In this case there is only one possible order for keys. This constraint on the order of the keys determines which valuations are allowed, which in turn determines the allowed schema. This means that operation O_i will be allowed only when h_i equals the required position of the key. So, $\text{pos}(O_i, h_i) = 1$ for all i; hence $p(n) = 1$ for all n.

Constraints that require keys to be sorted represent one extreme of the possibility spectrum. At the other extreme is when no constraints are placed on the order of the keys, for example, in an unsorted list. In this case $\text{pos}(O_1, h_0) = n$, $\text{pos}(O_2, h_1) = n - 1, \ldots, \text{pos}(O_n, h_{n-1}) = 1$. So, $p(n) = n!$.

In some data classes Equation (2.1) is equivalent to the more classical permutation formula of

$$P(n, r) = \frac{n!}{(n - r)!} \tag{2.2}$$

where n is the length of the history and r is the number of keys that have complete freedom in the relative position of the keys. For sorted lists there is no freedom in the relative positions of the keys, so $r = 0$ and $P(n, r) = 1$. For unsorted lists $r = n$ because keys can be in any order, so $P(n, r) = n!$ (remember that $0! = 1$ by definition).

2.1.8 Standard Probability

Every history in a complete set of histories E_k for a particular state has a probability of occurring. The collective probability, that is, the probability distribution, of all histories in E_k is called the "standard probability." The standard probability for state e is denoted $p_s(e)$.

Given this definition for the standard probability, how is it calculated? It begins with determining the probability of each history in E_k. Now, the probability of a particular history is given by the formula

$$p_i = \frac{\text{(possibility of history } i)}{\text{(number of histories in } E_k)} \tag{2.3}$$

If we then collect the probabilities for each history into an set ordered on i, we have a probability distribution, which is called the "standard probability."

The standard probability for a dynamic data structure can vary from a straight line with each history having the same probability to very complex shapes. The standard probabilities for specific data structures are discussed in more detail at the end of this chapter.

Stationary Structures

A dynamic data structure is said to be stationary [FFV80] if the probability distribution for the schema $I^{k+1}D$ and I^kQ is identical to that for I^k. In other words, a dynamic data structure is stationary if, after performing an insertion followed by a deletion, or after performing any type of query, the probability distribution remains unchanged.

When we say a dynamic data structure is "stationary," we are referring to its standard probability, not the dynamic data structure itself. This is an important distinction since the dynamic data structure may change significantly during any of the schema $I^{k+1}D$, I^kQ. This freedom of change without altering the probability distribution is termed "randomness" by Knuth [Knu77], and Bentley and Saxe [BS80] define it as a "steady state." Since our focus is on the probability distribution, we will use the term "stationary" in the rest of this book.

2.2 NOTATIONAL NOTES

Knuth, in [Knu77], developed a method of notation that conveys a great deal of information and yet is extremely compact. In [Knu77], Knuth dealt only with insertions (I) and deletions (D), and so his notation is limited to these two types of operations. However, in [FFV80] the notion of query (Q) operation was introduced.

So, the notational conventions presented here represent a merging of the work by Knuth and by Flajolet et al. [FFV80].

Our notational convention starts with the class of operation that is being performed. In dynamic data structures three basic operations are allowed: insertion, deletion, and query. We will represent an operation by the initial of the operation's name. So insertions are denoted by I; deletion, D; and queries, Q. Associated with each initial is a superscript and a subscript. The superscript denotes the number of times the operation is repeated, and the subscript identifies unique characteristics of the operation. The absence of a superscript is considered equivalent to a superscript of 1. If the subscript is omitted, no characteristics are implied. The prototypical operation employing this notation is

$$O \, ^{\text{repetition}}_{\text{characteristics}}$$

where O may be replaced by any operation initial. Some examples of operations with superscripts are as follows:

I^2D^3	Two insertions followed by three deletions
I^*	Any number of insertions
I^*D	Any number of insertions followed by a single deletion
I^*Q^*	Any number of insertions followed by any number of queries
$(I, Q)^*$	Any number of insertions and queries in any order

Insertions, deletions, and queries with specific characteristics are classified using the following notation:

I_r An insertion where the key is selected from a set of keys with a continuous distribution—for example, a set of real numbers equally distributed over the interval [0, 1]. The probability distribution for each key is the same and independent of all other keys.

I_o An insertion by relative order where the key is selected from any set of keys. The key is equally likely to be inserted in any interval within the data structure. The key's insertion point is independent of the number of insertions, deletions, or queries the data structure has undergone. This is equivalent to I_r when no deletions or queries have occurred.

I_b An insertion where the placement of the key is biased. The "bias" refers to the probability of the insertion of the key. One form of biased probability is an exponential distribution, where $1 - e^{-x}$ is the probability that X will be less than x. Another biased probability is if X is a real number in the interval [0, 1] and its probability is obtained by multiplying X by the key of the last deletion. This may seem rather artificial, but it's actually not. One such case where this kind of bias occurs is in priority queues where the key is time (or age) and the element with the smallest key is deleted.

D_r A random deletion. All elements have an equal probability of being deleted. This is the complement of I_r.

D_o A deletion by relative order such that the jth smallest element is deleted, given that there are d elements and j is between 1 and d. This is the complement of I_o.

D_q This is called the "priority queue" deletion. This is a special case of D_o where j is always equal to 1.

D_a A deletion by relative age where "age" is determined by the duration for which the key has been present. If there are d keys and k is between 1 and d, then the kth oldest element is the one for which there are $k - 1$ elements that are younger.

D_f A "first-in–first-out" (FIFO) deletion. This is a special case of D_a in which k always equals 1.

D_l A "last-in–first-out" (LIFO) deletion. This is a special case of D_a where k always equals d.

Q_- A query that fails; that is, a query for which no matching key was found.

Q_+ A query that is successful; that is, a query for which a matching key was found.

In cases where we are not concerned with the specific type of operation, the subscript may be a numeric value so that each operation may be distinguished from another. This type of notation was used earlier when we defined terms like "schema."

A final set of notational constructs is related to data structures, permutations, and the correlation that can be drawn between them.

If we have a sequence of keys $\{x_1\, x_2\, \ldots\, x_n\}$, then we define

$$\rho(x_1 x_2 \ldots x_n) \tag{2.4}$$

to be the canonical permutation of the subscripts so that the keys are placed in ascending order. For example, if $x_1 = \pi$, $x_2 = 2$, $x_3 = 3^2$, then $\rho(\pi\ 2\ 3^2) = 2\ 1\ 3$.

We also denote the data structure obtained by the sequence of operations $I(x_1)I(x_2) \ldots I(x_n)$ with $S(x_1 x_2 \ldots x_n)$, which is called the "S-function."

The notation for the deletion of the jth element from the data structure is defined as

$$R(x_1 x_2 \ldots x_n \backslash j) = y_1 y_2 \ldots y_{n-1} \tag{2.5}$$

provided that $1 \le j \le n$ and that the operation of removing the jth element from $S(x_1 x_2 \ldots x_n)$ and renumbering yields $S(y_1 y_2 \ldots y_{n-1})$. This is called the "R-function."

2.3 SPECIFIC STRUCTURES

Now let us explore some of the most common dynamic data classes using the terms defined above.

Linear lists Elements are accessed by position. Operations I and D are allowed without restrictions.

       Stacks Elements are accessed by position. Operations I and D are allowed, but restricted to operate on the element positioned "first" in the structure.

  LIFO queues Elements are accessed by position. Operations I and D are allowed, but insertions are restricted to operate on the element positioned "first" in the structure and deletions are restricted to operate on the element positioned "last" in the structure.

Priority queues Elements are accessed by value, and the keys belong to a totally ordered set. Operations are I and D; deletions are performed on the element with the highest priority defined as some relative value of keys. Insertions may occur anywhere.

  Dictionaries Elements are accessed by value, and the keys belong to a totally ordered set. The operations I, D, and Q are allowed without restrictions.

The preceding definitions do not mention how the dynamic data structure is implemented. In fact, each of these data classes may be implemented using linear (i.e., linked lists, arrays), nonlinear (i.e., trees, graphs) data structures or a decomposable structure. The choice of a specific implementation approach is application-dependent. Chapter 3 deals with the various methods for designing dynamic data structures and Chapter 4, with the performance analysis of dynamic data structures. In combination these chapters can help in making effective decisions about the implementation approaches.

2.4 SUMMARY

In this chapter a definition of a dynamic data structure was formally stated. Also defined were several terms that are used to describe dynamic data structures. This included the terms "operation," "key," "state," "schema," and "history." These terms and the others defined make in easy to describe a data class in a concise and precise manner. This was demonstrated in Section 2.3. Additional information on dynamic data structures can be found in [EO85] and [Kin88].

POINTS TO PONDER

2.1   Describe the difference between a key and an element in a data structure.

2.2   Describe the difference between a schema and a history.

2.3   What are the two combinatorial objects that constitute a sequence of operations?

2.4   Given the sequence of operations $I(2)I(3)I(1)D(2)$, what are its schema, valuation, and size?

2.5   How many permutations are possible on an unsorted list with four elements?

2.6   What is the probability distribution of an unsorted list with four elements?

Designing Dynamic Data 3
Structures

A dynamic data structure, by its nature, changes when an application executes. One distinguishing feature of a dynamic data structure is how it can change. In general, changes can be divided into the categories of "changes of content" and "changes in layout." A change in content is any change of the values stored in the elements of the dynamic data structure. Even ordinary read/write variables exhibit this feature. A change in layout is any change related to the size or schema of a dynamic data structure's state. Changes in content (or at least the possibility of change) are common to all variables, static and dynamic data structures included. It is the ability for a dynamic data structure to change its layout that distinguishes it from a static data structure. How to design data structures that have the ability to change their layout is the subject of this chapter.

The design of a dynamic data structure is an important subject since we should always be concerned with how effective a solution is. In Chapter 4 we will look at ways to determine the effectiveness of a dynamic data structure. In this chapter we will discuss how to design a dynamic data structure in such a way that it can be readily implemented and its behavior can be readily analyzed.

There are a variety of techniques for implementing dynamic data structures. One possible technique for creating dynamic data structures is to add new elements to a data structure by continually building bigger and bigger data structures, each with as many elements as are needed. While this would allow the data structure to adapt to any number of elements, as well as any other type of change, it certainly is not the most efficient approach. In fact, much more efficient approaches are possible with very little effort. Most techniques for designing dynamic data structures are based on the concept of divide and conquer. The phrase "divide and conquer" can sound deceptively simple; fortunately, it's not a deterrent to dynamic data structures.

In the design of a dynamic data structure two issues are central to the assessment of how applicable a specific design is: the extent to which changes in a dynamic data structure affect the dynamic data structure and the ease with which the design can be implemented. Secondary to this issue is how predictable the performance of the resulting dynamic data structure is. We'll begin with a look at how changes affect a dynamic data structure.

3.1 REBUILDING

In every dynamic data structure elements are maintained as a static data structure. So as elements are added, new static data structures must be created and added in some manner to the dynamic data structure. The creation of a static data structure is called a "build." When a new element is added to a dynamic data structure, the dynamic data structure must be altered in order to accommodate the new element. This "alteration" typically causes the dynamic data structure to reorganize itself. The process of change-induced reorganization is called "rebuilding."

Rebuilding is simply the creation of a new static data structure that will contain a set of elements that results from augmenting, changing, or eliminating members from the set of elements in a preexisting static data structure. The various approaches to rebuilding can be categorized according to the extent of the rebuilding process. In general there are three categories: local, partial, and global. We'll discuss each of them.

3.1.1 Local

Local rebuilding occurs when the extent of the rebuilding process is small in comparison to the data structure as a whole. That is, relatively few of the elements in a data structure are affected and manipulated as a result of the rebuilding process. Local rebuilding is probably the best known and most often used rebuilding procedure and is commonly used in maintaining a wide variety of structures.

Balanced trees are a common application in which local rebuilding occurs, and will serve as a good example. Trees may be balanced according to height, weight, degree, or path, but for the purpose of our example we'll look at height-balanced trees. With a height-balanced tree the distance from any node in the tree to any leaf below that node cannot differ by more than 1, with distance being measured as a count of the number of nodes you must pass through to get to the leaf. Now suppose we have the height-balanced tree depicted in Figure 3.1. Now let's insert a new leaf (node 5) at node 4. The only portion of the tree that this affects is node 4 itself. So the only portion of the tree that requires rebuilding is node 4 (one element). This is local rebuilding in the simplest case. Now suppose we insert a node, call it node 7, which displaces node 6 in such a way that it must now become a leaf of node 5. This might occur if the numbers we are using for the nodes represent the relative ranking of elements so that we maintain all leaves in sorted order. This would involve a local rebuild of node 5 to insert node 6 and the building of node 7 to replace the original node 6. Again this is local rebuilding, but at a slightly more expanded scale.

Conceptually we could also represent the tree in Figure 3.1 as a collection of nodes and subtrees with each subtree adhering to the same requirements as the entire tree. Figure 3.2 is a depiction of how this might be represented. While the subtrees in the example contain only a few nodes, they could contain any number of nodes and still the insertions of nodes 5 and 7 would not affect them. So, the rebuild is definitely local.

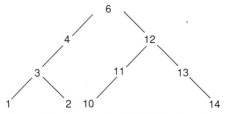

Figure 3.1   An example of a height-balanced tree.

3.1.2 Partial

In some situations any change you make to a dynamic data structure results in a need to rebuild an entire portion of a data structure. This is called "partial rebuilding." In general, partial rebuilding occurs when the extent of the rebuilding process involves a large portion of the data structure as a whole or involves entire substructures of the data structure.

To exemplify partial rebuilding, we'll look at trees again. In some trees, such as 2-3-4 trees, there are instances where it is impossible to restore balance to a tree using local rebuilding. The circumstances under which this is true is when a tree (such as a 2-3-4 tree) becomes unbalanced and all nodes below the first node at which the tree is unbalanced must be rebuilt. Take, for example, a 2-3-4 tree for which we need to insert the keys {C S F O R M E} and we wish to maintain all keys in sorted order. After inserting the first three elements we would have a node that looks like Figure 3.3*a*. When we go to insert the fourth element (O), we find that the node that contains the first three elements is full (we are allowed a maximum of three keys per node). So, in order to insert the new element, we must rebuild the structure into a binary tree as is shown in Figure 3.3*b*. This is a partial rebuild beginning at the node that contains the first three elements we've inserted. This does involve the whole tree (which is a global rebuild, which we discuss in the next section), but if we were looking at a subtree of some larger tree, it would be a less extensive rebuild.

After the rebuild we can insert the fourth element. This results in a tree like that in Figure 3.3*c*. When we insert the fifth key (R) no rebuilding is necessary since the

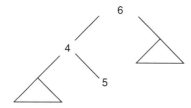

Figure 3.2   How a height-balanced tree would look depicted as nodes and subtrees.

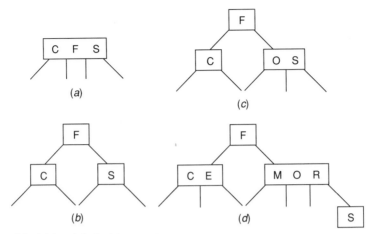

Figure 3.3 (*a*) A node in the 2-3-4 tree after inserting three elements. (*b*) The result of a rebuild before insertion of the fourth element {O}. (*c*) The tree after insertion of the fourth element. (*d*) The tree after the insertion of all elements.

node containing {O S} can accommodate it. When we insert the element {M} we find that it cannot be inserted without rebuilding the node that contains {O R S}. What needs to be done is that the {M} element must be inserted into the node that contains {O R S}, forcing {O} and {R} to be moved within the node and {S} to be removed from the node and placed below the node. This, by definition, is a partial rebuild. The resulting tree is depicted in Figure 3.3*d*.

3.1.3 Global

Global rebuilding occurs when, in order to alter, insert, or delete an element in the data structure, a replacement data structure must be constructed in order to accommodate the change. Since rebuilding an entire data structure each time an element is inserted or deleted can be very costly, global rebuilding is not a very good choice for creating dynamic data structure. However, there are some data structures for which local or partial rebuilding can be used part of the time, but which require global rebuilding at other times. The 2-3-4 tree in the previous section is one example. Typically, a dynamic data structure that requires global rebuilds is feasible in one of two instances. The first instance is where the dynamic data structure has a measure of tolerance for being "out of balance"—that is, where some number of insertions or deletions can be performed on the data structure without a need to rebuild the data structure at all. Some structures are tolerant of deletions, but intolerant of insertions. Other structures are just the opposite, and others still can tolerate both.

Typically, data structures that are tolerant of deletions but intolerant of insertions are ones that divide the element space in some fashion, for example, into quadrants as with pseudo–quad-trees. With pseudo–quad-trees it is possible to delete up to half the elements in the tree before the structure is considered out of balance [Ove83]. Insertions, on the other hand, will disturb the balance and force a rebuild.

To distinguish operations (insertions and deletions) for which a structure is tolerant from those that it is not, we say that an operation is "weak" if the structure is tolerant of it. We say that an operation is "strong" or "actual" if the structure is intolerant.

The second instance where dynamic data structures that require global rebuilds are feasible is where the dynamic data structure is updated by a combination of local, partial, and global rebuilds. Such dynamic data structures are also called "decomposable structure."

3.2 DECOMPOSABLE DATA STRUCTURES

While rebuilding is the process of accommodating changes to a data structure, there remains the question of how you can physically maintain a data structure in such a way that you can actually rebuild part of the data structure without affecting the rest of it. There are two issues to address: (1) how the data structure is physically stored and (2) the logical organization of the data structure. The issue of physical storage is addressed in later chapters. For now we'll concentrate on the logical organization.

To accomplish a subdivision of a data structure, we must look at the way in which the data structure may be broken into substructures that can be maintained separately without reducing the utility of the original data structure. The process of breaking a data structure into smaller substructures is called "decomposition" and a data structure that is divisible in this fashion is called "decomposable."

There are usually a variety of ways in which a decomposable data structure can be divided. For a given problem, certain decompositions are better than others and there is always some point at which the data structure is indivisible. A data structure may be indivisible because of physical limitations or because of functional reasons. Physical limitations arise when it is impossible to divide the data structure any finer. Functional reasons arise when an application never deals with an element of a data structure at a finer detail, even though the element may be divided further.

A ready example of how data structures may be divided can be found in computer processors. In the typical computer the binary bit is an indivisible entity. We group bits into bytes and bytes into words. In turn, certain combinations of bytes or words make up data types like integers or floating-point numbers, which have some structure imposed on the bits. This "grouping" continues into programming languages where structures consisting of specific combinations of data types are constructed. We are also free to embed structures within structures. If we reverse this grouping, we can look at the ways in which a data structure is decomposable.

Now suppose we have a monochrome bit map. The data structure that holds the bit map may consist of a series of elements that hold all the "pixels" for a single line of the bit map. If the application deals only with lines of a bit map, then the functional point to cease decomposing the bit-map data structure is at the line elements. However, we are typically concerned with the value of a single "pixel," and for the case of a monochrome bit map, this would be a single bit. Even though a bit map could be divided and maintained as a collection of bit elements (a physical limit), it's not something I would encourage.[1]

In general it is best to deal with decompositions at the functional level. The main motivation for this is that the data elements remain at a higher level of abstraction and therefore you are free to redefine the internal structure of the data element with a minimal effect on an application. This is the same kind of generalization provided by data encapsulation paradigms like object-oriented programming.

There has been theoretical work by various researchers to formalize the proper methods for subdividing a data structure. The primary focus of this research was in how to guarantee the proper extraction of information from a data structure after it has been subdivided. This research has its roots in set theory and focuses on the subject of decomposable problems. Specific attention has been paid to the related topics of decomposable set problems and order-decomposable problems.

3.2.1 Decomposable Problems

As mentioned earlier, any division of a data structure must not affect its utility. So, we must find a balance between how we divide the data structure and the preservation of its utility. This is the "conquer" dilemma of the divide-and-conquer axiom. If care is taken in how a data structure is divided, it is possible to easily yield results extracted from the resulting dynamic data structure. If we look at the problem in the other direction, we are concerned about finding a solution to a problem by dividing the problem into smaller problems, solving the smaller problems, and combining these solutions in order to find a solution to the original problem. This is called a "decomposable problem" (or a problem for which the divide-and-conquer axiom works.)

The subject of decomposable problems is an area of research in which considerable attention has been given. In 1980 Bentley and Saxe [BS80] built upon previous work and formalized a technique for designing dynamic data structures to solve a class of problems called "decomposable searching problems." It turns out that just about every searching problem is decomposable.

A comparable method was discussed by Overmars [Ove81] that deals with order-decomposable set problems. Overmars makes the observation that you can create dynamic data structures (he uses the term "dynamize") for most set problems for which a solution can be obtained by a divide-and-conquer strategy. Divide-and-conquer strategies are very prevalent for most problems, so it should be possible to create dynamic data structure in almost every situation.

In any software design project it's important to use the best technique for implementing a solution. The best choice depends on the nature of the problem. Techniques typically have conditions under which they may be applied. Both decomposable

---

[1] I knew a programmer, straight out of college, who spent a whole week looking for a bit bucket. He even asked the custodian if he had one.

searching problems and order-decomposable set problems have specific conditions, and so it's best to discuss the technique separately.

Decomposable Searching

One way in which dynamic data structures are used is to maintain a set of elements that are accessed according to some key. To obtain a specific element, it's typical to search the dynamic data structure for an element with a desired key. Once the element (or elements) with the desired key is (are) found, the element(s) is (are) returned for further processing. In this situation the operations on a dynamic data structure can be considered as a decomposable searching problem.

Not all searching problems are decomposable (but almost all are). If it is possible to create a dynamic data structure for a searching problem, then the searching problem must be decomposable. A searching problem is decomposable, for a given query Q, if there exists a binary operator (denoted by $\square$) that satisfies the condition

$$Q(x, A \cup B) = \square(Q(x, A), Q(x, B)) \tag{3.1}$$

What this condition states is that a query on a set that is formed by the union of two other sets must return the same result as the "union" of the results from performing the same query of the two individual sets, where the "union" is done by the binary operator. Implicit in Equation (3.1) is that the binary operator is both associative and cumulative. For example, the following statements are all equivalent:

$$Q(x, A \cup B \cup C) = \square(\square(Q(x, A), Q(x, B)), Q(x, C));$$

$$Q(x, A \cup B \cup C) = \square(\square(Q(x, C), Q(x, B)), Q(x, A));$$

which is a demonstration of the associative nature of $\square$. A cumulative example is

$$Q(x, A \cup B) = \square(Q(x, A), Q(x, B)) = \square(Q(x, B), Q(x, A)).$$

which simply means that the order in which subsets are queried is irrelevant.

Two subclasses of binary operators are important. The first subclass are the binary operators that have an inverse. That is, the operation of a specific binary operator can be "undone" by the application of another binary operator. A straightforward example is if the binary operator is addition, then its inverse is subtraction. An inverse binary operator is denoted $\square^{-1}$. An observation is that for binary operators that have an inverse, there is no need to actually delete requested elements from the original dynamic data structure. All that is required is that a copy of the elements that are to be deleted from the primary dynamic data structure be inserted into a "ghost" data structure. Then the results of a query are obtained by applying the inverse binary operator to the results of querying the "ghost" data structure and the results of querying the primary dynamic data structure—in other words, "subtracting" the results of the "ghost" data structure query from the results of the primary data structure query. This will be discussed in more detail in the next chapter.

The second subclass of binary operators are those that have zero or sticky elements. A sticky element is one in which, for every element x, $\square(z, x) = z$, where z is the sticky element. What gives rise to sticky elements depends a lot on the binary operator. For example, if z is false and $\square$ is the mathematical AND operation, then $\square(z, x)$ is false for all x. In such a case it doesn't matter what the content of the dynamic data structure is; the answer will always be the same.

Order-Decomposable Problems

A more general way in which dynamic data structures are used is to maintain sets of data for which the number of elements is maintained in some particular order—for example, ordered by time stamps, value, or some other characteristic of an element. A searching problem may also be an ordered set problem if the elements are ordered by the search key. This is sometimes done to aid in the searching of elements, but there are a variety of indexing schemes that can be used to locate elements, so not every searching problem is also an ordered set problem.

An order-decomposable problem P is any problem that has an ordering function, call it ORD, and a binary function $\square$, such that for each set $\{a_1, \ldots, a_n\}$ ordered by ORD the following holds:

$$P(a_1, \ldots, a_n) = \square(P(a_1, \ldots, a_i), P(a_{i+1}, \ldots, a_n)) \qquad (3.2)$$

for all i between 1 and n.

This definition is identical in form to that in Equation (3.1). What makes it different is the conditions. There's a little give and take. For an order-decomposable problem, the operation performed on the set to obtain a solution (the function P) can be anything. For a decomposable searching problem, the operation can only be a query. This is the "give"; the "take" is that there must be an ordering function.

The requirement for an ordering function is interesting because it does not restrict how the ordering of the elements is to be performed. If there is some required order for the elements based on some characteristic of the elements, there is most likely an ordering function that can order the elements. But suppose there is no required ordering. A collection of elements always has some overlying structure. This overlying structure always requires some order to the elements since elements must be stored in some fashion. So, even if there is not an internally required order for elements, there is always an external requirement. This means that the order-decomposable method for creating dynamic data structures has an even wider application, since it can be applied to any problem.

3.3 TRANSFORMS

Trees can be implemented very easily by using linked lists and building each node of the tree as needed, but not all data structures lend themselves to this simple model. Some require that other techniques of subdivision be used in order to retain a reasonable cost to the dynamic data structure. To achieve this a transform must be devised that will convert a static data structure into a dynamic data structure. A transform consists of a physical organization of a collection of static data structures and the algorithm for performing operations on the dynamic data structure. Thus, a transform is an algorithm for converting a static data structure into a data class (dynamic data structure). Typically the physical organization of a dynamic data structure is analogous to a particular counting scheme. For example, a linear linked list is analogous to integer counting.

When designing a transform, the cost of maintaining it must be considered. For example, a transform that triggers a global rebuild each time an element is altered, inserted, or deleted probably will not be a good transform. Because of this there is the notion of an "acceptable" or "admissible" transform. The actual definition of the criteria for admissibility is discussed in detail in Chapter 4. For now we will simply describe what an admissable transform is. In general, an admissible transform is one in which the increase in processing time and query time is kept within some reasonable bounds and that the storage requirements do not increase by an appreciable amount. When discussing admissible transforms it is said that a transform is "($F(N)$, $G(N)$) admissible" where $F(N)$ is the bound on the increase in processing time and $G(N)$ is the bound on the increase in query time.

There are a variety of well-understood transforms for which $F(N)$ and $G(N)$ have been determined. As mentioned earlier, these transforms are based on a particular counting scheme. In the process of designing a dynamic data structure consideration must be paid to certain implementation issues. One primary issue is the frequency with which elements will be inserted in relation to the frequency with which queries will be performed. Specific transforms can have different costs associated with the different operations. To help in the selection of an existing transform or the design of a new one we'll now look at the simplest and probably the most familiar transform, the geometric transform.

3.3.1 Geometric Transforms

A geometric transform is one in which the elements of the dynamic data structure are each placed in a separate static data structure. A geometric transform comes in two varieties. The first is a linear geometric transform, also called a "linear transform," in which each element has at most one decedent and one ancestor. A common example of a linear transform is a linear linked list, which is an admissable (N, 1) transform. The other variety of geometric transform is a nonlinear geometric transform, also called a "nonlinear transform." With a nonlinear transform, each element can have any number of ancestors or decedents. A common example of a nonlinear transform is a binary tree in which each element has at most one ancestor and two decedents. Most geometric transforms already have common names. Some examples of linear geometric transforms are linear linked lists, stacks, and queues. Some examples of nonlinear geometric transforms are trees, graphs, and other multilinked structures.

3.3.2 Binary Transforms

A binary transform is one in which the elements of the dynamic data structure are divided into static data structures such that the maximum number of elements in each static data structure is a power of 2. In addition, no two static data structures may have the same maximum number of elements. This is analogous to binary numbers and is the reason for the name of the transform.

Let's look at how dynamic data structure based on a binary transform would grow as elements are added. Let's begin with an empty structure. When the first element is added, a static structure that can contain one element is created and the first element is placed in that structure. When the second element is added, a new structure that can contain two elements is created and the first and second elements are placed in that structure. The structure that contained the first element is discarded. When the third is added, a new structure that can hold one element is created and the third element is placed in the structure. This would continue as we added each element so that after the 63rd element is added we would have five static data structures. One would contain 32 elements, one with 16, one with 8, one with 4, one with 2, and one with just one element.

When using a dynamic data structure based on a binary transform, the rebuilding will be global when N is a power of 2. The rebuilding will be partial when N is even and not a power of 2 and local when N is odd. This can be quantified further with the penalty functions since a binary transform is a admissible $(\log(N + 1), 1 + \log(N))$ transform.

3.3.3 Radix-k Transforms

A binary transform is a specific form of radix-k transform where $k = 2$. A radix-k transform (also called an "k-nary" or "base-k" transform) is one in which the count of the number of elements in each static data structure is based on radix-N counting. For example, suppose we have eight elements, with radix-3 counting (also called "tri-nary") there will be two static data structures, one containing six elements and the other containing two. If we were to add one more element, we would end up with one static data structure that contained all nine elements. A radix-3 transform is an admissible $(\log_3(N), 2\log_3(N))$ transform provided $N > 1$. In general, any radix-k transform is an admissible $(\log_k(N), (k - 1)\log_k(N))$ transform. Note that a binary transform is a radix-2 transform.

As the radix of a transform increases, the number of static data structures decreases for a given number of elements N. This has the effect of reducing both the query penalty and, to a lesser extent, the processing penalty. But this is not without a cost. As the radix increases there is an increase in wasted space, which becomes greater as N grows larger and reaches local maximums when N is to equal to $k^i + 1$, where k is the radix and i is some integer power. The wasted space consists of nonfilled elements in the static data structure and for a particular radix is equal to

$$(k - 1)(k^i - \sum_{0 \le j \le i-1} k^j) - 1 \tag{3.5}$$

Let's look at Equation (3.5) a little closer. The leading multiplier $(k - 1)$ is the number of possible states a digit with a particular radix may have. The value of $(k - 1)$ times the summation is the number of elements that must be filled before we need to go to the next radix digit, and the value of $(k - 1)k^i$ is the number of elements the next static data structure will have. The -1 arises because we need to go to the next radix when we need to add one more element than the current set of static data structures can hold.

Let's look at an example. If $k = 2$ (binary counting) and $i = 5$ then the number of "empty" elements is 0. This is true for any i. On the other hand, if $k = 3$ then the waste would be 27 "empty" elements. Table 3.1 contains a list of the waste for radix-k transforms for $k = 2$ through 5 and $i = 2$ through 5. One possible way to reduce the waste associated with the different radix transforms is to look at the number of elements and choose a radix that will minimize the waste. In turn, this will minimize the number of individual static data structures. This will have the effect of reducing the query penalty while increasing the processing penalty. This is feasible, but there is another type of transform that guarantees a fixed number of static data structures without a need to choose or switch the radix of the transform. This type of transform is the binomial transform.

3.3.4 k-Binomial Transforms

A k-binomial transform is one in which the elements of a dynamic data structure are divided into static data structures based on a binomial counting systems [Knu68]. Binomial transforms are described by the number of binomial coefficients in the counting scheme [BS80]. A k-binomial transform has k binomial coefficients. A nice feature of k-binomial transforms is that there are at most k static data structures, one for each binomial coefficient. Any k-binomial transform is an admissible $(k, (k!N)^{1/k})$ transform.

To exemplify k-binomial transforms, let's look at the 2-binomial transform. With a 2-binomial transform the number of elements in the dynamic data structure is represented by the formula

$$N = \binom{i}{2} + \binom{j}{2} \tag{3.6}$$

Table 3.1 List of Wasted Elements for Various Radix-k Transforms

Radix	Power				
	1	2	3	4	5
2	0	0	0	0	0
3	3	9	27	81	242
4	8	32	128	512	2048
5	15	75	375	1875	10475

where $i < j$ and i and j are both less than $(2N)^{1/2} + 1$. Table 3.2 contains a list of the number of elements in each static data structure for N from 1 to 20. With k-binomial transforms there are never any "empty" elements, and query times are quite good because of the limited number of static data structures. However, insertions are expensive since there is a high rebuild rate of the smallest static data structures. In addition, a global rebuild is required whenever the number of elements equals the next-largest binomial count.

3.3.5 Other Transforms

The types of available transforms are not limited to those just discussed. There are many others, and additional transforms will be discussed and analyzed in Chapter 4. A discussion of them in this chapter is premature since the key aspects of the transforms require an understanding of dynamic data structure analysis (the subject of Chapter 4). Even so, a few more words can be said about the design of transformations.

While binary, radix-k or k-binomial transforms are useful in a variety of situations, you may have a need to design a different type of transform. When designing new transforms you need to keep in mind how bounds on the costs associated with the dynamic data structure will be calculated (the topic in Chapter 4). In general, if the transform is isomorphic with a numbering system, then calculation of costs can be readily accomplished. If the transform is based on some heuristic approach, it might be difficult, if not impossible, to assess the effectiveness of the dynamic data structure.

3.4 SUMMARY

Choosing the right design for a dynamic data structure begins with understanding the requirements of the problem that the dynamic data structure will be used to solve.

Table 3.2 List of the Number of Elements in Each Static Data Structure Based on a 2-Binomial Transform

N	i	j	$\binom{i}{2}$	$\binom{j}{1}$	N	i	j	$\binom{i}{2}$	$\binom{j}{1}$
1	2	0	1	0	11	5	1	10	1
2	2	1	1	1	12	5	2	10	2
3	3	0	3	0	13	5	3	10	3
4	3	1	3	1	14	5	4	10	4
5	3	2	3	2	15	6	0	15	0
6	4	0	6	0	16	6	1	15	1
7	4	1	6	1	17	6	2	15	2
8	4	2	6	2	18	6	3	15	3
9	4	3	6	3	19	6	4	15	4
10	5	0	10	0	20	6	5	15	5

Some of the issues that must be considered in the design of dynamic data structures is the extent of rebuilding that will be required in order to maintain the dynamic data structure. The topics of local, partial, and global rebuilding were discussed.

Also of importance in designing dynamic data structure is maintaining the utility of the data structure. The subjects of decomposable searching problems and order-decomposable problems are quite pertinent to this subject and were also discussed. Finally, the various ways in which a dynamic data structure can be divided into static data structures was discussed. A method to do this using tranforms was discussed. The binary, radix-k, and k-binomial were discussed.

Additional information on designing data structures can be found in [AHU83], [Cle86], [Lin86], [SW87], and [Tre84]

POINTS TO PONDER

3.1 Name and characterize each style of rebuilding.

3.2 What is generally considered one of the primary drivers in the design of a dynamic data structure?

3.3 What are the two subjects of decomposable problems that serve as foundations for the design of dynamic data structures? Characterize and compare each of them.

3.4 What is a binary operator for decomposable problems?

3.5 How many distinct static data structures will there be for a 3-binomial transform? How many elements will be in each static data structure for $1 \leq N \leq 10$?

3.6 What do the binary transform and the radix-k transform have in common?

Dynamic Data Structure Analysis | **4**

After designing a dynamic data structure we would like to know what kind of performance to expect when we use the dynamic data structure. The analysis of an algorithm that gives rise to a dynamic data structure is done in essentially the same manner as the analysis of an algorithm that uses a static data structure. However, since most dynamic data structures are built as a collection of static data structures, the performance of a particular dynamic data structure is influenced by the performance associated with the underlying static data structures. The performance associated with static data structures has been studied extensively; as there are many good references on the subject, the analysis of static data structures will not be covered in this book. What we will explore is how to quantify the performance of a dynamic data structure and what additional costs are incurred when a static data structure is transformed into a dynamic data structure.

4.1 PERFORMANCE FACTORS

When a static data structure is analyzed, the expected performance is typically assessed by determining three quantities, called "cost functions":

$P(N)$—the preprocessing time
$Q(N)$—the query time
$S(N)$—the storage requirement

where N is some primary parameter, usually the number of elements in a data structure. When a dynamic data structure is analyzed, the expected performance is assessed by determining four cost functions:

$I(N)$—the insertion time
$D(N)$—the deletion time
$Q(N)$—the query time
$S(N)$—the storage requirements

The only difference between the quantities for the static data structure and the dynamic data structure is that the $P(N)$ in the static case is replaced by $I(N)$ and $D(N)$ in the dynamic case. The operations of insertions and deletions of elements each have a distinct impact on the performance of a dynamic data structure, and it is useful to assess the impact individually rather than to group the cost of the two operations into a single quantity.

It is sometimes useful to compare the performance of a static data structure to a dynamic data structure that performs the same function. To do this we need to define the relationship between $P(N)$ for static data structures and $I(N)$ and $D(N)$ for dynamic data structures. For a given schema, the preprocessing time $P(N)$ to build a dynamic data structure is the summation of the time required for each insertion $I(N)$ and deletion $D(N)$. This is true in general, but it's more typical to compare preprocessing times for a given state of a dynamic data structure. In this case the schema consists only of insertions and the preprocessing time for a given dynamic data structure is defined as

$$P(N) = \sum_{1 \le i \le N} I(i) \qquad (4.1)$$

We can invert this relationship and determine the "insertion time" for a static data structure. We determine this by amortizing the preprocessing time over N. Therefore, the insertion time is defined as

$$I(N) = \frac{P(N)}{N} \qquad (4.2)$$

When the performance of one algorithm is compared to another, it is conventional to give the functions $P(N)$, $I(N)$, $D(N)$, $Q(N)$, and $S(N)$ subscripts to uniquely identify them.

4.2 ADMISSIBLE TRANSFORMS

Just as there are algorithms that are better suited for a specific application than others, so are there transforms that are better suited than others. To help determine how effective a transform is, the notion of admissibility is introduced. In general, a transform is admissible [BS80] if the cost functions satisfy the relations

$$Q_B(N) \le Q_A(N) \cdot F(N) \qquad (4.3)$$

$$P_B(N) \le P_A(N) \cdot G(N)$$

$$S_B(N) \le S_A(N)$$

where N is the number of elements in the data structure and A is the static data structure from which the dynamic data structure B is derived; $F(N)$, referred to as the "query penalty," is related to the number of individual static data structures that exist, and $G(N)$, referred to as the "processing penalty," is the penalty function associated with the static data structure history associated with individual elements in dynamic data structure B.

For the relations in Equation (4.3) to hold, a further constraint that $Q_A(\ )$ is monotone nondecreasing and that $P_A(\ )$ and $S_A(\ )$ grow at least linearly is required. For most static data structures this is not hard to meet.

The relations in (4.3) are guidelines for the admissibility of transforms that were introduced by Bentley and Saxe [BS80] for dynamic data structures used in decomposable searching problems. However, they are general enough for use in determining the usefulness of transforms for other problems.

The penalty functions $F(N)$ and $G(N)$ warrant further comment. The functions provide some insight into the efficiency of the dynamic data structure. Because of this, a transform is usually referred to as an "admissible $(F(N), G(N))$ transform" to help convey this information about the efficiency. Specifically, an admissible transform is any transform for which the preprocessing time and query time for the dynamic data structure does not exceed some reasonable factor of the preprocessing time and query time of the equivalent static data structure and that the space requirements for the dynamic data structure does not exceed the space requirements of the static data structure with the same number of elements. Of course, in reality we may accept some leniency of these conditions. For example, a slight increase in the space requirements is often present owing to the addition of management information. Typically the overhead of maintaining the management information is ignored because it is considered negligible, so the condition of equivalent space usage is met.

The requirements for an admissible transform might seem to preclude the use of some dynamic data structures, such as those that use global rebuilding. In fact, dynamic data structures that require global rebuilding may still be admissible provided the global rebuilding occurs at such a frequency that the collective preprocessing time remains acceptable.

4.3 UPPER BOUNDS

A detailed analysis of a dynamic data structure can result in functions that involve continued fractions, power series, and other difficult-to-quantify formulas. Most of the complex mathematics required to analyze the costs associated with dynamic data structures can be avoided by looking at functions that define an upper bound on the costs. In many cases knowing just the upper bound on the efficiency of a dynamic data structure is sufficient to determine whether the performance is acceptable for a given application. In the design of a dynamic data structure we typically begin with a static data structure with some known properties. This means that we know the equation for $Q(N)$, $P(N)$, $S(N)$ for the static data structure. So, all that we need to calculate are the penalty functions $F(N)$ and $G(N)$. The study of specific static data structures is not within the scope of this book (it's a subject that entire books are made of).

The penalty functions that serve as the upper bound for a given dynamic data structure are calculated as follows. We begin by assuming that the dynamic data structure consists of one or more static data structures and that the functions $Q(N)$ are monotone nondecreasing and that $P(N)$ and $S(N)$ grow at least linearly. Given this, the query function for any dynamic data structure is

$$Q_B(N) = \sum_{1 \le i \le k} Q_A(n_i)$$

where k is the number of static data structures in the given dynamic data structure and n_i is number of elements in that data structure. Since $Q_A(\ )$ is monotone nondecreasing, then

$$Q_B(N) \le \sum_{1 \le i \le k} Q_A(\max(n))$$

where $\max(n)$ is the number of elements in the largest static data structure. The upper bound on $\max(n)$ is N since the number of elements in the static data structure cannot exceed the number of elements in the dynamic data structure. Therefore

$$Q_B(N) \le Q_A(N)k \tag{4.4}$$

So, the upper bound on $F(N)$ is the number of static data structures required to hold all the elements of the dynamic data structure.

The calculation of $G(N)$ is a little less straightforward and is dependent on the evolutionary stages a dynamic data structure must pass through in order to obtain a particular state. Every transform has its own characteristic evolution. What we need to determine is the maximum number of static data structures any particular element has been built into. To do this we begin with a dynamic data structure with zero elements and conclude with a dynamic data structure with N elements. As we go from the beginning state to the concluding state, we count the number of static data structures each element has been built into. The results of this calculation gives the value for $G(N)$.

4.3.1 Some Examples

As an example let's look at how to analyze a transform and determine both $F(N)$ and $G(N)$. To do this, let's look at the transform required to build linear linked lists (the linear geometric transform). With a linked linear list, each element that is added to the dynamic data structure is placed in its own static data structure. So a linked linear list with N elements has N static data structures; therefore, $F(N) = N$. Once an element is created, it is never rebuilt into another static data structure, so the maximum number of static data structures an element can be built into is 1; hence $G(N) = 1$. So, a linked linear list is an admissible $(N, 1)$ transform.

The analysis of the transform that gives rise to a linked linear list is rather trivial, so let's now look at a slightly more complex transform, the binary transform. With the binary transform there are at most $\log(N + 1)$ static structures (one for each bit in the binary number) at any point in time. This is a natural consequence of the binary counting scheme.

Now let's analyze the processing cost of the binary transform. The processing cost of inserting an element into a dynamic data structure based on a binary transform is dependent on which element is being inserted. For example, inserting the 127th element is relatively inexpensive since all that is required is the addition of a static structure with one element (this is true whenever N is odd). However, the insertion of the 128th element triggers a global rebuild since a static structure with 128 elements must be created and populated. In fact, global rebuilds are triggered whenever the 2/th element is inserted. Partial rebuilds occur whenever the number of elements is even and not a power of 2.

For a binary transform the first element inserted into the dynamic data structure will be built into the largest number of static data structures. The reason for this is that the first element inserted is involved in every global rebuild that the dynamic data will undergo. All other elements are involved in partial rebuilds until the point where they are included in the same structure as the first element, after which they are included in all subsequent global rebuilds. The number of partial rebuilds is always less than the total number of global rebuilds that occurred prior to the partial rebuild. So, for any given number of elements the first element inserted has been involved in at least $\log(N)$ global rebuilds (they occur only when N equals a power of 2). Also, when the first element is initially inserted into the dynamic data structure, it is inserted into a single-element static data structure. So, the total number of static data structures the first element has been built into is $1 + \log(N)$. This means that for a binary transform $G(N) = \log(N + 1)$. Therefore, a binary transform is an admissible $(\log(N + 1), 1 + \log(N))$ transform.

4.4 PERFORMANCE TRADE-OFFS

In Chapter 3 the binary, radix-k, and k-binomial transforms were mentioned. So far we have looked at linear geometric transform and binary transforms in some detail. The binary transform provides a quicker query time than does the linear geometric transform, but this is at the expense of the processing time. Typically, there is a trade-off between the query penalty and the processing penalty. A transform with a small query penalty will usually have a larger processing penalty. Likewise, a transform with a small processing penalty will usually have a larger query penalty.

Depending on the specific application, you might want to minimize one penalty over another. To help in selecting a particular transform, we will now take a look at various transforms that will provide faster query times than processing times, in a relative sense. Subsequently we will look at transforms that provide faster processing time than query times, again in a relative sense.

4.4.1 Fast Queries

A transformation's query penalty is influenced by the number of distinct static data structures that are maintained by the transform. The fewer the number of static data structures, the less the query penalty will be. A binary transform provides an improvement over a linked linear list since it reduces the number of static data structures. The best possible query times occur when there is a single static data structure. To achieve this would require a global rebuild every time a new element is added, which means that the processing penalty will be high, and for large problems this is impractical. So, a good question might be: How close can we come to maintaining one static data structure and still remain practical? Actually, surprising close, as we'll now see.

k-*Binomial Transforms*

A 2-binomial transform, also referred to simply as a "triangular transform" since it is based on the triangular counting scheme, is the simplest form of a k-binomial transform.[1] With a triangular transform the elements of the dynamic data structure are placed into two static data structures. One with $\binom{i}{2}$ elements and the other with $\binom{j}{1}$ elements. Because of the attributes of the triangular counting scheme, it is also true that $i > j$.

Determining the number of elements that exist at any one time is simple; it's 2, since by definition there is always at most two static data structures. So, $F(N) = 2$. Determining the number of structures any element may be built into is similar to the method we used to determine this quantity for the binary transform. Just as with the binary transform, the first element inserted into the dynamic data structure is the one that will be built into the most static data structures. The reason is that once an element is built into the larger static data structure [the ones with $\binom{i}{2}$ elements] it is involved in all global rebuilds. Any element inserted after the first element is first built into the smaller static data structures [the ones with $\binom{j}{1}$ elements] until a global rebuild occurs, at which point the elements are involved with subsequent global rebuilds. Since $i > j$ there will never be more smaller static data structures built than the number of larger static data structures that have been built. So all we need to determine is how many larger static data structures have been built. Now, the number of larger static data structures that have been built is the value of i. Therefore, we need to solve for i in terms of N.

Using a 2-binomial (triangular) counting scheme, a number is given by the formula

$$N = \binom{i}{2} + \binom{j}{1} \tag{4.5}$$

If we expand the binomials in Equation (4.5), we get

$$N = \frac{i(i-1)}{2} + j \tag{4.6}$$

Since $i > j$, then $2i > 2j$, and if we multiple both sides of Equation (4.7) by 2 and substitute for $2j$, we get

$$2N > i(i-1) + 2i$$

which reduces to $i < (2N)^{1/2}$. So, an upper bound on i and also on the maximum

---

[1]The design of the k-binomial transform was discussed in the previous chapter (honest, take a look).

number of static data structures any element can be built into is $(2N)^{1/2}$. So the triangular transform is an admissible $(2, (2N)^{1/2})$ transform.

The determination of the penalty functions for the triangular transform reveal that it is has an extremely good query time. However, this fast query time is achieved by incurring an additional cost to the processing time of building the dynamic data structure. Even so, the costs are reasonable and the triangular transform is quite practical.

4.4.2 Fast Insertion

The bulk of the costs associated with the processing times for dynamic data structures is associated with the partial and global rebuilds that occur during the insertion of elements. So in order to minimize the processing cost, we must reduce the frequency at which rebuilds occur. One method to achieve this is to implement a transform that mimics a particular counting scheme but does not maintain the static data structure strictly in accordance with the counting scheme. Such a transform is called a "dual transform" since it exhibits duality to more literal transformations of a counting scheme.

Dual Transforms
A specific example is the *dual triangular transform*, which is a case of the k-binomial transform where $k = 2$. With a dual triangular transform, elements are inserted into a single element dynamic data structure (a linear linked list will do fine) until there are $\binom{M}{2}$ elements, at which point the M elements are combined into a single static data structure and added to a second dynamic data structure. The dynamic data structure that contains the single-element static structures is termed the "small" structure, and the dynamic data structure that contains static structures with $\binom{M}{2}$ elements in each static data structure is called the "large" structure. If the number of elements in the small and large structures are added up, their values are the same as that for the two static data structures in the triangular (2-binomial) transform, thereby achieving the desired duality.

The analysis of the dual triangular transform is rather straightforward. First, each element is built into a static structure at most 2 times, once in the small structure and then again in the large. Therefore

$$P_D(N) \leq P_S(N)2$$

and the number of static data structures that exist at any given time is

$$Q_D(N) \leq QA(N) \cdot 2(2N)^{1/2}$$

since there are two dynamic data structures with up to $(2N)^{1/2}$ elements. So, the dual triangular transform is an admissible $(2(2N)^{1/2}, 2)$ transform.

The dual triangular transform can be generalized into a dual k-binomial transform. In a dual k-binomial transform there are k distinct dynamic data structures. Each static structure can contain static structures with $\binom{r}{i}$ elements, where $r \geq 1$ and $0 \leq i < k$.

An example is a dual k-binomial transform where $k \geq 3$. In this case the third dynamic data structure can contain

$$\binom{2}{2} = 1, \ \binom{3}{2} = 3, \ \binom{4}{2} = 6, \ \binom{5}{2} = 10$$

elements for $2 \leq r \leq 5$. Note that for the third dynamic data structure $i = 2$ and values of $r < 2$ are not allowed since the value of the binomial is undefined.

Now we shall proceed with the analysis of the dual k-binomial transform. Just as with the dual triangular transform, an element is built into dynamic data structure with the smallest k first, and then propagated into dynamic data structures with a larger k as enough elements are collected to fill the large static data structure. Since an element is built into a new structure only under these conditions, an element is built into at most k data structures, so $G(N) = k$. Also, each dynamic data structure contains at most $(k!N)^{1/2}$ static data structures. Since there are at most k dynamic data structures, $F(N) = k(k!N)^{1/2}$. Therefore, a dual k-binomial transform is an admissible $(k(k!N)^{1/2}, k)$ transform.

4.5 DELETION COSTS

So far we have discussed only the costs associated with building a dynamic data structure through a sequence of insertions. Even though insertions may be the most common use of dynamic data structures, there are many instances in which the deletion of elements is essential. Deletions can be very expensive operations in terms of the processing costs. The reason is that if a deletion affects the oldest (and usually the largest) static data structure, it typically triggers a global rebuild of the entire dynamic data structure. This could easily become unacceptable.

There are only a few practical approaches for dealing with deletions. One approach is to use only transforms that do not require global rebuilds at any point in time. Geometric transforms typically do not require global rebuilds since there is a one-to-one correspondence between elements and static data structures. This characteristic can be useful in designing hybrid dynamic data structures. One such design is to use a geometric transform in such a way that each "element" in the geometric transform is actually a static data structure that contains some number of elements stored according to any other transform. This is a relatively good alternative since the rebuilds will always be limited to the enclosing "element" of the geometric transform.

Another approach is to maintain all elements ever inserted into the dynamic data structure and simply mark the elements as "deleted." After a certain number of elements have been deleted, a global rebuild may be triggered to actually remove the elements. Since the timing of global rebuilds is up to the developer's discretion, you can choose whatever threshold is appropriate. This approach can be rather pervasive since all functions that access the dynamic data structure must always check to see if an element is valid. This approach does have some potential benefits since the complete processing history of a dynamic data structure can be maintained and there is the potential to recover from accidental deletions.

One other approach is to maintain two dynamic data structures. In one of the dynamic data structures, referred to as the "real" structure, elements are inserted. When a deletion of an element occurs, a copy of it is inserted into the second dynamic data structure, referred to as the "ghost" structure. When a query is applied to the dynamic data structure, it is applied to both the real and ghost dynamic data structures. Those elements that satisfy the query in the ghost structure are removed from the collection of elements that satisfy the query in the real structure. Since elements in the ghost structure also exist in the real structure, the removal of the matches in the ghost structure creates the proper results. When using real and ghost structures it is often advantageous to rebuild the real structure when some threshold of elements appears in the ghost structure. A good rule of thumb is that when the ghost structure is half as large as the real structure, perform a global rebuild.

In decomposable searching problems the operation of combining the results from the real and ghost structures is done with an inverse of the binary operator, which is used to combine results from each static data structure in the dynamic data structure. If an inverse does not exist, this approach cannot be used with decomposable searching problems. An example of a binary operator that has an inverse is the addition operation. The inverse is the subtraction operation.

4.6 SUMMARY

The penalty functions $F(N)$ and $G(N)$ give an indication of the efficiency of the transform. The query penalty function $F(N)$ is a measure of what it costs to use the dynamic data structure once it is built, and the processing penalty function $G(N)$ is a measure of what it costs to build up a dynamic data structure to a specific state. These penalty functions are used to state the admissibility of a transform using the phrase "an admissible $(F(N), G(N))$ transform."

The penalty functions for some transforms were mentioned in Chapter 3, with additional transforms discussed and analyzed in this chapter. The penalties for the various transformations reference in this book are summarized in Table 4.1.

For the interested reader a more mathematical rigorous treatment of the analysis of dynamic data structure has been done by Flajolet et al. [FFV80] and Francon et al.

Table 4.1 Summary of Penalty Functions for Various Transforms

Transform	$F(N)$	$G(N)$
Linear linked list	N	1
Binary	$\log(N + 1)$	$1 + \log(N)$
Radix-k	$\log_k(N)$	$(k - 1)\log_k(N)$
Triangular	2	$(2N)^{1/2}$
k-Binomial	k	$(k!N)^{1/k}$
Dual triangular	$2(2N)^{1/2}$	2
Dual k-binomial	$k(k!N)^{1/2}$	k

[FRS88]. In addition dynamic data structures have been devised to solve specific problems. One source of information is [Knu73]. The paper by Bentley and Saxe [BS80] greatly influenced the contents of this chapter.

POINTS TO PONDER

4.1   What are the cost functions that characterize the overall performance of a dynamic data structure? Describe each of them.

4.2   How does the insertion cost function and a dynamic data structure relate to the preprocessing costs function of a static data structure, and under what conditions?

4.3   What influences the value of the query penalty function? The processing penalty functions?

4.4   Which penalty function is affected the most by rebuilds?

4.5   What are three possible approaches for dealing with deletions?

4.6   Calculate the maximum number of static data structures any element would be built into for a k-binomial transform. Do this for any arbitrary $k > 1$.

Configuration Control | **5**

In the previous chapters dynamic data structures have been discussed in an abstract sense. While this is essential to exploring the theoretical and analytical aspects of dynamic data structures, it does not provide enough information to actually implement dynamic data structures. In this chapter we will explore what is needed in order to implement dynamic data structures.

There are three distinct implementation specific aspects to dynamic data structures. The first is how an application manages and tracks dynamic data structures; this is called "configuration management." The second is how a value contained in a dynamic data structure is converted into a static data type so that an application can use it. This is called "dynamic adaptation." The third is something you're already familiar with, and that's the concept of data structures. This chapter will concentrate on the first two aspects. The subject of data structures is left for outside study and, hopefully, you're already familiar with the subject.

5.1 METHODS OF CONFIGURATION CONTROL

Configuration control is the process of tracking and maintaining information about dynamic data structures so that information and values contained in the structures can be readily obtained. The configuration information describes the physical properties of each element and their structural relationship to one another. The physical properties of an element are size, type, and location.

Configuration information can be divided into two categories: explicit and implicit. Explicit configuration information is maintained within some control structure related to the data portion of the variable. A dynamic data structure must have such a control structure. Implicit configuration information is maintained in the executable image of the application and is fixed at the time of compilation. An example of implicit information is an atomic data type, or a static structure or union. In such data structures the type, size, and location are maintained and recorded by the compiler. Once the application is compiled, this information is encoded into the executable image of the application as rigid machine instructions.

At times it can be beneficial to manage a static data structure as a single dynamic data type, taking advantage of the implicit information related to the static data structure. The benefit of such an approach is to reduce the complexity of the configuration information maintained in the dynamic data structure.

I'll elucidate further with an example. Suppose you have a data structure called TIME that consists of two elements, hour and minutes.[1] If this structure is then considered to be a single dynamic data type, the only information you would have to maintain would be related to the data type TIME. This would include a type of TIME, a size equal to that of the TIME structure, and a location that would be the location of the first byte of the time structure.

Whenever a TIME variable is accessed, the (explicit) configuration information about the TIME variable would be used to extract the time structure. The TIME structure would then have to be assigned to a program variable for further value extraction since that information is implicit and the references will have to be resolved by the static structure information in the application.

If the information about each element in the TIME structure were maintained as a dynamic element, then the configuration information would double in volume. That is, you would have configuration information for each element, rather than for the structure as a whole. Since the elements of the TIME structure are coupled as a single object, it is more sensible to treat it as such.

Even though explicit and implicit configuration information are interrelated and share many of the same characteristics, we'll concentrate on ways to manage the explicit information. The implicit information is compiler-dependent and beyond the reach of applications. With this in mind, throughout the rest of this book the term "configuration control" is synonymous with "explicit configuration control."

There are two conceptual methods of configuration control: encapsulation and type databases. They differ in two respects. First is where the configuration information is maintained. With encapsulation it is maintained as part of the data structure itself, whereas with type databases the information is maintained in a separate location. The only difference is in accessibility of the control information. With languages like C, the encapsulated information is available to every portion of the code that comes into contact with the data structure. This availability can lead to improper changes to the configuration information. This potential for disaster can be averted in languages that support private data objects (like C++) by making the information available only to specific components of the application. The same sort of protection can be achieved by using type databases since the configuration information can be stored in protected system locations, separate and distinct from the data structures themselves.

Choosing between the methods of configuration control inherently involves issues of trade-offs and efficiency since each method has its own distinct merits. Also, because these two methods are so different, an appropriate combination of the two might provide the best solution. This provides for a great deal of freedom in the structure of the configuration information. What is important is that the configuration information be described in a logical, consistent, and concise manner.

In addition to choosing a conceptual method for configuration control, there is a

---

[1]Seconds pass too quickly to be of much importance.

choice of implementation method. There are two types of approaches: free access and indirect access. By the names of these approaches you've probably deduced that the choice hinges on issues of access to the configuration information.

5.1.1 Free Access

Free access is an approach that allows the developer direct and unlimited access to the configuration information. The developer can assign values to the various elements of the configuration information and have direct control over each dynamic data structure. Such an approach has the potential of allowing the type or size to be declared to be one thing and the actual data portion consist of something entirely different. This could have a disastrous effect on an application since the assignments to the dynamic data structure may affect portions of the application beyond the intent of the assignment.

Some characteristics that are important in determining whether this is an appropriate approach are the associated efficiency and size benefits. A free-access approach is efficient in terms of processing time because changes to the elements of the configuration information are done in-line, without the overhead of function calls. Free access can also be a more efficient method of implementation provided the developer thoroughly understands the configuration information and the structures he or she is dealing with.

For critical applications, a minor lapse by a developer to include an error check could be disastrous. In such cases, an indirect approach (which will be discussed later) would be more appropriate.

The aggregate size benefits of the free access approach are related to the amount of code and global data required with alternative approaches. With either approach there is a minimum amount of information a particular data structure requires to be fully defined. So most size benefits are code-related. In general, a free-access approach is beneficial in terms of efficiency and size if your need for dynamic data structures is limited to a few portions of the application and if the dynamic data structures are simple.

Free-access approaches are very problem-specific, and you should think of a free-access approach as you would assembly language. It should be used only when there are obvious size or performance gains to be made.

5.1.2 Indirect Access

The alternate approach for access to the configuration information is indirect access. With indirect access the developer is provided access to the configuration information only through a set of functions (methods in object-oriented languages). In order to assign or extract data from the structure, as well as change any of the configuration information, a function call has to be made. Within these functions, free access is allowed to part or all of the configuration information.

These functions should be part of a fixed, well-defined set of support functions that have been tested and change slowly (if at all) over the development of an application. They should also contain appropriate error checking. If they don't, they aren't much different from a free-access approach.

By using an indirect-access approach, the reliability of the configuration information is increased and can be verified more readily. It also means that the dynamic data structure and its associated configuration information are manipulated in a consistent manner regardless of the expertise of the developer. Since access is indirect and only through well-defined calls, it is possible to change the breadth of the configuration information and the extent of data types that can be managed without a need to alter the application. This is the more modular approach and is coherent with reliable development practices.

An indirect-access approach is (in general) more efficient then a free-access approach in terms of development time. The way to make indirect access efficient is by providing high-level support functions to reduce the burden on the developer. Just as free access is like assembly language, indirect access is like a high-level language. Most people would agree[2] that high-level languages are more efficient in terms of development time and portability than is assembly language. The same is true for indirect access.

Where the indirect method is less efficient than the free-access approach is in terms of the function call overhead. This can be high in some languages, but with C it can be minimized by reducing the number of arguments for each function and by passing pointers to variables. Almost by nature, using dynamic data structures means a reduction in function arguments. The main reason is that a dynamic data structure contains information that is sometimes passed as arguments to functions.

The aggregate size benefits of the indirect access approach are related to the number of times each function is called in an application. If the number of times an application uses a dynamic data structure is greater than one, then you will experience a size reduction of the application by not placing the support function in-line. If the application calls the functions once, then it's nominally the same as placing the function's code in-line, so there's no size benefit to preferring in-line inclusion.

There's another size benefit of indirect access. This benefit is related to how many applications use the support functions. Since the support functions are typically written to be generic (at least to a particular group of applications), they are placed in a library for use with all applications. If the operating system under which the application is developed supports shared libraries, then the machine code portion of the library is shared by all the applications; this reduces the size of the application. The actual gain is the size of the machine code divided by the number of applications simultaneously sharing the library. It's nominally zero if only one application is sharing the library at any one time.

There is no well-defined dividing line as to when to use a free-access approach or an indirect-access approach. The right choice depends on the specific application. In general, if the particular application has a specialized or unique type of data dynamic

---

[2]Those who program only in assembly language probably would not.

structure, and the dynamic data structure is used in a restricted portion of the application, then the free-access approach is best. The free-access approach might be best in cases where execution speed can be substantially increased by eliminating function calls. This is rare if the programming language is C and the indirect-access approach is implemented properly. In almost every other case the indirect-access approach is the right choice. The reason is simple; it provides the most overall benefit in terms of reliability, portability, development time, and application size.

5.1.3 Encapsulation

Encapsulation is a method of configuration control in which all the information pertaining to a dynamic data structure is passed from function to function within the application. The configuration information is bundled in such a way that it is treated as a single program variable by the application.

Encapsulation has many variations since some of the configuration information can be implicit rather than explicit. The purest form of encapsulation is one that consists of just the three configuration elements of size, type, and location. The actual storage location for the data portion of the variable (pointed to by "location") is maintained separate from the encapsulation structure. A variation of this is where the "location" portion is replaced by the actual data portion.

All other variations consist of allowing one or more elements of the configuration information to be implicit. If you allow all elements to be implicit, you have the type of data structure that is created with native constructs in the implementation language.

Potential Applications

Encapsulation is a very convenient method of tagging data with information. You can use this method to create typeless programming languages. Actually variables in a typeless language do have type; you (as a developer) don't have to think about it, and that's why its called "typeless." When an assignment is made to a variable, the compiler or the interpreter looks at the kind of value that is being assigned and then molds the variable to match the type. By doing this a variable may be a numeric value at one point and a function at another point. LISP is a good example of a typeless language.

Another common use of encapsulation is in hypertext applications. Within hypertext there are passive and active elements, and each element can be associated with other elements. As you navigate from element to element in a hypertext document, the system must decide how to display the element. It does this by referencing type information associated with the element.

An application of encapsulation that is becoming increasingly prevalent is message passing. A message is actually a union between what is called a "packet" and an encapsulated data type. A packet is simply a collection of data that has a source and destination associated with the data. When you encapsulate type information with the data, you have a message.

Tag	Allocated	Tag	Allocated	Sentinel

Figure 5.1 Memory utilization of e_malloc( ).

An Example

C has at least two functions that use encapsulation: **malloc( )** and **free( )**. With **malloc( )** you can request a block of memory of a specific size in bytes. If **malloc( )** can allocate the requested block, it returns a pointer to the memory block. If it is unsuccessful, it returns a NULL pointer. **Free( )** is the compliment of the **malloc( )** function. It takes a pointer to a data block that resulted from a call to **malloc( )** and removes the reservation of the memory, returning it for use through another call to **malloc( )**.

Malloc( ) and **free( )** share two elements of a dynamic data structure: location and size. The location is the area of memory allocated that is returned as a pointer from **malloc( )**. The size is the number of bytes requested. **Malloc( )** and **free( )** can be implemented using encapsulation.

Let's now implement an encapsulated **malloc( )** and **free( )**, which we'll call e_malloc( ) and e_free( ), respectively.[3] Figure 5.1 is a diagram of how memory will be utilized in such an implementation. For our purposes the tag contains information related to the size of the allocated memory it controls, a pointer to the start of the allocated memory, and a flag indicating whether the memory is currently reserved. The reason for the reserved flag is that it allows previously allocated memory that has subsequently been freed to be used at another time. This provides for more efficient use of memory. The sentinel tag at the end of the memory block defines the end of the memory pool. This allows an application to reserve memory in convenient blocks and use it piece by piece.

The procedural flow of e_malloc( ) and e_free( ) is presented in Listing 5.1. When this design is implemented, there are a few things to consider. The first is that a malloc function cannot call itself when it needs more memory; when a malloc( ) is out of memory, there is no more memory. The next consideration is the process by which malloc( ) extracts data. You could have several options here. One would be to have a reserved block or pool of memory in the application that can be subdivided and used. Another might be requesting memory from the operating system. Which method you choose depends on your ultimate application and your operating environment.

Listing 5.2 presents one possible implementation of the previously presented design. So that specifics of the operating system can be ignored, a memory pool approach is taken. There are some potential problems with such an implementation of malloc( ) and free( ). First, there is no way to protect the tag area of the memory

---

[3]If you were to call them malloc() and free(), then system calls may attempt to use your versions rather than the system versions. This could be disastrous.

Listing 5.1   The commented procedural flow of e_malloc() and e_free().

```
e_malloc(size)
{
  -- check pool for available block --
  if(none) return NULL
  if(block is more than needed) {
    allocate just the part you need, free the rest.
  return(pointer to reserved block)
}


e_free(ptr)
{
  check if pointer is within memory pool range.
  if so, mark the block as free.
  Now scan from beginning of pool and coalesce
  any free blocks which are contiguous.
}
```

block from inadvertent writes. If the calling application were to decrement the pointer returned by e_malloc( ) and write to the tag area, it could corrupt the information stored there and cause confusion when a free( ) was called.

To help avoid such problems, the tag area includes information about the location of the end of the tag in the MEM_TAG.cptr variable. This information is checked for consistency with the passed pointer to e_free( ) prior to freeing the block of memory. The passed pointer is also checked to make sure that it points somewhere within the memory pool. These validity checks will catch some alterations, but not all. One alteration that could slip past is if only the size information in the tag is altered. In such a case the "free memory" operation will be performed, and the system will be irreparably corrupted.

Another potential problem is related to the first. That is, if the information in the tag area is altered to the point that it does not pass the validity checks, then the reserved area of memory can never be freed. If the corruption occurs in a portion of the application that is called repeated, then eventually the entire memory pool will be consumed and the application will fail.[4]

5.1.4 Type Databases

A type database is a method of configuration control in which a database containing information related to a dynamic data structure is maintained separate from the data portion. This information remains in a fixed (or central) location in the application

---

[4]These potential problems actually exist in most C implementations of malloc( ) and free( ).

Listing 5.2   Malloc() and free() that use encapsulation.

```c
#include <stdio.h>

/* Dynamic data type for allocated memory */
typedef struct {
   unsigned int size;
   short int reserved;
   char *cptr;
} MEM_TAG;

#define MALLOC_MAX_POOL 2048
static char Malloc_pool[MALLOC_MAX_POOL];
static MEM_TAG *Mbase = NULL;

#define YES    1
#define NO     0

/*---------------------------------------------------------------------
 Allocate a specific amount of memory and return a
 pointer to the beginning of the allocated memory
 ---------------------------------------------------------------------*/
char *e_malloc(size)
unsigned size;
{
    MEM_TAG *mptr, *tmpptr;
    char *cptr;

/* Initialize the base pointer if it hasn't already been done */
   if(Mbase == NULL) {
      Mbase = (MEM_TAG *)Malloc_pool;
      Mbase->size = MALLOC_MAX_POOL - sizeof(MEM_TAG) * 2;
      Mbase->reserved = NO;
      /* Create a sentinel to mark end of block */
      tmpptr = (MEM_TAG *) (&Malloc_pool[MALLOC_MAX_POOL - sizeof(MEM_TAG)]);
      tmpptr->size = 0;
      tmpptr->reserved = YES;
   }

/* Search for an available part of memory large enough to hold the request
 */
   mptr = Mbase;
   while(mptr->size != 0) {
     cptr = (char *) mptr + sizeof(MEM_TAG);
```

(continued)

Listing 5.2   *(continued)*

```
      if(mptr->reserved == NO) {
        if(mptr->size >= size) { /* a find */
          if(mptr->size + sizeof(MEM_TAG) > size) { /* more than we need */
            tmpptr = (MEM_TAG *) (cptr + size);
            tmpptr->size = mptr->size - size - sizeof(MEM_TAG);
            tmpptr->reserved = NO;
            mptr->size = size;
            mptr->reserved = YES;
          }
          mptr->cptr = cptr;
          return(cptr);
    }
    }
    cptr += mptr->size;
    mptr = (MEM_TAG *) cptr;
  }
  return(NULL);
}


/*---------------------------------------------------------------------
 Deallocate a portion of memory allocated by a call
 to e_malloc(). Also coalesce free memory into contiguous
 blocks.
 ---------------------------------------------------------------------*/
e_free(ptr)
char *ptr;
{
   MEM_TAG *mptr, *tmpptr;

   mptr = (MEM_TAG *) ( ptr - sizeof(MEM_TAG) );

/* Sanity check *
   if (mptr < Mbase) { return(NO); }
   if (mptr - MEX_MEM_POOL > Mbase) { return(NO); }
   if (mptr->cptr != ptr) { return(NO); }

 /* Mark memory as free */
   mptr->reserved = NO;

/* Now coalesce all free memory blocks */
  mptr = Mbase;
   while ( mptr->size != 0 ) {
    tmpptr = (MEM_TAG *) ((char *)mptr + mptr->size + sizeof(MEM_TAG));
```

```
     if ( mptr->reserved == NO && tmpptr->reserved == NO) {
         mptr->size += tmpptr->size + sizeof(MEM_TAG);
     } else {
       mptr = tmpptr;
     }
   }
   return (YES);
}

/* Example calls */
main( ) {
  char *ptr1;
  char *ptr2;

  ptr1 = e_malloc(124);
  ptr2 = e_malloc(64);
  e_free(ptr1);
  e_free(ptr2);
}
```

and is not passed from point to point. The database serves as an information pool and is consulted each time the data variable is involved in any activity. Typically this is performed as a consequence of making a support-level function call.

Like encapsulation, a type database must contain information about the three properties of data: size, type, and location. Any number of these properties may be implicit or explicit, so there is a wide variety of possible implementation approaches.

What distinguishes encapsulation and type databases is the degree of dispersion between the configuration information and the data stores. With encapsulation the configuration information is adjacent to the data and is part of the data flow in the application. With type databases the configuration information is inherently maintained at a single location within the application.

Type databases can be implemented in several ways. One approach is to have a database with a fixed number of entries. For example, you could allow up to 256 dynamic data structures to be managed. In addition, you might place a limit on the sum total of the size of all the data structures. For some applications this might be a reasonable constraint. The benefit of this approach is that the memory needs of the application remain constant from the first moment of execution to the last. This means that if the program will load into memory, it will run without encountering a shortage of memory.

The main drawback to such an approach is the fixed size of the database and storage area for the dynamic data structure. As one alternative, you could lift the constraint on the storage area. The ultimate adaptive approach would be to allow the database and storage area to grow or shrink with program demands. To do this, you must be able to request resources (memory) from the system. This may not be possible in all environments.

Potential Applications

Type databases are most useful in situations where there is a collection of data that all share the same structure. The most prominent applications that have this characteristic are relational database management systems (DBMSs). In a relational DBMS data that shares the same structure is grouped into tables with an entry in the table (called a "tuple") for each data item. In a separate location in the DBMS (possibly in another table), a description of the structure of the data table is maintained. The DBMS then uses this information to determine how to deal with and manipulate the individual data items in the structure.

Another reason why type databases are used in DBMSs is space efficiency. Since every tuple in a table has the exact same structure, you need to describe that structure only once. If encapsulation were used, then every tuple would have additional information included with it that is identical for each tuple.

Type databases are also useful in situations where the data is stored separately from the configuration information. This might be by choice or simply a constraint. One type of application where this is true is called the Data Flow System[5] (DFS), which uses data flow processing techniques. With this system a series of applications, called "fittings", can tap into a data flow and perform a processing action on the data. The data within the flow is described by a type database that precedes the data. The data itself then consists of multiple tuples, one after the other.

Another noteworthy application of type databases is with variable binding. This is where an ordinary application variable is bound at run-time to another variable. Binding is usually performed at the pointer level. Since a pointer contains only location information, all other information must be maintained separately. This is the role the type database plays. Typically, type information is maintained in the type database. This information can be used to perform type translations during the variable update phase. This can greatly increase the usefulness of variable binding and make an application more versatile.

Examples

As an example application of the use of type databases, let's implement the malloc( ) and free( ) calls that are available in C. Ordinarily these calls are implemented using encapsulation (as discussed previously). The logical structure of the type database variants, which we'll call t_malloc( ) and t_free( ), is identical to that described in the previously discussed encapsulation example. Figure 5.2 is a diagram of how memory will be utilized. Figure 5.2 illustrates nicely the physical separation of the configura-

---

[5]Developed by the author at the University of California, Los Angeles, Institute of Geophysics and Planetary Physics (UCLA/IGPP).

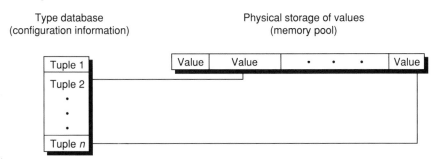

Figure 5.2   Diagram of memory utilization for the type database implementation of malloc( ) and free( ).

tion information and the actual storage location of data values. This physical separation is the main feature that distinguishes type databases from encapsulation.

An implementation of malloc( ) and free( ) using type databases is presented is Listing 5.3.

As discussed previously, a potential problem exists with the encapsulation variants of malloc( ) and free( ). This is because the configuration information is contiguous and embedded with the active variable. With a type database the control information is maintained separately from the active variables. This separation reduces the probability that the type database could be corrupted from improper use of the pointers to the memory pool.

In some environments the type database could be protected from corruption by placing the database in protected memory. A good example of such an environment would be an object-oriented system, like C++, which supports private data. In C++ you could make the malloc( ) and free( ) functions "friends" of the type database object. This would give these functions access to the type database and prevent uncontrolled alterations of the information. It would not be possible to do the same thing with the encapsulation versions because the tags are intermixed with the memory to which the application must be allowed unlimited access.

This does not mean that encapsulation is poorly suited to object-oriented approaches. In fact, object-oriented environments are based primarily on encapsulation. It's just that encapsulation is a poor approach for malloc( ) and free( ) since the security of the tag information cannot be adequately protected.

5.2 DATA STRUCTURE STORAGE

Dynamic data structures can be used to manage physical as well as virtual data structures. A physical data structure is one that is declared within the application using native constructs of the implementation language, in other words, an ordinary program variable. A dynamic data structure can be used to manage such a variable because it has a location associated with it. This location, along with its types and size, can become part of a dynamic data structure.

Listing 5.3   Malloc() and free() which use a type database.

```c
#include <stdio.h>

/* Dynamic data type for allocated memory */
typedef struct {
   unsigned int size;
   short int reserved;
   char *cptr;
} MALLOC_ITEM;

#define MAX_MALLOC_POOL 2048
static char Malloc_pool[MAX_MALLOC_POOL];
#define MAX_MALLOC_ITEMS        128
static MALLOC_ITEM Malloc_item[MAX_MALLOC_ITEMS];
static unsigned Malloc_cnt;

#define YES    1
#define NO     0

/*-------------------------------------------------------------------
Allocate a specific amount of memory and return a
pointer to the beginning of the allocated memory
-------------------------------------------------------------------*/
  char *t_malloc(size)
unsigned size;
{
   unsigned i;
/* Initialize the base pointer if it hasn't already been done */
   if(Malloc_item[0].cptr != Malloc_pool) {
      Malloc_item[0].cptr = Malloc_pool;
      Malloc_item[0].size = sizeof(Malloc_pool);
      Malloc_item[0].reserved = NO;
      Malloc_cnt = 1;
   }

/* Search for an available part of memory large enough to hold
   the requested number of bytes
 */
   for(i = 0; i < Malloc_cnt; i++) {
     if(Malloc_item[i].reserved == NO) {
       if(Malloc_item[i].size <= size) {  /* A valid candidate */
         if(Malloc_item[i].size > size) { /* Split */
           if(Malloc_cnt >= MAX_MALLOC_ITEMS) return(NULL);
           Malloc_item[Malloc_cnt].size = Malloc_item[i].size - size;
```

```
        Malloc_item[Malloc_cnt].cptr = Malloc_item[i].cptr + size;
        Malloc_item[Malloc_cnt].reserved = NO;
        Malloc_item[i].size = size;
        Malloc_cnt++;
      }
      Malloc_item[i].reserved = YES;
      return(Malloc_item[i].cptr);
    }
  }
}
return(NULL);
}


/*--------------------------------------------------------------------
  Deallocate a portion of memory allocated by a call
  to e_malloc(). Also coalesce free memory into contiguous
  blocks.
  ------------------------------------------------------------------*/
t_free(ptr) char *ptr;
{
  unsigned i, j, m;
  unsigned pack_start;
  unsigned pack_offset = 0;

  for(i = 0; i < Malloc_cnt; i++) {
    if(ptr == Malloc_item[i].cptr) { /* The entry to free */
      Malloc_item[i].reserved = NO;
      if(i < MAX_MALLOC_ITEMS) { /* See if next item is unreserved */
        if(Malloc_item[i + 1].reserved == NO) { /* coalesce */
          Malloc_item[i].size += Malloc_item[i + 1].size;
          pack_start = i + 1;
          pack_offset++;
        }
      }
      if(i > 0) { /* Check is previous item is unreserved */
        if(Malloc_item[i - 1].reserved == NO) { /* Coalesce */
          Malloc_item[i].size += Malloc_item[i + 1].size;
          pack_start = i;
          pack_offset++;
        }
      }
      if(pack_offset > 0) {  /* Need to compact list */
        m = pack_start;
```

(continued)

Listing 5. *(continued)*

```
      for(m = pack_start, j = pack_start + pack_offset;
          j < Malloc_cnt - 1; m++, j++) {
        Malloc_item[m].size = Malloc_item[j].size;
        Malloc_item[m].cptr = Malloc_item[j].cptr;
        Malloc_item[m].reserved = Malloc_item[j].reserved;
      }
    }
    Malloc_cnt -= pack_offset;
    return(YES);
    }
  }
  return(NO); /* Not pointing to an area which was malloc()ed */
}


main() {
  char *ptr1;
  char *ptr2;

  ptr1 = t_malloc(124);
  ptr2 = t_malloc(64);
  t_free(ptr1);
  t_free(ptr2);
}
```

The usefulness of doing this is limited. First, the character and structure of the data portion is fixed at compile time. Second, if you were to manage several such variables, the data portion of each variable might not be contiguous. Because of this you cannot treat the collective dynamic data structures in any bulk sense. Each structure must be dealt with individually. This can be costly in terms of processing time.

In certain situations, associating physical variables with dynamic data structures is beneficial. One such situation is where an application variable is bound to either another physical variable or a dynamic data structure. In this case you can mix the use of ordinary program variable with dynamic data structures. You can then work directly with the data variable when assigning values to it and use the benefits of group management offered by dynamic data structure techniques.

Remember, dynamic data structure is a data structure that is formed and shaped from a portion of raw memory and managed by the run-time environment. In contrast, a physical data structure is a data structure that is defined at the time of compilation and is managed only during compilation. After compilation all references to the data structure are resolved and fixed. The fundamental purpose of virtual data structures is to place control, and provide well-managed control, over the raw memory available to an application at run-time. Normally this raw memory is managed indiscriminately.

5.3 SUMMARY

Static and dynamic data structures share many characteristics. Where they differ is that the layout and types of each element in a dynamic data structure can change with time and conditions while a static data structure is fixed at compilation time. This characteristic of time and environmental dependence gives rise to more versatile methods of application development.

It is almost inevitable that increased versatility is accompanied by increased complexity. This is also true with the implementation of dynamic data structures. Fortunately, this increased complexity is not overburdening and can be hidden in libraries or toolkits so that the end developer never needs to be concerned with it. In fact, with a proper implementation of the libraries or toolkits the complexity at the application level can be considerably less than with alternate approaches.

What dynamic data structures do provide that static data structures do not is well-defined control over memory that is shaped at run-time. To support dynamic data structures you need an environment that will provide control over specific configuration information, which consists of size, type, and location. This information may be defined implicitly or explicitly.

There are two methods of configuration control: encapsulation and a type database. Both of these methods may allow free or indirect access to the configuration information they contain.

POINTS TO PONDER

5.1 What are the elements of a data item that define its configuration?
5.2 (a) What combination of configuration control and method of access is most vulnerable to corruption? (b) Which is least vulnerable?
5.3 What is the most significant difference between type databases and encapsulation?
5.4 Which method of configuration control inherently has the greatest dispersion between the configuration information and the data stores?

Dynamic Adaptation | **6**

Dynamic adaptation is self-adjustment by the application to external conditions or configuration information. The adjustment performed by the application, called an "adaptive response," results in reducing some or all of the dynamic data structure into a usable type by the application. External conditions can be just about anything, such as information maintained in external files, maintained separately within the application, or communicated from application to application.

6.1 DATA INTERPRETER

Whenever you work with dynamic data structures you also must deal with dynamic adaptation. Any portion of an application that performs the task of dynamic adaptation is called a "data interpreter." In some cases the data interpreter portion may not be obvious. Take, for example, the malloc( ) and free( ) functions presented in Chapter 5. The data interpreter portion of these functions is relatively hard to distinguish. The reason is that these functions use a very specialized method of dynamic adaptation that accomplishes just the task they are to perform. The fact that dynamic adaptation exists in these functions was simply a natural consequence of the particular task; that is, one could not exist without the other.

You could allow the natural adaptive approach to take shape in all dynamic portions of your application. If you did, you would end up with a specialized method for each dynamic portion in your application. This would make things unnecessarily complex. The best way to avoid undue complexity is to develop a set of functions that will manage all your dynamic data structures. This set of functions collectively constitutes the data interpreter.

A data interpreter, like its language counterpart, translates descriptions of data into immediately usable forms. A data interpreter differs from its language counterpart only with respect to the environment in which it is used. A data interpreter is an embedded interpreter that is included in a compiled, machine-executable application.

With a data interpreter the instruction set may be fixed, but it may also be changed while an application runs. This ability to alter the instruction set is essential in some applications (as we'll see later) since you may not be able to ascertain all possible forms that a dynamic data structure is to have. If the configuration information is tokenized (compiled) so that immediate interpretation can be performed, the data interpreter is more like a hardware processor.

The instruction set for a data interpreter may be tokenized, natural-language-like, or anything in between. Regardless of the semantics of the instruction set, the design of a data interpreter involves the same concepts as the design of a language compiler or interpreter. The steps a data interpreter must go through are

1. Obtain an instruction.
2. Determine action.
3. Perform action.

These steps can be executed once, iterated as long as there is another instruction, or iterated until an instruction to stop is reached. Figure 6.1 depicts the various portions of a data interpreter.

A data interpreter can obtain an instruction in a variety of ways. One way is as arguments to a function call that invokes the interpreter for a single loop. This would result in a single action being performed according to the specific instruction. The interpretive loop may also be invoked as a result of some other action. For instance, suppose you have a block of dynamic data structures and would like a collection of program variables updated every time the block is changed (the program variables are bound to the block). In this case the interpreter loop would be called in conjunction with any call that makes a change to the block.

Typically a data interpreter is stateless. This allows the interpreter to be called in a variety of ways by different portions of the application. The dynamic data structure itself is where any state information is maintained.

The action performed by the data interpreter can be anything ranging from the creation of a new dynamic data structure, adding an element to an existing dynamic data structure, extracting a value, or assigning a value to elements in a dynamic data

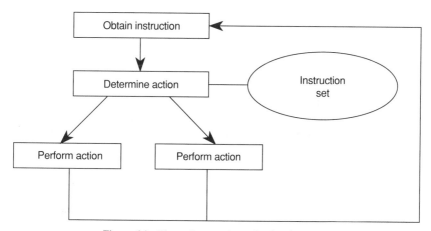

Figure 6.1 The various portions of a data interpreter.

structure. In some instances the action performed is one of translation (as we'll see in the section on binding) such as converting from one type to another. The set of actions an application may have at its disposal can vary from application to application. There is a minimum set that should be available to all applications. These are creating a dynamic data structure, assigning a value to an element, and extracting a value from an element.

6.1.1 Context Switching

Context switching is a relatively straightforward way to implement a data interpreter. With context switching the particular task that is performed is based on the object on which the task is to be performed. Context switching is common in structured programming and is essential to object-oriented programming.

With context switching the instruction set for the data interpreter is the context pool. In the simplest context switching data interpreters, this set is fixed at compile time. This is called a "closed-set context pool." However, the adaptability of an application can be greatly increased if we allow the instruction set for the data interpreter to be altered (typically expanded) at run-time. This is called "set expansion."

To implement context switching, you need some form of conditional execution. Almost all computer systems support this in hardware, so almost all programming languages support it, too. Examples are IF ... ELSE ... ENDIF constructs, calculated GOTOs in FORTRAN, and switch( )/case: constructs in C. You could use any of these constructs to implement context switching. The switch( )/case: construct reflects the ideology of context switching the closest.

A code snippet that exemplifies context switching is presented in Listing 6.1. This piece of code accepts a pointer to a dynamic data structure (of type DDS), a textual name of an element in a dynamic data structure, and a pointer to a double variable in which the element's value is returned. In this case a double type variable is all you need since it is the atomic data type of the highest resolution and all values can be represented by it without a loss of information.

The configuration information for a field, which is used in this snippet, is returned as a pointer to a structure of type CONFIG_INFO by the function element_info( ). The structure contains at least two elements. The first is **type**, which contains a token that identifies the type of the field, and **value**, which is a union that has elements for each possible type. Only element_info( ) knows whether the configuration information is encapsulated or kept in a type database. It could be implemented in either way.

The instruction set in the snippet consists of just those types identified with case statements, namely, INT, FLOAT, and DOUBLE. Since each instruction must have an associated case statement, the instruction set is closed. This results in a rigid instruction set that cannot be changed. In some applications this is quite acceptable or even preferred. In others it is not, and so techniques that allow set expansion must be used.

Listing 6.1   Snippet which exemplifies context switching.

```
element_value(dds, name, value)
DDS *dds;
char name[];
double *value;
{
    CONFIG_INFO *cinfo;

    if((cinfo = element_info(dds, name)) == NULL)
      return(ERROR);
    switch(cinfo->type) {
      case INT:
        *value = cinfo->value.ivar;
        break;
      case FLOAT:
        *value = cinfo->value.fvar;
        break;
      case DOUBLE:
        *value = cinfo->value.dvar;
        break;
    }
    return(OK);
}
```

6.1.2 Set Expansion

Set expansion is a technique that allows the application to register dynamic data structure types and associated functions at run-time. These functions are then called as necessary during execution of the application when their respective actions are needed. These functions are quite analogous to what is called a "method" in an object-oriented system, since they describe how a data abstraction can be converted into a usable item. Because these functions share many of the same properties as methods, we will use the same name when referring to set expansion functions.

The registering of methods and their subsequent use requires certain services to exist. These can be included in the application itself (probably as part of a library) or could be provided by the operating environment. In either case, there is a minimum set of services that must exist. These services are registration of a method and invocation of the method. Optional services might include deactivating a method or printing lists of currently registered methods.

The registration of a method results in a type being entered into the instruction set for the data interpreter. Once this is accomplished, the method can be used by any other portion of the application to interpret a data element of the associated type. The actual use of a method (its invocation) is accomplished by a context switch, just as with an ordinary interpreter. Where things differ is that there needs to be a way to provide context switching with a variable number of cases. This means that the conventional switch( )/case: type of context switching is inadequate because of its rigidity. Flexible context switching can be accomplished by a proper structuring of the instruction set information and effective management. One data structure that would serve to do this is

```
typedef struct _INSTRUCTION_ {
   int type;
   char *get_value( );
   char *set_value( );
   struct _INSTRUCTION_ *next;
} INSTRUCTION;
```

A set of functions that provides minimum services and data interpretation is detailed in Listing 6.2. The flexible context switching portion of this snippet is contained in the while( ) loops in the functions get_element_value( ) and set_element_value( ). Within this loop the instruction set is searched for a type token that matches that for the element in question. If a match is found, then the methods for getting a value and setting the value are also located. This is because the INSTRUCTION structure bundles all the type and method information together.

In an object-oriented language like C++, the minimum services are provided as part of the basic language. If the native services of a language are used, a simplified and more powerful interpreter can be built. As an example, let's look at how the previous code snippet might be written in C++.

In C++ the registering of a method can be accomplished by use of virtual functions in a base class. The extraction and assignment of values can then be accomplished by simply referring to the member functions of the derived class. Listing 6.3 exemplifies how this can be accomplished. Listing 6.3 contains just one class that is to be used for defining objects. It is GENERIC_DDS. This a dynamic data structure that can contain any number of elements. The get_element_value( ) and set_element_value( ) member functions could be implemented with a normal switch( )/case: type interpreter, or they can contain set expansive interpreters similar to those presented in the previous listing. Note also that these member functions lack the dynamic data structure argument found in their data structure counterparts presented in Listing 6.2. The reason is that the data they are to operate on is part of the same object the member functions are part of and a pointer to the parent object is passed by default to all member functions, so there is no need to explicitly declare the argument.

The make_element( ) is unique to the GENERIC_DDS class and allows the addition of elements to an object of this class.

The approaches presented here are just two of the many possible. For the languages they are written in they are concise and efficient. In other languages or in other applications different approaches might prove to be better.

Listing 6.2   One way to implement set expansion and flexible context switching.

```
/*---------------------------------------------------------------
 Register a type and the methods for setting and
 getting its value.
 ------------------------------------------------------------ */
register(type, get, set)
int type;
char *get();
char *set();
{
    extern INSTRUCTION *Last_in_set;

    INSTRUCTION *new;

    if((new = (INSTRUCTION *)malloc(sizeof(INSTRUCTION))
     == NULL) return(ERROR);
    new->next = NULL;      /* Sentinel */
    new->type = type;
    new->get_value = get;
    new->set_value = set;
    last_in_set->next = new;
    return(OK);
}


/*---------------------------------------------------------------
 Get the value associated with a given field name
 in a given dynamic data structure.
 ------------------------------------------------------------ */
get_element_value(dds, name, value)
DDS *dds;
char name[];
double *value;
{
  extern INSTRUCTION First_in_set;

  INSTRUCTION *current;
  char *valloc;
  int type;

  current = first_in_set;

/* Get information about element */
  if((valloc = dds_valloc_type(dds, name, &type))
```

(continued)

Listing 6.2   *(continued)*

```
      == NULL) return(ERROR);
 /* Search instruction set for methods to convert
   value */
  while(current != NULL) {
    if (type == current->type) {
      *value = current->get_value(valloc);
      return(OK);
   }
   current = current->next;
  }
  return(ERROR);
}
/*-------------------------------------------------------------
 Set the value associated with a given field name
 in a given dynamic data structure.
 -----------------------------------------------------------*/
set_element_value(dds, name, value)
DDS *dds;
char name[];
double value;
{
  extern INSTRUCTION First_in_set;

  INSTRUCTION *current;
  char *valloc;
  int type;

  current = first_in_set;

/* Get information about element */
  if((valloc = dds_valloc_type(dds, name, &type))
     == NULL) return(ERROR);

/* Search instruction set for methods to convert
   value */
  while(current != NULL) {
    if (type == current->type) {
      current->set_value(valloc, value);
      return(OK);
    }
    current = current->next;
  }
  return(ERROR);
}
```

Listing 6.3   C++ code defining an expandable class for use with dynamic data structures.

```
/* The base class for all dynamic data structures */

class BASE_DDS {
  public:
   virtual
    int get_element_value(char name[], double *value);
   virtual
    int set_element_value(char name[], double *value);
};

/* Generic field type */

typedef struct _ELEMENT_ {
    char name[MAX_NAME];
    int type;
    union {
      double dvar;
      int ivar;
      float fvar;
      } value;
    _ELEMENT_ *next;
} ELEMENT;

/* A generic and expandable dynamic data structure */
class GENERIC_DDS : BASE_DDS {
    ELEMENT elist;
  public:
      int get_element_value(char name[], double *value);
      int set_element_value(char name[], double *value);
      int make_element(char name[], int type);
};
```

6.2 VALUE REALIZATION

Value realization is the process of how values are extracted or assigned to elements within a dynamic data structure. Value realization is the interface between the dynamic data structure and the application. It is used by the data interpreter while performing actions on a dynamic data structure. The methods, used in flexible context switching, are a form of value realization. Whether standard switch( )/case: or flexible context switching is used, value realization must be employed.

There are two types of value realization: expression evaluation and binding. Both methods may be used simultaneously in an application. In some cases binding must rely on expression evaluation to realize a value.

6.2.1 Expression Evaluation

Expression evaluation is probably very familiar to you. It is the calculation of a formula or evaluation of a function, resulting in one or more new values. Type casting is also considered to be expression evaluation. The results of an expression evaluation can be used in a variety of ways. In C things such as

```
x = y * 3;
x++;
y = sin(x);
```

are "expressions," and the act of calculating the result is called "evaluation."

In expressions like those in the previous example, equality evaluation is used to make assignments to variables. An equality evaluation is performed in two steps. The first step is an evaluation of the portion of the expression on the right-hand side of the equality sign. This value is then converted to the same type as the destination value and then assigned to the destination variable. The destination variable is the variable on the left-hand side of the equality sign.

One restriction to equality evaluation is that only one value can be returned. An equality expression can indirectly return multiple values by returning a pointer to a structure. This structure can contain any number of values.

Another type of evaluation that can return any number of values is argument evaluation. Argument evaluation is where some of the arguments to a function are for returning values. The function may also have any number of input arguments. Typically the number of arguments a function may have is fixed. It is possible, especially in C, to write functions that can have a variable number of arguments.

An argument list may vary in two directions. The first is vertically. This is a common approach and is accomplished using arrays or linked lists. The first item of the list is passed as the argument to the function. The number of items in the list is indicated either by a second argument indicating how many elements are in the list or with a sentinel item placed at the end of the list.

The other direction in which an argument list can be altered is horizontally. This is a less common approach, but functions such as printf( ) use it. With horizontal expansion a function can accept one or more arguments. How many arguments a particular call of a function will have is fixed at compile time. This is more limiting than vertically variable argument lists since vertical lists can change while the application is executing. The real benefit of horizontally variable argument lists is that the arguments are not of fixed type. This allows a single function to deal with all variable types. Again printf( ) is a prime example.

In most versions of C[1] a portable, environment-independent way of dealing with variable argument lists is supported. To demonstrate how to build a variable argument list function, let's construct a function that will return a value of an element in a dynamic data structure. One way to do this is illustrated in Listing 6.4. Essentially, this is identical in functionality to the example presented in the section on context

---

[1]This is a requirement in ANSI C.

Listing 6.4 Example of a variable argument list function that returns the value of an element in a dynamic data structure.

```
/*------------------------------------------------------------
 Variable argument list function that will
 return the value of an element in a dynamic
 data structure.
 ------------------------------------------------------------*/
get_element_value(dds, name, ...)
DDS *dds;
char name[];
{
    va_list argptr;
    CONFIG_INFO *cinfo;

    va_start(argptr, name);
    if((cinfo = element_info(dds, name)) == NULL) {
      va_end(argptr);
      return(ERROR);
    }
    switch(cinfo->type) {
      case INT:
        va_arg(argptr, (int *)) = cinfo->value.ivar;
        break;
      case FLOAT:
        va_arg(argptr, (float *)) = cinfo->value.fvar;
        break;
      case DOUBLE:
        va_arg(argptr, (double *)) = cinfo->value.dvar;
        break;
    }
    va_end(argptr);
    return(OK);
}
```

switching. The only difference is that it expects the argument for assigning the value (which follows the argument: **name**) to be of the same type as the element in the dynamic data structure. This variable, which is a pointer, is assigned the value of the element without any conversion or promotion to the type of highest resolution.

This function is much more versatile then it might appear. By allowing the value argument to be of any type, you could add support for new types, as you have a need for them, without affecting existing applications. For example, you could add a string type or even newly defined types like a date or time type. Since changes such as this would not affect the entry requirements for the function, all changes would be backward-compatible.

There are a few guidelines you could follow to make expression evaluation simpler. For values returned as an evaluated expression, all numeric values should be returned as the numeric type with the most range. This value can then be type-cast into the proper type for the destination variable. Typically the compiler does this for you as part of the assignment, so you don't have to worry about it. For argument evaluation the guidelines are even simpler: Use expandable argument lists where appropriate. Following these guidelines should minimize the number of individual functions and simplify the developer's interface.

6.2.2 Binding

Expression evaluation is one method of value realization; binding is another. In the most broad term, binding is any act that results in the direct association of two or more units of information.

At the application level there are four units of information that can be bound: the name, description, and location of an object and the value that is assigned to the object. The name of an object can be the name of a variable, function, or any other application element. A description of an object includes structural and constraint-related information. For example, an integer has a specific structure and range of values it can contain. The location of an object is the physical storage location of the object's values. These four classes of information are identical to the information that a dynamic data structure must manage, so binding and dynamic data structures tend to be found in the same applications.

The process of binding can be categorized according to the classes of the items being bound. The categories are type–description, name–type (called a "declaration"), declaration–declaration, and location–value. You can find applications for each of these when you work with dynamic data structures. Almost by nature, you will always use type–description, name–type and location–value binding. These are analogous to the size, type, and location of unknown components of a dynamic data structure. These terms are not used to describe dynamic data structures because they are used to describe much broader concepts related to programming and procedural language implementation. The one category that has not yet surfaced is "declaration–declaration."

For our purposes declaration–declaration binding is defined as the association of one or more application variables so that a change in one variable affects a change in all other variables that are associated with it. It's common to refer to declaration–declaration binding as simply "variable binding" or just "binding." The same will be done from here on.

Variable Binding
Variable binding can be used to realize the values in dynamic data structures by associating an ordinary application variable with a portion of the dynamic data structure. Then whenever a value within the dynamic data structure is changed, this change is reflected in the application variable. There is no need to make a call every

time you need to extract a value from the dynamic data structure (as is true with expression evaluation). This can result in a substantial savings in execution time if the application relies heavily on dynamic data structures.

To implement variable binding all you need is some mechanism to obtain the address of a variable and some means to use this address. In C, this is directly available using pointers and the address operator (&). In other languages you may be able to obtain the address, but using it would require functions written in some other language since the implementation language may not support it.

Referential Binding   There are two ways the address of a variable can be used to implement variable binding. The first is through the use of referential variables. A referential variable is a variable that has as its value the address of another variable. The term "referential variable" is used here to distinguish it from a pointer, even though, in C, for example, a pointer could be used as a referential variable. A referential variable is actually an ordinary program variable and can be manipulated and passed as arguments to functions just like ordinary variables. What distinguishes it from an ordinary variable is that its value is interpreted in a special way.

The role a referential variable plays in variable binding is that the address of an ordinary variable is assigned to the referential variable. The ordinary variable is the base variable for the binding and is the only member of the bound variable set that contains a real-world value. When ever the real value of a referential variable is desired, it must be dereferenced. If you think this sounds a lot like the role and use of pointers in C, you're right. The reason its described in these terms is that not every language has pointers, but every language can have referential variables. To exemplify this point (and others), let's look at three ways to implement variable binding using referential variables. As the first example let's use pointers in C. Listing 6.5 contains an example of how variable binding can be accomplished using referential variable. Even though bind( ) and eval( ) are implemented as macros in this example, it is not required that this be true. The reason this was done was to demonstrate how simple variable binding using referential variables can be. It also allows the base variable to be of any type without altering the eval( ). If eval( ) were a function, there would have to an eval( ) for almost every base variable type. This would require the developer to remember a larger vocabulary. There is one benefit to this possibility: since the name of the eval( ) function could reflect the type of evaluation, the type argument could be eliminated.

Now let's explore how we can achieve the same functionality in a programming language that does not support pointers directly. The language we'll use is FORTRAN.[2] The way to implement referential pointers with FORTRAN is to employ carrier variables. A carrier variable is a variable whose value is a memory address, but in order to use the address, a function written in another language must be called. Listing 6.6 is a direct translation of the previous example into FORTRAN with carrier variables used instead. Because FORTRAN does not support pointers at the applica-

---

[2]I apologize for using FORTRAN. However, this does demonstrate why it is a language to avoid.

Listing 6.5 Example of variable binding using pointers as referential variables in C.

```
/*-------------------------------------------------------------
  REFVAR: A referential variable type.
  bind(r, b): Binds a referential variable "r" to a
             base variable "b".
  eval(r, t): Extracts the value of the base variable
             that the referential variable "r" refers
             to. The type of the base variable must be
             known and is passed in "t".
  ------------------------------------------------------------- */
#define bind(r, b)      r = (REFVAR)&b
#define eval(r, t)      (*(t *)r)
typedef char * REFVAR; /* A referential variable type */

main() {
  float base_var;
  REFVAR rvar;

  bind(rvar, base_var);

  base_var = 123.678;
  printf("Base value: %f\n", base_var);
  printf("Referential variable: %f\n", eval(rvar, float));
}
```

tion level, the implementation of bind( ) and eval( ) will have to be slightly different than in the C example. Here they will have to be actual functions, written in C. Listing 6.7 contains source for one way in which bind( ) and eval( ) may be written. These functions are written assuming Berkeley C and Berkeley FORTRAN calling conventions. This is why the functions written in C have underscores appended to the function name. This may be different in other C and/or FORTRAN implementations. Another feature of FORTRAN that is evident in these functions is its convention of passing variables as pointers.

There are a couple of noteworthy comparisons between the C and FORTRAN examples. First, in the FORTRAN example eval( ) will return numeric values only, whereas in the C example any type may be returned, even derived types. The parity of functionality could be increased if more eval( ) type functions were added to the FORTRAN example. Second, each approach is both simplistic and effective. The support functions for binding are therefore easy to maintain and readily verifiable.

Update Lists   The other approach to variable binding is the use of update lists. This approach provides greater transparency at the application level than does the use of referential variables. An update list consists of a list of types and addresses of variables that are to be assigned the value of a base variable. Commonly the base

Listing 6.6 Example of variable binding using pointers as referential variables in FORTRAN.

```
C Constants
      integer float
      parameter (float = 1)

C Function declarations
      real eval

C Interval variables
      real base_var
      integer rvar

      call bind(rvar, base_var)
      base_var = 123.456
      print *, 'Base value: ', base_var
      print *, 'Referential variable:',
    &  eval(rvar, float)
      end
```

variable's value is assigned to the variables in the update list as a related action. This action, called a "symbiotic trigger," can result from a call to change the base variable's value or as a result of performing some form of input/output (I/O). In general, a symbiotic trigger occurs in response to a change of state. So, just about any event can be used as a trigger.

The most notable aspect of update lists is that once a variable is bound, you can be assured that the variable contains the most recent value of the base variable. There is never a need for functions like eval( ) that will extract the variable's value. The value is readily available by using the native operators in the implementation language.

Step by step, this is how an update list works. First, a base variable is designated. This is usually a dynamic data structure. Then application variables are bound to all or part of the dynamic data structure. The process of binding results in the address of the application variable being placed in an update list along with the information about which part of the dynamic data structure it is bound to. Typically the variable type of the application variable is also recorded to assist in type conversions. Then each time the symbiotic trigger occurs, the update list is processed and the values of the portion of the dynamic data structure that is bound to any application variable are copied into the application variable.

Now let's look at how an update list might be implemented in C. From the list of requirements mentioned in the preceding paragraph, we can determine that we need a function to bind an application variable to a base variable. We also need an event that will serve as the symbiotic trigger. For this example we'll require that assignments to the base variable be made through a function call. The invocation of this

Listing 6.7 The bind( ) and eval( ) functions to support variable binding in FORTRAN.

```
/*------------------------------------------------------------
  BIND - Take the address of the second argument
  and assign it as the value of the first argument.
  ----------------------------------------------------------*/
bind_(rvar, basevar)
char *rvar;
char *basevar;
{
  *rvar = basevar;
  return(0);
}


/*------------------------------------------------------------
  EVAL - Return the value pointed to by the first
  argument. The type of the value is defined by the
  second argument.
*/------------------------------------------------------------
double eval_(rvar, vtype)
char *rvar;
int *type;
{
  switch(*type) {
    case FLOAT:
     return( (double)(float *)*rvar )
     break;
  }
}
```

function call will serve as the symbiotic trigger. Listing 6.8 contains source for one way to meet these requirements. This particular implementation of an update list employs an array to hold the application variable information (which is fine in some cases, as in this example). Because of this there is maximum number of application variables that can be bound to the base variable. A link list would eliminate this artificial limitation. Also, this example is limited to the binding of numeric variables.

Notice that assign( ) uses a switch/case: construct to perform the type conversion. This is fine in those situations where the set of application variable types is a closed set. If you allow an open set, then expansive set context switching should be employed (this was discussed earlier in the chapter).

It's worth noting that a "union" is one form of variable binding that employs a common addressing scheme.

Timing Two aspects of variable binding are related to when an event occurs. One event is the actual binding of the application variable to the base variable. This is

Listing 6.8 Example of how to implement an update list in C.

```
#define DOUBLE 1
#define FLOAT  2
#define INT    3

#define MAX_UPDATE_LIST 10

typedef struct {
   char *var_ptr;
   int type;
} UPDATE_LIST;

typedef struct {
   double value;
   ulist_cnt;
   UPDATE_LIST ulist[MAX_UPDATE_LIST];
} BASE_VAR;

main() {
   double dvar;
   int ivar;
   BASE_VAR basevar;

   bind_clear(&basevar);
   bind(&basevar, &dvar);
   bind(&basevar, &ivar);

   assign(&basevar, 123.456);
   printf("dvar (should be 123.456): %lf\n", dvar);
   printf("ivar (should be 123): %d\n", ivar);

   assign(&basevar, 456.123);
   printf("dvar (should be 456.123): %lf\n", dvar);
   printf("ivar (should be 456): %d\n", ivar);
}

/*------------------------------------------------------------
 Clear all bindings to a base variable. Also called
 to initialize a base variable to a known state.
 ----------------------------------------------------------*/
bind_clear(bvar)
BASE_VAR *bvar;
{
```

(continued)

Listing 6.8   *(continued)*

```
    bvar->ulist_cnt = 0;
}


/*------------------------------------------------------------
 Places the passed information in an update list.
 Returns ERROR if no more entries can be placed in
 the update list.
------------------------------------------------------------*/
bind(bvar, var_ptr, var_type)
BASE_VAR *bvar;
char *var_addr;
int var_type;
{
   if(bvar->ulist_cnt == MAX_UPDATE_LIST) {
     return(ERROR);
   }

   bvar->ulist[bvar->ulist_cnt].var_ptr = var_addr;
   bvar->ulist[bvar->ulist_cnt].type = var_type;
   bvar->ulist_cnt++;
   return(OK);
}


/*------------------------------------------------------------
 Assigns a value to a base variable.
------------------------------------------------------------*/
assign(bvar, value)
BASE_VAR *bvar;
double value;
{
   int i;

   bvar->value = value;
   for(i = 0; i < bvar->ulist_cnt; i++) {
     switch(bvar->ulist[i].type) {
       case DOUBLE:
         (*(double *)bvar.ulist[i].var_ptr) =
            bvar.value;
             break;
           case FLOAT:
             (*(float *)bvar.ulist[i].var_ptr) =
               bvar.value;
             break;
```

```
        case INT:
          (*(int *)bvar.ulist[i].var_ptr) =
             bvar.value;
          break;
      }
   }
}
```

referred to as the "bind time." The other event is the reflection of the base variable's value in all bound variables. This is referred to as the "realization time." It is important that the timing of events is considered during the development of applications.

There are two epochs in which the timing of variable binding are placed. These are called "early" and "late," with the reference time being the running of an application. Early binding is when all binding actions are performed during the compilation process. Late binding is when the binding actions are completed during the execution of the application.

All the examples presented in this section use late binding, except for the referential C example (Listing 6.5.) This is the most commonly used epoch when dealing with dynamic data structures since the actual form and interrelationship of elements in the dynamic data structure are not fully defined at compilation time.

There are situations in which early binding is used with dynamic data structures. One is when unions are used. A union, such as the native C union, is a binding of all elements of the union at compile time.

It's also possible (even though rare with dynamic data structures) to bind a referential variable at compile time. Listing 6.5 is an example of this. The reason the bind times are early in this listing is because they are macros that are evaluated in line at the time of compilation. One benefit of these macros is that the returned value of eval( ) can be of any variable type.

Realization time is divided into three epochs: instantaneous, delayed, and coaxed realization. "Instantaneous realization" is when the value of the base variable is reflected in all bound variables immediately. With instantaneous realization there is never a possibility that the value in a bound variable can be different from the base variable. A referential variable has an instantaneous realization time since all bound variables "share" the memory occupied by the base variable by pointing to it.

"Delayed realization" is when all bound variables are updated to reflect the value of the base variable sometime after the base variable's value has changed. This usually occurs in conjunction with the changing of the base variable. With delayed realization it's possible that a bound variable can have an incorrect value. This possibility exists only if the symbiotic trigger does not occur at the time the base variable is changed.[3] An update list is a method of realization that exhibits delayed realization.

[3]Also in parallel processing environments.

"Coaxed realization" is when the value of the base variable is updated as a result of a specific request. The actions performed in response to a symbiotic trigger represent a form of coaxing. At the application level coaxing is the invocation of a specific function whose sole purpose is to update all bound variables. Realization by expression exhibits coaxed timing, and so would the update routine of a symbiotic trigger if it were called independent of the trigger.

6.3 SUMMARY

Dynamic adaptation is the process of value realization of elements within a dynamic data structure. This process is performed by a data interpreter and is implemented using context switching. The context pool that supports the interpretation may be fixed or expandable. Value realization may be accomplished by either expression evaluation or binding. Each type of value realization has various approaches, each of which have different bind times.

POINTS TO PONDER

6.1   Describe what dynamic adaptation is.
6.2   Explain the role of the data interpreter.
6.3   What is the relationship between methods and value realization?
6.4   What are the various methods of variable binding, and how do they relate to one another?
6.5   Contrast expression evaluation and variable binding methods of value realization.
6.6   Describe the differences between a carrier variable and a pointer when they are used in variable binding.
6.7   What are the epoches of bind time, and to what epoch does each method of binding typically belong?
6.8   Describe which epoch of realization each realization method falls in. The realization methods are expression, referential, and update list.
6.9   Describe the effect of binding more than one application variable to a single element in a dynamic data structure. (Which value will the element have on output?)

Data Description Standards | 7

In the examples in the previous chapters a casual approach to data description was taken to facilitate the presentation of other concepts. Ordinarily you should take a more formal approach to describing dynamic data structures. There is one thing to be said of any appropriate method of data description: it should be concise, precise, and nice. Depending on the scope of the dynamic data structures you plan to use, this could be quite an undertaking.

With this in mind, you could embark on designing a data description language of your own. Before you do this, it's prudent to evaluate other preexisting methods, especially standard approaches. Throughout this chapter we'll look at some approaches that have been adopted as "standard" by ANSI as well as others that have gained enough acceptance to be considered standards of one form or another.

7.1 C STRUCTURES

The syntax for defining C structures is probably the most widely used standard (ANSI) for structured data descriptions. All except the most novice C programmers know what a C structure is and how to use it. C structure definitions are also easy to read, use, and define. A grammatical definition of C structures can be found in Listing 7.1. There are several benefits to using the same syntax that is used to describe C structures for describing the form of dynamic data structures. First, you can describe the data in a form that is a natural extension of the implementation language (that is, if you program in C). Second, you will have an almost direct means of converting any dynamic data structure into a data structure with a static form. And third, most developers are already quite familiar with C structure syntax and capabilities.

Given so many good reasons why would you choose any other approach? The answer lies in the limitations of C structure definitions. That is, they don't provide all the information you need, for instance, textual descriptions of the data item or other notational items. You could provide a means to do this by requiring a comment block after each variable definition (preferably in-line with the declaration), but this can make the declaration look cluttered and reduce the readability.

Listing 7.1 Grammar definitions for a C-style structure.

```
Terminal Symbols:


NAME       := A series of alphanumeric characters, the
              first character of the name must be
              alphabetic.


Non-terminal Symbols:


struct_specifier : 'struct' '{' struct_dec_list '}'
                 | 'struct' NAME '{' struct_dec_list '}'
                 | 'struct' NAME
struct_dec_list  : declaration
                 | declaration struct_dec_list
declaration      : type name_list ';'
name_list        : NAME
                 | NAME ',' name_list
type             : 'char'
                 | 'short'
                 | 'int'
                 | 'long'
                 | 'unsigned'
                 | 'float'
                 | 'double'
                 | struct_specifier
```

7.2 FLATTENED-FORMAT DESCRIPTORS

Flattened-format descriptors strive to provide sufficient data documentation while pursuing C's minimalist style for data description. This type of data description method is used in most relational database management systems (DBMSs) to describe the tables (or relations) of data maintained in the system. It has also been used for documenting the structure of data sets in various "home brewed" data management and analysis systems. The UCLA/IGPP Data Flow System (DFS) is one such system.

To further exemplify what flattened-format descriptors are, we'll look at the Data Flow Systems approach in more detail. The specification for the DFS flattened-format descriptor is depicted in Figure 7.1. As you can see in Figure 7.1, each field in an item definition is fixed in length. This provides for rapid parsing of the definitions. Another feature is that the length of a single definition is less than 80 characters. This is intentional so that the definitions can be easily viewed on screen and easily worked with in an editor.

An individual
field descriptor:

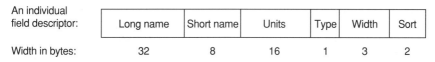

Width in bytes: 32 8 16 1 3 2

Figure 7.1 Representation of the Data Flow Systems' flattened-format descriptor.

The purpose of each field in a flattened-format descriptor is as follows:

Long name A name for the item that is as descriptive as possible. This field is used to document exactly what the item is.

Short name A terse name which is used as a handle for extracting the data item. Typically the user specifies this name in all interactions.

Units Provided to further describe the contents of the field; also used when labeling graphs or other forms of output.

Type A single-letter code for the data type of the item. The types are limited to those listed in Table 7.1.

Width The size of the field in bytes. This is used to calculate the location of each field in the data record.

Sort The order in which data fields have been sorted. This is used to optimize searches and retrieval of data records. A value of 0 means that the field has not been sorted.

The last two fields in this definition (width and sort) are considered "system" fields and are modified and defined by applications that create the data set. This control is necessary because the accuracy of the "width" field is crucial to locating the actual data item.

When a data set is stored in a disk file by the Data Flow System, two more flat meta–data files are created. The first is called an "abstract file." In this file is simple text that consists of any number of lines. The text in the file usually contains detailed descriptions of the data set, such as where the data originated from. It may also include processing histories of the data set and any other information that might be useful for future users of the data set. The second meta–data file is called a "header file." This file is similar to the descriptor file in that it contains fixed fields. Within

Table 7.1 Letter Codes and Their C Equivalents

Code	C equivalent
I	int
R	float
D	double
T	double
A	char

the fields is information such as the number of records in the data set, the number of columns (which can also be determined by counting the number of descriptors), as well as the date when the data set was created and other bits of information.

One of the major benefits of using flattened-format descriptors is that they can readily migrate from DBMS to DBMS, without any change in the basic definition style. This is due to its tabular nature and the limitations that one data item is defined with each line of the definition. This tabular nature also makes them easy to read by humans (people like you and me).

There are other variations of this particular style of data description. One variation of this form is used by the Planetary Plasma Interactions Node of the Planetary Data System (NASA), and another is used by the Atmospheres Node, also of the Planetary Data System. In each variation, as well as all others, the basic approach remains the same: namely, flat descriptors with homogeneous structure. Where they differ is in the extent of information that is required.

You should feel free to define your own flattened-format structure definition. One thing to keep in mind is the word "flattened," that is, two-dimensional. If you fail to do this, you will be reducing the portability of the definition among data management systems.

7.3 OBJECT DEFINITION LANGUAGE

SPIDS, which is an acronym for Standards for the Preparation and Interchange of Data Sets, is a collection of specifications and recommendations for documenting and storing data sets so that they can be readily utilized by others. It was developed under the auspices of the Planetary Data System [a NASA-funded project administered by Jet Propulsion Laboratory (JPL)].

One aspect of SPIDS that is useful in relation to dynamic data structures is its Object Definition Language (ODL). This language was developed to provide high-level descriptions of the structure of data sets and can be used to describe anything from a simple text file to digital images to complex multidimensional data. For all its capability, the syntactic specifications for ODL can be described with the grammar definitions in Listing 7.2. Basically all this lexicographical magic means is that an object is defined with a series of keyword–value pairs with the keyword and value separated by an equality sign (this = that, for example), and the value may optionally be followed by a units specification. Values can be anything including integers specified in any radix, literals, strings, floating-point numbers, dates and/or times, or an array of any combination of these.

An object definition begins with the keyword of "OBJECT" and the value associated with it is the class name for the object. Between this "OBJECT" statement, until there is a matching "ENDOBJECT" statement, is a series of statements (keyword–value pairs) that define the structure of the object. Objects may also be defined

Listing 7.2   Grammar definitions for the Object Definition Language.

```
Terminal Symbol:


DIGIT                  := The numbers 0-9.
LETTER                 := The letters A-Z and a-z
PRINTABLE              := Any printing ASCII character plus
                          tab, but not a LETTER or DIGIT.
SEPERATOR              := space, tab, comma


Non-terminal Symbols (Lexical elements):


alphanum               : DIGIT
                       | LETTER
character              : alphanum
                       | PRINTABLE
word                   : letter
                       | word alphanum
name                   : word
                       | name word
text                   : character
                       | text character
integer                : sign unsigned_integer
unsigned_integer       : DIGIT
                       | integer DIGIT
extended_integer       : alphanum
                       | extended_integer alphanum
real                   : unscaled_real | scaled_real
unscaled_real          : integer '.' unsigned_integer
                       | sign '.' unsigned_integer
scaled_real            : unscaled_real
                       | unscaled_real 'E' integer
                       | unscaled_real 'e' integer
date                   : year_doy
                       | year_month_day
min_sec                : unsigned_integer
                       | unsigned_intger '.' unsigned_integer
time                   : min_sec
                       | unsigned_integer ':' min_sec
                       | unsigned_integer ':' unsigned_integer
                       ':' min_sec
date_time              : date '-' time
year_doy               : year '/' doy
```

(continued)

Listing 7.2   *(continued)*

```
year_month_day       : year '/' month '/' day
year                 : unsigned_integer
month                : unsigned_integer
day                  : unsigned_integer
day                  : unsigned_integer
sign                 : '+'
                     | '-'


Non-terminal Symbols (Syntactic Elements):

statement            : structural
                     | value_assignment
                     | pointer
structural           : object
                     | endobject
                     | end
object               : 'OBJECT' '=' name
endobject            : 'ENDOBJECT'
end                  : 'END'
value_assignment     : name '=' value
value                : integer_value
                     |real_value
                     | date_time_value
                     | literal_value
                     | text_string
                     | value_list
integer_value        : integer
                     | integer units_expression
                     | radix '#' extended_integer
radix                : unsigned_integer
real_value           : real
                     | real units_expression
date_time_value      : date_time '<' time_units '>'
literal_value        : name
                     | ''' text '''
text_string          : '"' text '"'
value_list           : '(' v_list ')'
v_list               : value
                     | v_list SEPERATOR value
units_expression     : '<' units_definition '>'
units_definition     : units
                     | units_definition units_operator units
```

```
units               :  name
units_operator      :  '*'
                    |  '/'
                    |  '^'
time_units          :  'UTC'
                    |  'GMT'
                    |  'PST'
                    |  'MST'
                    |  'CST'
                    |  'EST'
                    |  'PDT'
                    |  'MDT'
                    |  'CDT'
                    |  'EDT'
pointer             :  '^' name '=' pointer_value
pointer_value       :  unsigned_integer
                    |  text_string
```

as being part of other objects. This can be done either in-line between another "OBJECT"/"ENDOBJECT" pair or by referencing another object by name (with a "CLASS" keyword).

An object description without an enclosing OBJECT/ENDOBJECT pair is considered the master object and is used as the highest-level description of the data set. Typically this object is the first one defined in the set of descriptions. This is analogous to the **main**( ) function in C with all delineated objects being analogous to all other functions.

The end of all the object definitions is marked with an "END" statement. The actual data set that is described can be included in the same file (or stream) as the object definitions and must begin immediately after the END statement. The data set can also be maintained in a distinct and separate location from its description. If this is done, there must be a "TABLE_POINTER" statement defining the name of the file that holds the data set.

The usefulness of the SPIDS Object Definition Language is hinged on having a closed set of keywords. SPIDS uses keywords to set the context of how the value assigned to it will be interpreted. It therefore follows that a keyword may restrict the kinds of values that may be assigned to it. PDS has defined a set of keywords it uses; the most common are listed in Table 7.2. There are many more keywords defined as part the SPIDS application of the Object Definition Language. The most numerous groups are related to the specification of image-based data sets.

As always (since you are an analyst and developer), to define any set of keywords, the important point is that it should be standardized and everyone who intends to share data defined with the Object Definition Language should use the same set.

Table 7.2   Some of the Most Commonly Used Keywords of the Object Definition Language

Keyword	Interpretation of its value
FILE_TYPE	A description of the overall characteristics of the data file; allowed values are TEXT, TABLE, IMAGE, CUBE and QUBE
TABLE_TYPE	A description of how the data is stored; allowed values are ASCII and BINARY
RECORD_TYPE	A description of the method in which records are stored; it can be STREAM or FIXED_LENGTH
RECORD_BYTES	A count of the number of bytes in a record
TABLE_ROWS	A count of the number of entries or records in the data table
ROW_COLUMNS	The number of individual items or fields in a single row
COLUMN_NAME	A list of names, one per field in data record; the number of names should match the value assigned to ROW_COLUMNS
COLUMN_TYPE	A list of data types, one per field in the data record; allowed types are INTEGER, REAL, DOUBLE, LITERAL, STRING, and TIME
FILE_NOTE	A textual description of the contents of the file
TABLE_POINTER	The name of the file that contains the actual data

7.4 SFDU

An SFDU, which is an acronym for Standard Formatted Data Unit, is a method of data encapsulation that can be used to identify general properties of data items. It was designed by the Consultative Committee for Space Data Systems (CCSDS), which consisted of members from the following space agencies: Centre National D'Etudes Spaciales (CNES) of France; Deutsche Forschungs-u. Versuchsanstalt fuer Luft und Raumfahrt e.V (DFVLR) of Germany; European Space Agency (ESA) of Europe, Indian Space Research Organization (ISRO) of India; Instituto de Pesquisas Especiais (INPE) of Brazil; National Aeronautics and Space Administration (NASA) of the United States; and National Space Development Agency (NASDA) of Japan. Even though the SFDU specification is not a standard approved by any international standards organizations, it can be considered an international standard among space agencies.

The structure of an SFDU is depicted in Figure 7.2. Basically an SFDU consists of a fixed-length label that contains coded information about the Control Authority, which has jurisdiction of the formats that describe the data contained in the SFDU, a version ID for the version of the SFDU employed, a class ID that provides a high-level description of the SFDU contents, and a data description package identifier. There is also an area reserved for future use.

The effectiveness of the SFDU methodology lies in the concept of a Control Authority. The Control Authority is an entity that assigns format identifiers and maintains the definitions of the formats for which the identifiers refer to. Control Authorities are established in a hierarchical sense; that is, there is one main Control Authority that gives other groups the authority to establish their own data definition package identifiers (DDPI). In turn, this group can give authority to other groups to define DDPI under their control authority ID.

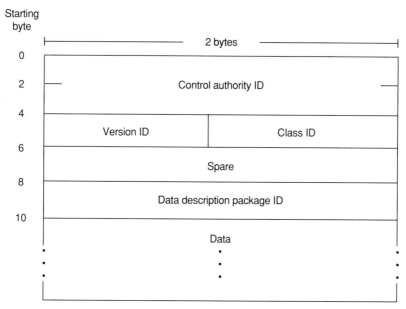

Figure 7.2   The structure of a Standard Formatted Data Unit (SFDU).

SFDUs can be used in one of two ways. The first method is by "envelope" and the other is by "marker." With the envelope method you must know the length of the entire SFDU before the SFDU label is written. With the marker method the data is contained in a series of SFDUs beginning with a main SFDU and ending with a special marker SFDU. The main SFDU, the marker SFDU, and the intervening data SFDUs are distinguished from one another by their respective DDID. It is the DDID in the main SFDU that identifies whether the aggregate SFDU is an envelope type or a marker type.

One drawback to the use of the SFDU methodology is that there is a tendency to describe the entire format of a data set with a single DDPI. This would be analogous to defining a data type for each type of data set you will deal with. This is a very high-level abstraction and leads to situations in which the structure of all possible data sets an application might deal with is hard-coded into the application. This is in contrast with the C structure definition, flattened-format descriptors and the object definition language methodologies, which define a data set's structure as a collection of atomic data types.

7.5 ANSI X12

The problem of moving data from one system to another has been an issue that many groups have had to deal with. In order to address this issue an ANSI committee was formed to develop a standard method of describing data and the methods of inter-change. This committee is called the Electronic Business Data Interchange[2] (EBDI) committee, or Accredited Standards Committee X12. There are several subcom-mittees of X12. The one which relates most closely with the topic is this book is Subcommittee C. This subcommittee is charged with communication and control structure standards.

ANSI X12.6-1986 [X12.6] details a formal method for the description of data. This standard identifies a "data element" as the smallest named item. A data element can be represented as a value, text, or qualifier. A data element has two attributes: length and type. (For dynamic data structures, location is also an attribute; see Chapter 3.) The length of a data element is specified as a range, that is, a minimum and a maximum. If the minimum and maximum are the same, the data element is fixed in length; if they differ, the data element is variable in length. The type of a data element can be one of the following: numeric, decimal, identifier, string, date, or time. Each type has a specific symbol that is used to represent it. These are presented in Table 7.3. A numeric data type is a fixed decimal-point number where the value of n (included in its symbol name) specifies the number of decimal places to the right of the decimal point. The decimal point is not included in the representation of the data value. A decimal data type is similar to a numeric. Where they differ is that with a decimal data type the decimal point is embedded in the representation of the data value and is optional when integer values are represented. Both numeric and decimal types may have an optional + or − sign. The absence of a sign is the same as having a plus sign precede the number. The presence of a plus sign, minus sign, or decimal point does not count against the maximum length of the data element. (Why? I don't know.)

An identifier data type is a special data class in which the allowed value of the data element is chosen from a predefined list and can be composed of a sequence of letters, digits, special characters, or spaces.

A string data type has a value that is composed of a sequence of any printable characters other then those reserved as separator characters.[3]

There are two remaining data types: date and time. The value contained in either of these data types must adhere to the ISO standard formats. For dates this is YYMMDD, where YY is the last two digits of the year, MM is the month number (1 to 12), and DD is the day. For times the format is HHMM, with HH representing the hour in a 24-hour cycle and MM the minutes.

The X12.6 standard also defines higher-level abstractions to aid in the description of data. These abstractions are built up with data elements. The first three of these abstraction are the element group, the data segment, and the transaction set. The

---

[2]Don't let the words "Business Data" in the committee's name lead you to believe that the standards that were generated can be applied only in the business world. It just so happens that a bunch of business types took the lead.

[3]The X12.6 standard states that delimiters (terminators and separators) are part of a standard now being developed.

Table 7.3   Symbols Used to Specify a Data Element's Type

Type	Symbol
Numeric	Nn
Decimal	R
Identifier	ID
String	AN
Date	DT
Time	TM

interrelationship between these abstractions and data elements is depicted in Figure 7.3.

In simple terms, an element group begins with a group separator, an optional element qualifier (which is an element ID extracted from the Data Element Dictionary, discussed later) and a unit separator, and then one or more data elements delimited with unit separators. A unit of measure ID (also found in the Data Element Dictionary) can optionally follow the last data element, and a descriptive string may optionally follow the unit of measure ID. Both the unit of measure ID and the descriptive string are delimited by preceding them with a unit separator.

A data segment consists of a segment ID (which can be found in the Data Segment Dictionary), one or more group elements, and a terminator.

A transaction set is a collection of data segments, some with special meanings and

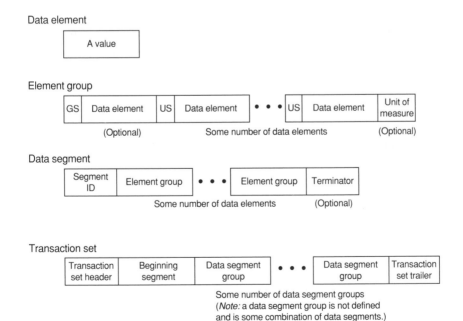

Figure 7.3   Interrelationship between the ANSI X12.6 abstractions for data descriptions.

applications. It begins with a transaction set header, followed by what is called a "beginning segment," followed by one or more data segment groups and ending with a transaction set trailer. What we've discussed so far is sufficient for using the ANSI X12.6 approach for describing dynamic data structures. The actual ANSI X12.6 standard has specifications for higher-level packaging of data, as well as complex repeating and looping data element group definitions. You should read the actual X12.6 standard if you are interested in more details.

The ANSI X12.6 standard also specifies that all data, including any packaging information (e.g., segment ID) are represented as American Standard Code for Information Interchange (ASCII) characters selected from the uppercase characters, numbers, and a few special characters (punctuating and arithmetic). If you wish to use lowercase letters and other special characters (angle, square, and curly braces for example) in your data, you can do so only if the receiver of the data agrees to accept them. If you communicate only with yourself, this should be an easily obtained agreement. The only other allowed characters are the delimiters. The actual characters to use for delimiters are set in the interchange control header (not discussed here.) By convention, the characters used are the new line for the terminator and the asterisk (*) for the data element separator. The remaining delimiter, the unit separator, is seldom used, and there is no convention (as near as I can tell). The reason seams to be that the standard data dictionary (ANSI X12.22 [X12,22]) defines all segments so that data elements are positional rather than delimited.

There are two companion standards to ANSI X12.6 that are essential. The first is ANSI X12.3 [X12.3], which defines a Data Element Dictionary. Each element in the dictionary is assigned a unique ID number. These ID numbers are used in element group specifications to define what is contained in the element group's data elements. An element's definition consists of a length specification (minimum and maximum), a type, and a brief description, as discussed earlier in this section. Specific groups and organizations have the responsibility of maintaining groups of element definitions, so ANSI X12.6 will be reissued as changes are made.

The other companion standard is ANSI X12.22. This is the Data Segment Dictionary. This document defines various data segments that are commonly used in the business world.

The ANSI X12.6 standard might be easier to understand if you think of a Data Element Dictionary ID as a type declaration, a data element as a specific variable, and a data segment as a structure.

7.6 COMPARISONS

Each data description approach presented in this chapter has unique features that distinguish it from the others, but there are also many similarities between the approaches. For example, the C structure, flattened data descriptor, and the object description language are all self-contained methods of describing data. All the information you need to understand the structure and type of the data is contained in its description. This is contrasted with the SFDU and ANSI X12.6 approaches, where you must have either a Data Description Package Dictionary for an SFDU or a Data Element Dictionary when you use an ANSI X12.6 approach.

Another general feature of data description approaches is how intermingled the data and its descriptions are. With the SFDU and ANSI X12.6 approaches the data is intermingled with the description itself, whereas with the C structure, the flattened data description, and the object description language the data is maintained in a distinct form, separate from the description.

So, what approach should you use? Well, that depends on the actual application. The C structure, flattened-format descriptors, and object definition language are very efficient, in terms of both processing time and volume of descriptive information, in situations where moderate to large amounts of data with the same structure or form are processed. In such situations descriptions are sent ahead of the data itself. If you have situations where the form of the data changes rapidly, it might be better to use the SFDU or the ANSI X12.6 approach since these utilize self-contained data packets. Of course, the same can be accomplished with any other approach simply by requiring a data description followed by one data item.

There is one major detractor with the SFDU and the ANSI X12.6 approaches: you must have some external information in order to interpret the description, in particular, the Data Description Package Dictionary for an SFDU and the Data Element Dictionary for an ANSI X12.6 description. The requirements for these dictionaries arise out of the desire to make the data descriptions as compact as possible. What this means to you is that you have to worry about having a current dictionary. The ANSI X12.6 and SFDU approaches have dealt with this by developing standard dictionaries. In those applications I've seen that use one of these approaches I've found that the dictionaries (actually a small subset) are hard-coded into the application. This severely limits the dynamic capabilities of the application.

7.7 SUMMARY

Adopting a standard approach to data description can be a very beneficial choice. One reason is that it provides a means to describe data in unambiguous terms. Another reason is that it broadens the pool of expertise from which you can draw on. This is especially true if others outside your group or company adopt the same standard. Yet another reason is that if you use a standard approach, you should be able to transmit your data to other people, groups, or applications and your data can be read and understood. There are other reasons, but they become increasingly altruistic. Regardless of the reasons, if you use dynamic data structures you must have some means of describing the data's structure in order to access it and use it within any application you develop. Additional information on building translators can be found in [Cal79] and [Els73].

POINTS TO PONDER

7.1 What purpose does data description serve for dynamic data structures?

7.2 Describe as many data description characteristics of each approach presented in this chapter as you can. This should include C structure definitions, flattened-format descriptors, the object definition language, the standard format data unit (SFDU), and the ANSI X12.6 standard.

7.3 Which approach would be best if the data you typically deal with is two-dimensional? Diverse in structure? In small discrete samples?

7.4 Which approaches are self-contained, and which require external references in order to fully resolve data descriptions?

A Software Engineering *8*
Perspective

There are many approaches to software engineering, and each typically focuses on a particular aspect of the development process. Some focus on the transactions involved, or the transformations that are to be performed, while other approaches focus on the data that must be dealt with. Each approach has its own set of merits, and no single approach can apply to all projects.[1]

Typically projects are initiated to solve a particular need, but a project whose scope is too broad may result in an unviable project, as a result of either excessive cost or deadline limitations. In some cases you can make the project viable by limiting or scaling back its scope, but this could result in an application that falls short of what is actually needed. A more preferable solution is not to scale back the scope, but find other ways to make the project viable. One way is to use dynamic data structures, and in this chapter we'll look at why this is so.

Since this book's focus is on dynamic data structures, we'll concentrate mainly on data-oriented approaches to software engineering. There are several formal data-oriented approaches to software engineering, such as the "Warnier–Orr approach" (more generically called "data structured systems development"), the "Jackson system development methodology," a technique called "logical construction of software," and object-oriented design (which is a mix of data and procedural definitions). Each of these approaches have distinct features that make them worthy of study. I won't describe any of these in detail since the specifics of each approach are better left to books and papers dedicated to the topic.

8.1 PROJECT PLANNING

Every project, small or large, begins with planning. This can be formal or informal, but nevertheless it occurs. During a project's planning phase there are many decisions to be made, and these decisions can have a large influence on the viability of the project as a whole. Aside from the basic functionality of an application, there are decisions to be made that relate to the hardware platform the system will run on, the human considerations (interface, syntax, etc.), and database considerations.

Following these decisions you must decide on issues related to the actual imple-

---

[1] I know of some salespeople who will disagree.

mentation, such as the implementation language, implementation approaches (like using dynamic data structures), what preexisting software will be used (libraries, etc.), and which development tools to use. These decisions, and others as well, affect several aspects related to the project. These aspects include the size, complexity, degree of structure, and maintainability of the resulting application. Since these decisions occur early in the project and are sometimes difficult to change, we'll look at just how dynamic data structures can and do influence these aspects.

8.1.1 Size

In some respects the most controllable portion of an application is its size. This is due mainly to the fact that most applications must maintain information (data) as part of its functionality. When you deal with database considerations, you are confronted with issues such as memory limitations, the extent of which data types will be handled, interdependence among data items, and the association between data items. These issues form a powerful combination that influence other aspects of an application's implementations.

This can be significant especially in relation to database issues. One measure of size is the shear volume of an application—that is, how large it is as measured in bytes. For example, an application that can deal with a maximum of 10 tuples of information will have a size that is measurably larger than if the maximum number of tuples were 5. In some cases this could be significant enough to limit the application's usefulness.

The count of the number of lines of code in an application is another measure of an application's size. In a rather crude fashion the count of the lines of code measures the manageability of a project. I think very few people would disagree that a 10-line application is more manageable than a 1000-line application, provided both are written with a similar coding structure.[2]

Dynamic data structures can contribute to a reduction in the size of a project, if applied properly. Rather than try and prove this with words, let's look at an example. In this situation, we have a spacecraft that is orbiting the earth. From this spacecraft we obtain some measurements, say, its velocity. From a ground-based source we also obtain the position of the spacecraft. The requirements for the system are to be able to view each set of data individually and also aggregately. A conventional approach of using ordinary data structures is presented in Listing 8.1. A dynamic data structure approach to the same problem is presented in Listing 8.2. The metrics for each approach is presented in Table 8.1.

Overall these metrics reveal that the dynamic data structure approach should result in a significant reduction in the size of the application. This reduction does not sacrifice any functionality. In fact, the dynamic data structure approach is more

---

[2]Any 1000-line C program could be made into a 10-line C program by removing 990 new lines. Doing this would not be considered good coding structure. Besides, what would your mother think of you if you did?

Listing 8.1   Conventional approach to spacecraft problem.

```
typedef struct {
  TIME tick;
  SPEED velocity;
} MOVEMENT;

typedef struct {
  TIME tick;
  LOCATION location;
} POSITION;

/* A simple program to display the data in all
   required fashions.
*/
main()
{
  POSITION p_data;
  MOVEMENT m_data;

  while(read_movement(&m_data)) {
    display_movement(&m_data);
  }

  while(read_position(&p_data)) {
   display_position(&p_data);
  }

  while(read_movement(&m_data) && read_position(&p_data)) {
   display_pos_move(&m_data, &p_data);
  }
}
```

functional since it can handle a wider variety of data structures. Overall, this reduction in size translates into easier maintenance and reduced development costs.

This, of course, is my opinion. In order for you to make your own decisions, I'll detail the rationale behind each metric. First, the size of the resulting object files is a measure of the shear volume of the application. The reason the size of object files, and not the executable images, is measured is that once an application is rendered executable, it includes all portions of system libraries it needs. These can be considerable in size and obscure the measure of that portion of the application you actually wrote.

Another source of shear volume not included in the object file size metric is the size of nonstandard functions that each example expects, for instance, **make_dds( )**

Listing 8.2 Dynamic data structure approach to spacecraft problem.

```
#include <dds.h>

main()
{
  DDS *p_data;
  DDS *m_data;

  p_data = make_dds(DDS_POSITION, ITEM_TIME, ITEM_LOCATION,
          ITEM_END);
  m_data = make_dds(DDS_MOVEMENT, ITEM_TIME, ITEM_SPEED,
          ITEM_END);

  while(read_dds(m_data)) {
    display_dds(m_data, NULL);
  }

  while(read_dds(p_data)) {
    display_dds(p_data, NULL);
  }

  while(read_dds(m_data) && read_dds(p_data)) {
    display_dds(m_data, p_data, NULL);
  }
}
```

in the dynamic data structure example and **read_movement**( ) in the conventional example. Since the functions expected in the dynamic data structure are generic, they would probably be part of a system-wide library. If this is true, then they should be considered in the same fashion as standard libraries are considered. That is, their contributions to the application size should not be included in the shear volume measurements. The same should be true for the conventional example. However, since the functions the conventional example expects are highly specialized, they probably would not be part of some system-wide library, and therefore their contributions to the shear size of the application should be included in the measure of the application's shear size. If this were done it would make the size reduction due to using dynamic data structures even greater.

The next metric in the table is the count of the number of lines of code. For the lines of code metric the include file (dds.h) required by the dynamic data structure example is not counted. The reasons for not doing so are analogous to the reasons why the contributions of system libraries are not included in the object size metric; that is, it is presumed that this is a system-wide include file and therefore not authored by the developer of the example.

Table 8.1 Chart of the Metrics for a Conventional and a
Dynamic Data Structure Approach to a Specific Problem

	Approach	
Metric	DDS	Conventional
Size of object file	644	733
Lines of code	23	29
Number of functions	3	5

Finally, a function count metric is included in the table. A function count does not measure the size of an application; it is more a measure of an application's complexity. The topic of complexity will be discussed in the next section. The metric is included in this table for easy comparison of all metrics.

It's quite possible to devise situations where a dynamic data structure approach would result in an increase in the project's size. In such situations you should use whatever approach minimizes the size unless a unified approach to all development is foremost important. You should never consider a single approach to be the only approach in all situations.

8.1.2 Complexity

Complexity is often difficult to quantize because it depends on the expertise and past experiences of the developer and the tools and libraries that are available. Complexity is a measure of the convolution of the control flow or control path, the number of operations that are performed (function calls, arithmetic, . . .), and the number of operands (variables) that exist. Typically the greater the measure of any one of these items, the greater the complexity of an application. The greater the complexity, the more difficult it is to thoroughly test an application and maintain it.

It seems that the basic requirements imposed on today's applications (windowing interfaces and broad utility) force an application to be far more complex than can be easily dealt with. This is one of the reasons why computer-aided software engineering (CASE) exists. A good set of CASE tools can greatly reduce the burden on a developer with regard to managing a complex application. CASE tools can also help guide the developer in the creation of well-structured, easily maintained applications. Even so, an application should be kept as simple as possible.

Dynamic data structures can help to reduce the complexity of an application and thereby make an application easier to deal with. The truth in this statement can be seen by looking at the examples presented in Section 8.1.1. By counting the number of individual functions we can get a comparative measure of the complexity of the two examples. As shown in Table 8.1, the dynamic data structure example is less complex then the conventional example since it requires fewer functions to do the same task.

Another aspect of an application that can contribute to its complexity is the extent or repertoire of data types the application must deal with. Closely related to this is how easily new data types can be integrated into the application. In some conventional languages (like FORTRAN or BASIC) this is not an issue since you cannot create new data types. In languages like C it is a real issue. This same issue arises when you use dynamic data structures since you are free to define any data types you like, regardless of what language you implement in. This issue typically becomes important during a project's maintenance phase, rather than during its planning phase, and is also important during prototyping activities. The reason it should be considered during the planning phase is that if a project is planned properly, you can minimize certain aspects of the application's maintenance. Again the examples in Section 8.1.1 exemplify this. If we were to add another type of data set to the requirements it would be simpler and less time-consuming to extend the dynamic data structure version than to extend the more conventional version.

Other aspects of an application that bear on its complexity are the interdependence and associativity between data items. In Chapter 4 we looked at how associativity between application variables and elements of a dynamic data structure could be established. In the most recommended techniques (variable binding), functions are used to establish this associativity. This is a prudent approach from a software engineering perspective since it provides a mechanism for accountability, consistency, and structured control. Without this it could be difficult to assure yourself that data integrity is fully maintained.

8.1.3 Degree of Structure

The degree of structure in an application—that is, the measure of how easy the application's task can be divided into discrete functions and how well the information that the application must deal with can be organized—also contributes to the project's viability and its future maintainability. It has been found through practice that what you should seek in an application's design is a hierarchical structure with minimal breadth, that is, with the least number of fundamental (atomic) functions. You should also strive to hide as much information from the developer as is reasonable.[3] Data hiding typically reduces the degree of structure with regard to the data domain of the application while minimizing the functional breadth, hence simplifying the application's functional domain. Dynamic data structures can help to reduce the complexity of both of these domains and is worthy of more detailed discussion.

Functional Structure

Determining a good functional structure for an application begins with the division of a goal into functional domains. These domains then become actual functions or procedures in your application. Ideally domains are included in other domains in a fashion so that the net functionality in any domain is simply an augmentation or a

---

[3]People who pay income tax usually take this point of view with the IRS.

combination of other domains or just a single domain. Also, there should be a minimum set of domains that are included in all other domains.

A good example of a such a function set is the standard I/O functions in C. At the lowest level are the functions **read( )** and **write( )**, which read and write one or more bytes from a source that is specified as an integer number (a file descriptor). Layered on top of these calls are other, more powerful functions. On the **write( )** side of the family tree are **putc( )**, then **printf( )**, and **fwrite( )**. A similar lineage exists on the **read( )** side.

Dynamic data structures provide a similar minimalistic foundation for effective dynamic memory management. The various approaches to implementing dynamic data structures (discussed in the previous chapters) is hierarchical, beginning with simple, basic elements and building up to complex operations. So, from both a practical and software engineering perspective the use of dynamic data structures provides a proper basis for good applications.

Data Hiding

In general, the more information that can be hidden (concealed from, but useful to or used by the developer), the better. C's standard I/O functions are again a good example. When you make a call to **fopen( )**, it returns a pointer, called a "file pointer," and you use this file pointer in all references to the file. This file pointer actually has associated with it a "buffer," information about the current location in the file, and other things. As a developer you never need to concern yourself directly with this information. In addition, access to this information is made through other function calls [e.g., **ftell( )**, **ungetc( )**]. This data hiding makes working with files not only easier, but more efficient.

Dynamic data structures provide a similar kind of data hiding for working with and managing raw memory. With dynamic data structures you can create data structures at run-time and specify their configuration at a very high level. The actual storage location and all the configuration information can be hidden from the developer, thus simplifying the task of effective memory utilitization.

8.1.4 Miscellaneous Contributions

There are a few areas where the development costs of a project are affected favorably by using dynamic data structures. The first is that data definitions are at the procedural or functional level. This allows for the preservation of configuration and type information even if the implementation language does not support this. In turn, this allows for more powerful libraries to be constructed that are even more generic than would otherwise be possible. The function display_dds( ) in Listing 8.2 (Section 8.1.1) is a good example. Since functions like display_dds( ) are so generic, they should be readily usable in a variety of applications, therefore spreading the development costs of the libraries over the various projects and reducing the individual cost of each project.

Other areas where dynamic data structures make constructive contributions is that they can reduce function count without reducing the functionality. In most cases the functionality is actually increased. This is a developer's heaven since it makes for a simpler application that is easier to manage and understand. In turn, this reduction of the number of functions results in a reduction in the lines of code. This, too, makes managing an applications easier.

8.2 APPLICATION DESIGN

Following the planning phase of a project, you enter into the design phase. It is during this phase that certain aspects related to the extent of use and character of dynamic data structures are decided. Specifically, these are

- Definition syntax
- Representation of dynamic data structures
- Realization methods
- The data types that will be supported in the dynamic data structures

Each of these topics where discussed in detail in previous chapters. You should refer to those chapters for a thorough understanding of the choices that are available and the merits of each choice.

In addition to the merits mentioned in the previous chapters, there is the issue of reusability. As you design an application you should keep in mind that your functions or procedures should be reusable. This same design goal should also extend to the data structures used in an application; that is, can they serve a useful purpose in more than one place. Dynamic data structures provide the highest level of data reusability since they all are created from the same source (raw memory), which can be recycled during the execution of the application.

The support functions used in conjunction with dynamic data structures are also reusable. This is a direct consequence of the nature of dynamic data structures and is especially true if you use the most formal approach to implementing dynamic data structures. These same support functions provide for the creation of dynamic data structures in a rigorous fashion. Formal definitions and rigorous constraints are important since they make the definition of an application's design more concise and straightforward.

8.3 IMPLEMENTATION

The next step in a project's development cycle is its implementation, and there are some distinct benefits related to the use of dynamic data structures that can influence an application's implementation strategy. The first is related to the data structures that an application uses. Prior to dynamic data structures, data structures in an application had to be defined during the design phase of the product life cycle. When dynamic data structures are used, only the limits and extent of a data structure need to be defined during the design phase. The actual complexity and structure of the data can be defined as the application evolves.

This is a significant deviation from ordinary software engineering procedures and can unnerve some system analysts. The reason is something called "baselining," which is just another name for freezing something in a particular configuration. Some system analysts prefer to baseline data structures early in the project's life cycle, mainly because the data structures have such a profound effect on the rest of the project. This can lead to a product that is not implemented in the best fashion because the data structures that were defined early in the project imposed poorly chosen constraints. With dynamic data structures, what you should baseline are the low-level designs of the data structures used to manage the configuration of the dynamic data structures and the dynamic data structure support functions. Then delay the baselining of the actual data structures (dynamic ones in this case) until later in the development cycle.

This approach could also be beneficial if used in rapid prototyping. In place of fixed data structures, dynamic data structures could be used. Since dynamic data structures can carry more information than can ordinary structures (such as type information), support functions tend to be very generic. For example, functions that print a dynamic data structure to the screen are quite generic and work with any dynamic data structure. Therefore, you can change and improve upon the data structure without the need to constantly rewrite the support functions. Once the best design for the data structure is determined through the prototyping process, you can baseline the portion of the code that defines the dynamic data structures. This should lead to the best overall application in the least amount of time since there's no need to consider the prototype as a throwaway version. In fact, most of the prototype (especially the data structures) should be good-quality code.

Another benefit of using dynamic data structures is when the scope of the project is difficult to define early in the project (at the time of requirements analysis). Some instances where this might be true include situations where the people who are requesting the software (or have a need for it) cannot adequately define their needs. If you kept trying to ascertain all requirements, you could delay the project, pushing it past its best market window, or you could end up with a requirements list that does not really meet the user's needs since decisions were forced. In such circumstances it is better to develop some quick prototypes, allow the user to interact with the prototype, and provide feedback to refine the requirements. By using dynamic data structures in prototyping situations, you should be able to provide quicker turnaround between prototypes.[4]

8.4 CONTRIBUTIONS TO QUALITY

Software quality is a measure of many things, some of which are difficult to quantize. Collectively, software quality is a measure of an application's reliability, efficiency,

---

[4]This should please the user who typically wanted the application before (s)he asked for it.

flexibility, reusability, and maintainability. Dynamic data structures can actually contribute to software quality in each of these areas. Let's look at these areas individually.

Reliability is typically a measure of how many problems or failures occur per line of code in an application. When you use dynamic data structures, much of the code related to data, which would otherwise reside in the application, is shifted into the support functions. Typically, these functions are slowly varying in form and content, mainly because they are lower-level functions, but also because they are versatile enough to serve almost all required purposes. This "low-level" nature of the functions means that they are used heavily and therefore any bugs that might exist in them are flushed out early in a project. Consequently, once an application is complete, the reliabilty of these routines is very high.

Efficiency is a measure of how many resources are required by an application. This includes general resources like memory, disk space, and the amount of code. As detialed in the Section 8.1.1, the use of dynamic data structures can reduce the amount of code required to implement an application. On the other hand, dynamic data structures typically require more memory per data item than do ordinary data structures simply because more information is maintained in them. Because of this "give a little, take a little" nature in some situations, it will be less efficient to use dynamic data structures. However, in the majority of cases it would be more efficient.

It has been mentioned at several places in this book how easy it is to change and modify dynamic data structures. In fact, many changes can and do occur when an application is run. It has also been mentioned that the support routines are general in character. This also means that the flexibility of an application that uses dynamic data structures is very high, which is a good thing.

The versatility of the support functions of dynamic data structures means that they are very reusable.

The remaining factor is "maintainability." Since this is such an important factor, the next section is dedicated to the topic.

8.5 MAINTENANCE AND ENHANCEMENT

Maintenance of software has continued to demand more and more resources as the years progress. Approximately 80 percent of an applications total cost can be attributed to maintenance, with the remaining percentage attributed to actual development costs. The majority (50 percent) of software maintenance is directed at perfecting the application, which includes improving an application's features and general enhancements. One quarter (25 percent) of all maintenance is adaptive, that is, modifying the application so that it will work on new hardware platforms or in new or improved environments [Pre87]. The remaining quarter consists mostly of corrective maintenance (fixing bugs). Consequently, keeping maintenance costs down has become a major concern.

In many applications if you can understand how the data structures in an application work, you can understand the application itself.[5] A key factor in understanding the data structures (even if you were the original author) is having the data structures properly documented. The best place for this documentation is in the application itself. Since most of today's programming languages do not require any sort of data documentation as part of the data declaration, it is sometimes difficult to even understand what a single variable is used for. By using dynamic data structures for the storage and management of key data elements, you can impose documentation requirements by simply making it a necessary part of describing a dynamic data structure. This will provide personal, readily accessible information on maintenance and will reduce maintenance costs by reducing the time spent understanding (or deciphering) the data structures. It's worth noting that in some CASE systems data descriptions are required and maintained separately from the application code itself.

Another aspect of maintenance and enhancement that contributes to maintenance costs is the side effects changes can have. There are instances where the change of a data structure can have serious repercussions throughout an application. If dynamic data structures are used, this perturbation can be minimized since dynamic data structure support functions are typically generic and therefore will work with any structure you can define. In addition to data side effects there are documentation side effects. As mentioned previously, dynamic data structures can be self-documented entities, so it is possible that a change to a data structure definition will always have a corresponding change in its documentation (or vice versa, given a set of tools to translate a description into data structure definitions).

A couple of other areas in which the use of dynamic data structures helps reduce maintenance costs is that dynamic data structures can reduce the complexity of an application (as discussed in Section 8.1.1 and 8.1.2). A simpler application is easier to maintain since it is easier to understand. Dynamic data structures also allow you to encapsulate data and functionality (as do object-oriented systems) in an organized way (we'll see more of this later). This raises the abstraction of what is "data" to a higher level and once again makes an application easier to comprehend.

CASE tools also strive to reduce the costs of a project's maintenance, as well as the development costs. However, a project can still be inflicted with increased costs related to change side effects, especially those related to operations performed on data structures. The same protections against change side effects provided by the use of dynamic data structures can apply when you use CASE tools for developing dynamic data structure–based applications. The benefits of using dynamic data structures from within a CASE system is magnified even more if the CASE tool understands and can utilize dynamic data structures as part of its conversion of application description into application code. With such a situation a developer would have to supply only a small amount of code glue to generate fully functional applications.

Object-oriented systems and programming languages provide some of the same maintenance benefits that dynamic data structures do. The areas in which they

---

[5]Obviously, applications written by deranged individuals are not included.

overlap is in data hiding, type-specific system response, and standardization of data (object) descriptions. The main area where they differ is that with dynamic data structures the functions and the data can be maintained separately, cleanly, and distinctly. This is not the case with object-oriented systems. To some this is an all-important philosophical as well as design criterion.

8.6 SUMMARY

Dynamic data structures contribute in a positive way to all aspects of software engineering. During the development phase of a project, the use of dynamic data structures can reduce the size, complexity, and degree of structure of an application. This can result in reduced development costs while at the same time increasing the functional potential of an application. Dynamic data structures continue to contribute constructively even as you enter the maintenance phase of a project. One contribution is a potential reduction in the number of failures in the system, due mainly to dynamic data structure's contributions to quality. Another contribution is in the increased ability to enhance an application with a minimal amount of side effects due to code changes.

These benefits can be realized even if you develop your project with a CASE system or if your chosen implementation language is object-oriented. Overall, the role of dynamic data structure is to allow an application to have an extensible design that can readily adapt to specific situations, all with a minimum of programmer effort and in some cases automatically at run-time.

POINTS TO PONDER

8.1 In what approaches to software engineering does the use of dynamic data structures play a focal role?

8.2 In what ways does the use of dynamic data structures contribute to a software project? Address the facets of size, complexity, and degree of structure.

8.3 What aspects related to the use of dynamic data structures must be decided in the initial design phase of a project?

8.4 How does the use of dynamic data structures affect the implementation phase of an application's development?

8.5 In what way does the use of dynamic data structures contribute to software quality?

8.6 How is the use of dynamic data structures beneficial during the maintenance phase of a project's life cycle?

Part II
Application

Basic Toolkit | **9**

In the chapters that will follow we'll take a look at how dynamic data structures can be used in a variety of environments. Some of the environments we'll be looking at range from network communication to programming languages to database management applications. This range is quite broad, and you might think that the application of dynamic data structures in each environment would have to be a "from-scratch, development. This needn't be the case. In fact, what makes each environment unique is the highest level of the applications. At the lowest levels dynamic data structures can be implemented the same.

The implementation of a basic toolkit of dynamic data structure functions is presented in this chapter. In addition, a set of general functions that will be used at various times in some applications is also presented.

9.1 DESIGN CONSIDERATIONS

As detailed in Chapter 8, there are some decisions to be made before we can begin to implement the two sets of functions:

- What dynamic data structure definition syntax to use?
- What method of configuration control?
- What realization methods to use?
- Which data types to be supported in the dynamic data structures?

For the definition syntax we'll use a C-style syntax for defining dynamic data structures (as discussed in Chapter 5; just in case you've forgotten). Many of the reasons for this choice were outlined in Chapter 5.

The choice for the method of configuration control will be encapsulation as detailed in Chapter 3. The main reason for this choice is that it is the most efficient method for a majority of the applications that will be presented.

As for the realization methods, support will be available for both variable binding and extraction by function call; these were detailed in Chapter 4. The reason is so that the method that is most appropriate can be used.

The basic data types that will be supported are the same as those available in C, namely: int, float, double, and char. In addition to these types, there will also be the types of date, time, and bit. With these seven basic data types, it should be possible to build up any other object you might desire.

9.2 BASIC FUNCTIONS

We'll begin the development of the basic support functions by defining a basic structure and related items that will serve as the generic building block for dynamic data structures. These structures and definitions will also be used in all the functions that create, use, and manage dynamic data structures. The basic structure should contain ample information so that any data item can be resolved into an actual value. It should also have sufficient flexibility so that it can be used as part of abstract data structure definitions. That is, it should be possible to group any number of building-block data structures together to form other structures. It is also desirable to have a place holder for data documentation.

A collection of specifications that should meet all the requirements is presented in Listing 9.1. The definitions in Listing 9.1 are mostly type definitions. There is a reason for this; it allows for the enhancement of the basic dynamic data structure building block without resulting in repercussions that affect all aspects of any applications that use dynamic data structures.

Some items in Listing 9.1 have obvious purposes. For instance, DDS_MAX_ DESC and DDS_MAX_NAME are constants that are used to define the maximum length of certain variables. Another part of Listing 9.1 that requires no more than mentioning its existence is the section that defines the types of functions. In between the constants and the function declarations are several typedefs and one enumerated type declaration. Each of these warrant some discussion. The enumerated type declaration (DDS_TYPE) defines the "names" for all the allowed data types. There should be a one-to-one correspondence between elements in DDS_TYPE and elements in the typedef DDS_VALUE. There are three nonnative C types defined in DDS_TYPE; these are DDST_DATE, DDST_TIME, and DDST_BIT. Each of these has corresponding typedefs and declarations in DDS_VALUE.

The typedef DDS_ELEMENT declares what constitutes a single dynamic data structure element. DDS_ELEMENT is designed so that referential realization (detailed in Chapter 6) and explicit type declaration and encapsulation configuration control (detailed in Chapter 5) are employed. The final typedef is DDS. This declares the structure that is used as the seed for the declaration of dynamic data structures. A variable of type DDS serves as the handle for the management of a dynamic data structure.

The following basic functions are required for the use of dynamic data structures: create a data structure, destroy a data structure, add an element, remove an element, extract the value of an element, set the name of the element, and set the description of the element. In order to help maintain data integrity, all functions will employ encapsulation configuration control with explicit type specification, as detailed in Chapter 5. What this means at the function level is that the portion of the dynamic

Listing 9.1   The include file dds.h, which contains specifications for data types used in the creation
and management of dynamic data structures.

```
#ifndef _DDS_
#define _DDS_   1


#include <stdio.h>
#include <alloc.h>


#ifdef __BORLANDC__
/* Do not do a free(). There appears to be a bug in Version 2.0
   of the compiler.
*/
#define free(x)
#endif


#define DDS_MAX_DESC          256
#define DDS_MAX_NAME          128


#define DDS_READ          1
#define DDS_WRITE         2


enum DDS_TYPE { DDST_DDS = 1, DDST_ELEMENT, DDST_INT,
                DDST_FLOAT, DDST_DOUBLE, DDST_CHAR, DDST_BIT,
                DDST_DATE, DDST_TIME, DDST_STRING, DDST_PTR };

typedef struct {
   char *ptr;
   int len;
   int malloced;
} DDS_STRING;

typedef struct {
  short year;
   short month;
   short day;
} DDS_DATE;

typedef struct {
  short hour;
  short minute;
  short sec;
  short msec;
} DDS_TIME;
```

(continued)

Listing 9.1   *(continued)*

```
typedef struct {
   unsigned int bits;
   unsigned int n;
} DDS_BITS;

typedef union {
   int i;
   float f;
   double d;
   char *ptr;
   char c;
   DDS_STRING s;
   DDS_DATE date;
   DDS_TIME time;
   DDS_BITS b;
} DDS_VALUE;

typedef struct {
   DDS_VALUE value;
   enum DDS_TYPE type;
} DDS_DATA;

typedef struct DDS_ELEMENT {
  DDS_DATA data;
  char name[DDS_MAX_NAME + 1];
  char desc[DDS_MAX_DESC + 1];
  struct DDS_ELEMENT *left;
  struct DDS_ELEMENT *right;
} DDS_ELEMENT;

typedef struct DDS {
  DDS_ELEMENT *first_element;
  DDS_ELEMENT *last_element;
  struct DDS *bindlist;
  unsigned e_count;
} DDS;
/* Function decalrations */
DDS_ELEMENT *dds_make_element();
DDS_ELEMENT *dds_get_element();
DDS_ELEMENT *dds_add_element();
DDS_ELEMENT *dds_clone_element();
void dds_set_element_name();
void dds_set_element_desc();
```

```
DDS *dds_create();
void dds_destroy();
char *dds_type_str();
DDS *dds_compile_C();
DDS *dds_str_compile_C();


#endif _DDS_
```

data structure on which a function is to operate is passed as one of the arguments to the function.

We'll begin the development of the basic functions with a function for creating a dynamic data structure. This action consists of creating a DDS structure from raw memory and initializing its elements. A pointer to the newly created DDS structure is then returned. Listing 9.2 contains the source for such a function, which is called dds_create( ). If dds_create( ) returns a NULL pointer, then the function was unable to create the dynamic data structure. The only condition under which this would be valid is if the function were unable to acquire memory from the system [**malloc( )** failed].

In order to destroy a dynamic data structure, two operations must be performed. Both of these operations relate to returning all memory extracted from the system

Listing 9.2 Source for the function dds_create(), which creates an instance of a dynamic data structure.

```
#include "dds.h"


/*------------------------------------------------------------
    Creates a seed for the definition of a dynamic data
    structure. It returns a pointer to the seed.
-----------------------------------------------------------*/
DDS *
dds_create()
{
  DDS *dds;

  if((dds = (DDS *)malloc(sizeof(DDS))) != NULL) {
    dds->first_element = NULL;
    dds->last_element = NULL;
    dds->bindlist = NULL;
    dds->e_count = 0;
  }
  return(dds);
}
```

memory pool. In order to destroy a dynamic data structure properly, memory must be freed in a specific order. The reason is that some portions of the dynamic data structure are dependent on others. You must remove all dependent portions of the dynamic data structure before removing the nondependent portions. The dependent portion of the DDS structure is each element in the dynamic data structure. So all elements must be freed before freeing the memory allocated for the DDS structure. The DDS structure must be freed only after the last element in the DDS structure is freed. Listing 9.3 contains the source for a function, called dds_destroy( ), to perform this operation.

Once you've created a seed for the dynamic data structure [with a call to dds_create( )], you can define the actual elements of the structure. To do this you simply need to add the definition of an element to the current list of elements in the dynamic data structure. Listing 9.4 contains the source for a function called dds_add_element( ), which performs this operation. The function dds_add_element( ) is called with four parameters. The first is the pointer to the dynamic data structure, the second is the data type for the element to add, the third is the name for the element, and the final argument is a textual description for the element. The first thing dds_add_element( )

Listing 9.3 Source for the function dds_destroy( ), which destroys a dynamic data structure.

```
#include "dds.h"

/*------------------------------------------------------------
   Destroys a dynamic data structure in an orderly
   way.
   -----------------------------------------------------------*/
void
dds_destroy(dds)
DDS *dds;
{
  if(dds == NULL) return;

  if(dds->bindlist != NULL) {
     dds_destroy(dds->bindlist);
     dds->bindlist = NULL;
  }

  while(dds->first_element != NULL) {
   dds_remove_element(dds, dds->first_element);
  }

  free(dds);
 return;
}
```

Listing 9.4 Source for the function dds_add_element, which adds elements to a dynamic data structure.

```c
#include "dds.h"


/*-------------------------------------------------------------
    Adds an element to a dynamic data structure
    given the type, name, and description of the
    element.
----------------------------------------------------------*/
DDS_ELEMENT *
dds_add_element(dds, type, name, desc)
DDS   *dds;
enum DDS_TYPE type;
char name[];
char desc[];
{

    DDS_ELEMENT *dds_element;

    if(dds == NULL) return(NULL);

    if( (dds_element = dds_make_element()) == NULL) {
      return(NULL);
    }

    dds_element->data.type = type;
    dds_set_element_name(dds_element, name);
    dds_set_element_desc(dds_element, desc);
    if(type == DDST_STRING) {
      dds_element->data.value.s.ptr = NULL;
      dds_element->data.value.s.len = 0;
      dds_element->data.value.s.malloced = 0;
    }

    dds_append_element(dds, dds_element);
    return(dds_element);
  }


/*-------------------------------------------------------------
    Appends a predefined dynamic data structure element
    to a dynamic data structure.
----------------------------------------------------------*/
dds_append_element(dds, dds_element)
```

(continued)

Listing 9.4   *(continued)*

```
DDS *dds;
DDS_ELEMENT *dds_element;
{
   if(dds == NULL || dds_element == NULL) return(0);

   if(dds->first_element == NULL) {
      dds_element->left = NULL;
      dds->first_element .= dds_element;
   } else {
      dds->last_element->right = dds_element;
      dds_element->left = dds->last_element;
   }
   dds_element->right = NULL;
   dds->last_element = dds_element;

   dds->e_count++;
   return(dds->e_count);
}


/*----------------------------------------------------------------
   Creates an element for use in a dynamic data structure.
   It initializes variables in the element structure.
   It returns NULL if it can not make a new element; this
   occurs only if memory can not be allocated.
   ------------------------------------------------------------*/
DDS_ELEMENT *
dds_make_element()
{
   DDS_ELEMENT *dds_element;

   dds_element = (DDS_ELEMENT *)malloc(sizeof(DDS_ELEMENT));
   if(dds_element != NULL) {
      dds_element->left = NULL;
      dds_element->right = NULL;
   }

   return(dds_element);
}


/*----------------------------------------------------------------
   Assigns an actual character array to the
   character pointer in a DDS element.
   ------------------------------------------------------------*/
```

```
dds_seed_string(dds_element, cptr, clen)
DDS_ELEMENT *dds_element;
char *cptr;
int clen;
{
   if(dds_element == NULL) return(0);
   if(dds_element->data.type != DDST_STRING) return(0); /* not proper
  type */
   if(cptr == NULL) {
     if((cptr = (char *)malloc(clen)) == NULL) {
      return(0);
     }
     dds_element->data.value.s.malloced = 1;
   } else {
     dds_element->data.value.s.malloced = 0;
   }

   dds_element->data.value.s.ptr = cptr;
   dds_element->data.value.s.len = clen;

   return(1);
}
```

does is make a new element. This new element is populated with the values passed. It then calls dds_append_element( ) to add the element to the given dynamic data structure. On completion, dds_add_element( ) returns the count of the number of elements in the dynamic data structure. If the count is 0, then dds_add_element( ) was unable to create the new element.

The function dds_append_element( ) in Listing 9.4 requires two arguments. The first is a pointer to a dynamic data structure, and the second is a pointer to an element to add to the dynamic data structure. It returns a count of the number of elements in the dynamic data structure or zero if it was impossible to do so.

On occasion you might have a need to modify a dynamic data structure by removing elements in the structure. The source for a function, called dds_remove_element( ), that will perform such an action is presented in Listing 9.5.

The function dds_remove_element( ) is called with two arguments; the first is a pointer to a dynamic data structure, and the second is the pointer to the element in the dynamic data structure to remove. The first operation dds_remove_element( ) performs is to ensure that both the dynamic data structure pointer and the element pointer are valid. If they both are, then two actions are performed. The first is that any reference to the element in the dynamic data structure is removed and the dynamic data structure link list is adjusted to close up any gaps that may have resulted from removing the element. The second action is to call dds_free_element( ), which ac-

Listing 9.5 Source for the function dds_remove_element(), which removes an element from a dynamic data structure, and dds_free_element( ), which frees all memory associated with an element.

```c
#include "dds.h"


/*-------------------------------------------------------------------
    Removes an element from a dynamic data structure.
    The element to remove is passed by pointer. If the
    dynamic data structure pointer or the element
    pointer is NULL, nothing is done.
    -------------------------------------------------------------*/
dds_remove_element(dds, dds_element)
DDS *dds;
DDS_ELEMENT *dds_element;
{

    if(dds == NULL || dds_element == NULL) return(0);

    if(dds_element->left != NULL) {
        dds_element->left->right = dds_element->right;
    }

    if(dds_element->right != NULL) {
        dds_element->right->left = dds_element->left;
    }

    if(dds_element->left == NULL && dds_element->right == NULL) { /* no
    more */
        dds->first_element = NULL;
        dds->last_element = NULL;
    } else if(dds_element->left == NULL) {
        /* Its the first element */
        dds->first_element = dds_element->right;
    } else if(dds_element->right == NULL) { /* Its the last element */
        dds->last_element = dds_element->left;
    }

    dds_free_element(dds_element);
    dds->e_count--;

    return(dds->e_count);
}
/*-------------------------------------------------------------------
    Frees all memory associated with a dynamic
    data structure element. This works on an
```

```
    independent dynamic data structure element
    that differs from dds_remove_element(), which
    works on elements in a dynamic data structure.
--------------------------------------------------------------------*/
dds_free_element(dds_element)
DDS_ELEMENT *dds_element;
{
    struct heapinfo hi;

    if(dds_element == NULL) return(0);

    if(dds_element->data.type == DDST_STRING) {
        if(dds_element->data.value.s.malloced) {
          free(dds_element->data.value.s.ptr);
      }
    }

    free(dds_element);
    return(1);
}
```

cepts one argument, a pointer to a dynamic data structure element. The action that dds_free_element( ) performs is that all memory associated with the element is returned to the system. This includes the memory occupied by the element itself as well as any memory allocated for the purpose of storing element values.

One potential deficiency in dds_remove_element( ) is that it requires a pointer to the element to remove. This can be a little troublesome, since it is similar to having to remember which element in an array represents a specific quantity. The existence of a function to return the pointer to an element in a dynamic data structure given just the element's name can eliminate this potential deficiency. Listing 9.6 contains the source for such a function. This function, dds_get_element( ), is called with two arguments; the first is a pointer to a dynamic data structure and the second is the reference name of the element. It locates the element in the dynamic data structure by comparing the given name to the names of each element and returns a pointer to the first element with that name. If the name could not be found, a NULL pointer is returned.

The final basic functions are dds_set_element_name( ) and dds_set_element_desc( ). The source for these functions is given in Listing 9.7. These functions accept two arguments. The first is a pointer to the element to operate on and the second is a string. For dds_set_element_name( ), the string contains the name that is to be associated with the element. For dds_set_element_desc( ), the string contains a description to be associated with the element. Each function takes precautions to ensure that no memory is overwritten as the string is copied into the element's

Listing 9.6 Source for the function dds_get_element( ), which obtains information about a specific element in a dynamic data structure.

```
#include "dds.h"


/*------------------------------------------------------------
    Returns a pointer to the element in the given dynamic
    data structure that has the given name. Returns NULL
    if there does not exists an element with the given
    name.
------------------------------------------------------------*/
DDS_ELEMENT *dds_get_element(dds, name)
DDS *dds;
char name[];
{
    DDS_ELEMENT *dds_element;

    if(dds == NULL) return(NULL);

    dds_element = dds->first_element;
    while(dds_element != NULL) {
        if(strcmp(name, dds_element->name) == 0) { break; }
        dds_element = dds_element->right;
    }

    return(dds_element);
}
```

variable by using the function **strncpy( )**. The functions also ensure that strings are properly terminated [which is not guaranteed by **strncpy( )**] by always placing a zero byte at the absolute end of the element's variable.

9.3 GENERAL FUNCTIONS

Now that a functional foundation for the management of dynamic data structures has been laid, we should develop a set of functions that will simplify the application interface for using dynamic data structures. One such function is related to the realization method for extracting values from dynamic data structures. Possible realization methods were detailed in Chapter 6. Because of the variety of applications that will be presented, we need functions that will allow value realization by either expression evaluation or binding methods.

Listing 9.8 contains the source for two functions: one that extracts and one that sets the value of an element in a dynamic data structure. Each of these tasks are performed

Listing 9.7   Source for the function dds_set_element_name( ), which sets the name of an element, and dds_set_element_desc( ), which sets a description of an element in a dynamic data structure.

```
#include "dds.h"

/*-------------------------------------------------------------
   Sets the name of a dynamic data structure element.
-------------------------------------------------------------*/
void dds_set_element_name(dds_element, name)
DDS_ELEMENT *dds_element;
char name[];
{
   if(dds_element != NULL) {
      strncpy(dds_element->name, name, DDS_MAX_NAME);
      dds_element->name[DDS_MAX_NAME] = '\0';
   }
}


/*-------------------------------------------------------------
   Sets the description of a dynamic data structure
   element.
-------------------------------------------------------------*/
void dds_set_element_desc(dds_element, desc)
DDS_ELEMENT *dds_element;
char desc[];
{

   if(dds_element != NULL) {
      strncpy(dds_element->desc, desc, DDS_MAX_DESC);
      dds_element->desc[DDS_MAX_DESC] = '\0';
   }
}
```

by expression evaluation. Both functions in Listing 9.8 require three arguments. The first is a pointer to the dynamic data structure element from which to extract the data value. The second argument is a pointer to the application variable. If the function called is dds_get_element_value( ), then the element's value will be transferred to the application variable. If the function called is dds_set_element_value( ), then the value associated with the element is set to the value in the variable. The third argument specifies the data type of the application variable. The allowed types are those found in the enumerate type DDS_TYPE found in Listing 9.1.

A special feature of both functions in Listing 9.8 is that they perform type conversion if the application variable and the dynamic data structure element differ in type. This type conversion is accomplished with a call to dds_convert_value( ), which

Listing 9.8   Source for the functions dds_set_element_value( ), dds_get_element_value( ), and a variety of type conversion functions that set and get the value of an element in a dynamic data structure.

```c
#include "dds.h"


/*------------------------------------------------------------
   Extracts the value of an element in a dynamic data
   structure.
   ---------------------------------------------------*/
dds_get_element_value(dds_element, ap_var, ap_var_type)
DDS_ELEMENT *dds_element;   .
char *ap_var;
enum DDS_TYPE ap_var_type;
{
   int success = 0;
   DDS_DATA dds_data;

   if(dds_element == NULL) return(success);

  dds_data.type = ap_var_type;
   if(ap_var_type == DDST_STRING) {
     dds_data.value.s.ptr = ap_var;
   }

   success = dds_convert_value(&dds_element->data, &dds_data);
   if(!success) { return(0); }

   if(ap_var_type != DDST_STRING) {
     memcpy(ap_var, &dds_data.value, dds_sizeof(ap_var_type));
   }
   return(success);
}


/*------------------------------------------------------------
   Sets the value of an element in a dynamic data
   structure to be the same as that of the passed
   application variable.
   ---------------------------------------------------*/
dds_set_element_value(dds_element, ap_var, ap_var_type)
DDS_ELEMENT *dds_element;
char *ap_var;
enum DDS_TYPE ap_var_type;
{
   int success = 0;
   DDS_DATA dds_data;
```

```
    if(dds_element == NULL) return(success);

  dds_data.type = ap_var_type;
   memcpy(&dds_data.value, ap_var, dds_sizeof(ap_var_type));
   success = dds_convert_value(&dds_data, &dds_element->data);
   return(success);
}

/*----------------------------------------------------------------
   Returns the size of a dynamic data structure data
    type.
   -------------------------------------------------------------*/
dds_sizeof(dds_type)
enum DDS_TYPE dds_type;
{
    switch(dds_type) {
        case DDST_DDS:
         return(sizeof(DDS));
        case DDST_INT:
         return(sizeof(int));
        case DDST_FLOAT:
         return(sizeof(float));
        case DDST_DOUBLE:
         return(sizeof(double));
        case DDST_CHAR:
         return(sizeof(char));
        case DDST_PTR:
         return(sizeof(char *));
        case DDST_STRING:
         return(sizeof(char));
        case DDST_BIT:
         return(sizeof(DDS_BITS));
        case DDST_DATE:
         return(sizeof(DDS_DATE));
        case DDST_TIME:
         return(sizeof(DDS_TIME));
    }
}

/*----------------------------------------------------------------
   Copies the contents of one DDS_VALUE variable to   another perform-
   ing type conversion as necessary.
   -------------------------------------------------------------*/
```

(continued)

Listing 9.8 *(continued)*

```c
#include <dos.h>
dds_convert_value(from, to)
DDS_DATA *from;
DDS_DATA *to;
{
  int success = 0;

    switch(to->type) {
      case DDST_DDS:
        success = dds_convert_to_dds(from, &to->value);
        break;
      case DDST_INT:
        success = dds_convert_to_int(from, &to->value);
        break;
      case DDST_FLOAT:
        success = dds_convert_to_float(from, &to->value);
        break;
      case DDST_DOUBLE:
        success = dds_convert_to_double(from, &to->value);
        break;
      case DDST_CHAR:
        success = dds_convert_to_char(from, &to->value);
        break;
      case DDST_PTR:
        success = dds_convert_to_ptr(from, &to->value);
        break;
      case DDST_STRING:
        success = dds_convert_to_string(from, &to->value);
        break;
      case DDST_BIT:
        success = dds_convert_to_bit(from, &to->value);
        break;
      case DDST_DATE:
        success = dds_convert_to_date(from, &to->value);
        break;
      case DDST_TIME:
        success = dds_convert_to_time(from, &to->value);
        break;
    }
    return(success);
}
```

```
/*----------------------------------------------------------------
   Converts the contents of the passed element into
   a variable of type dds.
   ----------------------------------------------------------- */
dds_convert_to_dds(data, dds)
DDS_DATA *data;
DDS **dds;
{
   int success = 1;

   switch(data->type) {
      case DDST_DDS:
       *dds = (DDS *)data->value.ptr;
       break;
      default:
       success = 0;
       break;
   }
   return(success);
}
/*----------------------------------------------------------------
   Converts the contents of the passed element into
   a variable of type int.
   -----------------------------------------------------------*/
dds_convert_to_int(data, ival)
DDS_DATA *data;
int *ival;
{
   int success = 1;

   switch(data->type) {
     case DDST_INT:
       *ival = data->value.i;
       break;
     case DDST_FLOAT:
       *ival = data->value.f;
       break;
     case DDST_DOUBLE:
       *ival = data->value.d;
       break;
     case DDST_CHAR:
       *ival = data->value.c;
       break;
     case DDST_PTR:
```

(continued)

Listing 9.8 *(continued)*

```
      *ival = *data->value.ptr;
      break;
   case DDST_STRING:
     sscanf(data->value.s.ptr, "%d", ival);
     break;
   case DDST_BIT:
     *ival = data->value.b.bits;
     break;
   default:
     success = 0;
     break;
  }
  return(success);
}


/*-----------------------------------------------------------
  Converts the contents of the passed element into
  a variable of type FLOAT.
  ---------------------------------------------------------*/
dds_convert_to_float(data, fval)
DDS_DATA *data;
float *fval;
{
   int success = 1;

   switch(data->type) {
     case DDST_INT:
       *fval = data->value.i;
       break;
     case DDST_FLOAT:
       *fval = data->value.f;
       break;
     case DDST_DOUBLE:
       *fval = data->value.d;
       break;
     case DDST_CHAR:
       *fval = data->value.c;
       break;
     case DDST_PTR:
       *fval = *data->value.ptr;
       break;
     case DDST_STRING:
       sscanf(data->value.s.ptr, "%f", fval);
```

```
        break;
      case DDST_BIT:
        *fval = data->value.b.bits;
        break;
      default:
        success = 0;
        break;
   }
   return(success);
}


/*-----------------------------------------------------------
  Converts the contents of the passed element into
  a variable of type DOUBLE.
  -----------------------------------------------------------*/
dds_convert_to_double(data, dval)
DDS_DATA *data;
double *dval;
{
   int success = 1;

   switch(data->type) {
     case DDST_INT:
       *dval = data->value.i;
       break;
     case DDST_FLOAT:
       *dval = data->value.f;
       break;
     case DDST_DOUBLE:
       *dval = data->value.d;
       break;
     case DDST_CHAR:
       *dval = data->value.c;
       break;
     case DDST_PTR:
       *dval = *data->value.ptr;
       break;
     case DDST_STRING:
       sscanf(data->value.s.ptr, "%lf", dval);
       break;
     case DDST_BIT:
       *dval = data->value.b.bits;
       break;
```

(continued)

Listing 9.8 *(continued)*

```
      default:
        success = 0;
        break;
   }
   return(success);
}


/*-------------------------------------------------------------
   Converts the contents of the passed element into
   a variable of type STRING.
   -------------------------------------------------------*/
dds_convert_to_string(data, s)
DDS_DATA *data;
DDS_STRING *s;
{
int success = 1;

   switch(data->type) {
     case DDST_INT:
       sprintf(s->ptr, "%d", data->value.i);
       break;
     case DDST_FLOAT:
       sprintf(s->ptr, "%f", data->value.f);
       break;
     case DDST_DOUBLE:
       sprintf(s->ptr, "%lf", data->value.d);
       break;
     case DDST_CHAR:
       sprintf(s->ptr, "%c", data->value.c);
       break;
     case DDST_STRING:
       strcpy(s->ptr, data->value.s.ptr);
       break;
     case DDST_BIT:
       sprintf(s->ptr, "%x", data->value.b.bits);
       break;
     case DDST_DATE:
       sprintf(s->ptr, "%2d/%02d/%02d",
         data->value.date.month,
         data->value.date.day,
         data->value.date.year);
       break;
     case DDST_TIME:
```

```
          sprintf(s->ptr, "%d:%02d:%02d",
            data->value.time.hour,
            data->value.time.minute,
            data->value.time.sec,
            data->value.time.msec);
          break;
      default:
        success = 0;
        break;
    }
    return(success);
}


/*-----------------------------------------------------------
    Converts the contents of the passed element into
    a variable of type DATE.
    ------------------------------------------------------*/
dds_convert_to_date(data, date)
DDS_DATA *data;
DDS_DATE *date;
{
    int success = 1;
    switch(data->type) {
      case DDST_DATE:
        memcpy(date, &data->value, sizeof(DDS_DATE));
        break;
      default:
        success = 0;
        break;
    }
    return(success);
}


/*-----------------------------------------------------------
    Converts the contents of the passed element into
    a variable of type TIME.
    ------------------------------------------------------*/
dds_convert_to_time(data, time)
DDS_DATA *data;
DDS_TIME *time;
{
    int success = 1;
```

(continued)

Listing 9.8   *(continued)*

```
  switch(data->type) {
    case DDST_TIME:
      memcpy(time, &data->value, sizeof(DDS_TIME));
      break;
    default:
      success = 0;
      break;
  }
  return(success);
}


/*-------------------------------------------------------------
   Converts the contents of the passed element into
   a variable of type BIT.
   -----------------------------------------------------------*/
dds_convert_to_bit(data, bit)
DDS_DATA *data;
DDS_BITS *bit;
{
  int success = 1;
  switch(data->type) {
    case DDST_INT:
      bit->bits = data->value.i;
      bit->n = sizeof(unsigned int) * 8;
      break;
    case DDST_FLOAT:
      bit->bits = data->value.f;
      bit->n = sizeof(unsigned int) * 8;
      break;
    case DDST_DOUBLE:
      bit->bits = data->value.d;
      bit->n = sizeof(unsigned int) * 8;
      break;
    case DDST_CHAR:
      bit->bits = data->value.c;
      bit->n = sizeof(char) * 8;
      break;
    case DDST_PTR:
      bit->bits = *data->value.ptr;
      bit->n = sizeof(char *) * 8;
      break;
    case DDST_STRING:
      sscanf(data->value.s.ptr, "%u", &bit->bits);
```

```
      bit->n = sizeof(unsigned int) * 8;
      break;
    case DDST_BIT:
      memcpy(bit, &data->value, sizeof(DDST_BIT));
      break;
    default:
      success = 0;
      break;
  }
  return(success);
}


/*------------------------------------------------------------
   Converts the contents of the passed element into
   a variable of type PTR.
   ----------------------------------------------------------*/
dds_convert_to_ptr(data, ptr)
DDS_DATA *data;
char **ptr;
{
int success = 1;
switch(data->type) {
    case DDST_INT:
      *ptr = (char *)data->value.i;
      break;
    case DDST_CHAR:
      *ptr = (char *)data->value.c;
      break;
    case DDST_PTR:
      *ptr = data->value.ptr;
      break;
    case DDST_STRING:
      sscanf(data->value.s.ptr, "%u", ptr);
      break;
    case DDST_BIT:
      *ptr = (char *)data->value.b.bits;
      break;
    default:
      success = 0;
      break;
  }
  return(success);
}
```

(continued)

Listing 9.8   *(continued)*

```
/*-----------------------------------------------------------
    Converts the contents of the passed element into
    a variable of type CHAR.
    ---------------------------------------------------------*/
dds_convert_to_char(data, c)
DDS_DATA *data;
char *c;
{
int success = 1;
switch(data->type) {
    case DDST_INT:
      *c = data->value.i;
      break;
    case DDST_FLOAT:
      *c = data->value.f;
      break;
    case DDST_DOUBLE:
      *c = data->value.d;
      break;
    case DDST_CHAR:
      *c = data->value.c;
      break;
    case DDST_PTR:
      *c = *data->value.ptr;
      break;
    case DDST_STRING:
      sscanf(data->value.s.ptr, "%c", c);
      break;
    case DDST_BIT:
      *c = data->value.b.bits;
      break;
    default:
      success = 0;
      break;
   }
   return(success);
}
```

can be thought of as a conversion clearinghouse from which the appropriate conversion function is called. In a sense the action taken by dds_convert_value( ) is similar to looking up the row index of the conversion matrix. It then calls the conversion function for that row. The conversion function then determines the column index and performs the specific conversion that is required.

A complete set of conversion functions can also be found in Listing 9.8. The entry requirements for each of these functions is a pointer to the dynamic data element's value element and a pointer to the application variable. The data type of the application variable must match the data type expected by the specific conversion function. This is ensured by dds_convert_value( ). The return value of these functions is true (1) if a conversion was performed and false (0) otherwise.

One of the difficulties of allowing conversions from any type to any other is that you end up with an $N \times N$ matrix of possibilities. Typically, you end up with fewer than $N \times N$ possibilities because in some cases there is no logical conversion between data types. One such conversion is between a DDS_DATE variable and a DDS_TIME variable.[1]

Realization by binding can be a much more compact way of using dynamic data structures. The reason is that you need to make only one function call to establish a link between an application variable and an element in a dynamic data structure, after which the value of the application variable always reflects the value of the element. This is in contrast to expression evaluation, in which you must make a function call every time you need the value of an element. Listing 9.9 contains the source for a set of functions that will bind an application variable to an element in a dynamic data structure and ensure that the application variable is automatically updated. The first function in Listing 9.9, dds_bind( ), takes three arguments. The first is a pointer to the dynamic data structure element to bind to, the second is a pointer to an application variable that is to be bound to the element, and the third is the type code for the application variable.

So as to minimize the number of similar functions and also to use dynamic data structures to their fullest extent, the list of bound variables is maintained in a dynamic data structure. In order to do this a variation of the meaning of certain values in the dynamic data structure element must be applied. The first of these is that all variables are referred to by reference so that only the character pointer variable is assigned a value. The second is that the value in the "type" variable indicates the type of variable pointed to by the character pointer. All other variables maintain their original interpretation.

One final requirement on the bind list dynamic data structure is that there must exist paired elements. The first element of the pair defines the pointer to the dynamic data structure element that is part of the bind. The second element defines the application variable that is participating in the bind.

The second function in Listing 9.9, dds_do_bind( ), performs the action of transferring information between bound variables. It is called with a pointer to the bind

---

[1]Converting a FORTRAN programmer to a C programmer is another conversion that is just as tough.

Listing 9.9   Source for dds_bind( ) and dds_do_bind( ), which bind an application variable to an element in a dynamic data structure and synchronize the content of the dynamic data structure and the application variable.

```c
#include "dds.h"


/*-----------------------------------------------------------
   Establishes a binding between a program variable and
   and element in dynamic data structure.
   ------------------------------------------->----------------*/
dds_bind(dds, dds_element, ap_var, ap_var_type)
DDS *dds;
DDS_ELEMENT *dds_element;
char *ap_var;
enum DDS_TYPE ap_var_type;
{
   DDS_ELEMENT *bind_to;
   DDS_ELEMENT *bind_ap;

   if(dds->bindlist == NULL) {  /* First time, create it */
      dds->bindlist = dds_create();
      if(dds->bindlist == NULL) { return(0); }
   }

   if(dds_add_element(dds->bindlist, DDST_ELEMENT, "", "")
         == 0) {
      return(0);
   }
   bind_to = dds->bindlist->last_element;

   if(dds_add_element(dds->bindlist, ap_var_type, "", "")
         == 0) {
      dds_remove_element(dds->bindlist, bind_to);
      return(0);
   }
   bind_ap = dds->bindlist->last_element;

 /* now tweek the actual values in the DDS elements */
   bind_to->data.value.ptr = (char *)dds_element;
   bind_ap->data.value.ptr = (char *)ap_var;

   return(1);
}
```

```
/*------------------------------------------------------------
    Performs the actual copying of information between
    bound variables.
--------------------------------------------------------------*/
dds_do_bind(dds, direction)
DDS *dds;
int direction;
{
    DDS_ELEMENT *dds_element;
    DDS_ELEMENT *ap_element;

    if(dds->bindlist == NULL) { return(0); }

    dds_element = dds->bindlist->first_element;
    while(dds_element != NULL) {
        ap_element = dds_element->right;
        if(direction == DDS_READ) {
          dds_get_element_value(dds_element->data.value.ptr,
              ap_element->data.value.ptr, ap_element->data.type);
        } else if (direction == DDS_WRITE) {
          dds_set_element_value(dds_element->data.value.ptr,
              ap_element->data.value.ptr, ap_element->data.type);
        }
        dds_element = ap_element->right;
    }
    return(1);
}
```

list (which is a dynamic data structure) and a specification of the direction of the transfer. The direction is from the perspective of the application variable, so that a "read" means "copy the information in the dynamic data structure element into the application variable." A "write" means "copy the information in the application variable into the dynamic data structure element."

Another set of general-purpose functions are those that aid in the creation of a dynamic data structure based on specifications written in some data description language. As mentioned earlier in this chapter, we will use the a C-style structure definition syntax as the basis for a data description language. Our C-style syntax will be identical to C's definitions, with the exception that each element must be defined by a type–variable name pair. Any comment (which begins with a "/*" and ends with a "/*") that follows such a definition is considered a description for that element. A nice attribute of this approach is that if the dynamic data structure description were placed in a file, that file could be included in an application at compile time (with an

"#include" statement) to define a hard-coded structure identical to the dynamic data structure it defines.

The source for a parser that meets the lexicographical definitions presented in Listing 7.1 and the requirements just presented is given in Listing 9.10. Running this source through lex will result in a function that, when called, will scan a source of text and tokenize any structures it recognizes. The source of text is accessed through the function yygetc( ), which in this case is customized so that the source can be defined by the calling application.

Recognizing the structural elements in a description is only half of what is needed in order to convert the description into a dynamic data structure. The next task to perform is to translate the tokens into actions that will create the dynamic data structure. You could write a function to serve this purpose or use yacc to do the job for you. Listing 9.11 presents the source for a compiler that integrates with the lexicographical analyzer defined in Listing 9.10. An important element of the inter-dependence between Listings 9.10 and 9.11 is that the output of running Listing 9.10 through lex (which is placed in the file lex_yy.c[2]) must be included in Listing 9.11, which is then run through yacc. The reason is that in order for the output of lex to work with the output of yacc, it must know about the tokens used by yacc in generating its output. This can be done only at the time yacc processes its source file.

After you run Listing 9.11 through yacc you will end up with a file called ytab.c.

---

[2]This is the name when you use MKS lex running under DOS. On a UNIX system the name is typically lex.yy.c, and may be different on other systems.

Listing 9.10 Specification for a lexicographical analyzer for a C-style structure definition language (written for use with lex).

```
/* Lexicographic definitions to tokenize a C style declaration */

/* Declrations of external functions - must be preceeded by spaces */

static FILE *Dds_fptr;

dds_init_C_parser(fptr)
FILE *fptr;
{
  Dds_fptr = fptr;
}

#ifdef yygetc()
#undef yygetc()
#endif yygetc()
```

```
yygetc() {
  int c;

  c = fgetc(Dds_fptr);
  return(c);
}

yywrap()
{
  return(1);
}

/* Beginning of lex macros - must not be preceeded by any spaces */

%%

struct          { return(STRUCT); }
";"             { return(';'); }
"{"             { return('{'); }
"}"             { return('}'); }
"*"             { return('*'); }
"["             { return('['); }
"]"             { return(']'); }
float           { return(FLOAT); }
double          { return(DOUBLE); }
char            { return(CHAR); }
int             { return(INT); }
[ \n\t\r\f]+    { /* ignore white space */ }
[a-zA-Z_]+      {
                    strncpy(var_name, yytext, DDS_MAX_NAME);
                    var_name[DDS_MAX_NAME] = '';
                    return(WORD);
                }
[0-9]+          {
                    var_size = atoi(yytext);
                    return(NUMBER);
                }
"/*".*"*/"      {
                    strncpy(var_desc, yytext, DDS_MAX_DESC);
                    var_desc[DDS_MAX_DESC] = '';
                    return(COMMENT);
                }
                { /* ignore everyting else */ }
%%
```

Listing 9.11 Specification for a compiler for C-style structure definition language (written for use with yacc).

```
/* Compiler for a simple C type definition lanaguage */
%{
#include <string.h>
#include "dds.h"

static char var_name[DDS_MAX_NAME + 1];
static char var_desc[DDS_MAX_DESC + 1];
static int var_size;
static DDS_ELEMENT *element;
static int type;
%}

%union {
   int ival;
   char *cptr;
}

%token <ival> STRUCT TERM
%token <ival> INT DOUBLE FLOAT CHAR WORD COMMENT NUMBER
%type <ival> decl_type
%type <cptr> vname desc

%start struct_decl
%%
struct_decl : STRUCT '{' item_list '}'
            {
               YYACCEPT;
            }
      ;

item_list : item_decl
          | item_list item_decl
      ;

item_decl : decl_type vname ';'
            {
               if($1 == DDST_CHAR) {      /* Check about refining type */
                 if(var_size > 0) {
                   type = DDST_STRING;
                 } else if(var_size == 0) {
                   type = DDST_PTR;
                 }
```

```
                } else {
                  type = $1;
                }

                element = dds_add_element(Dds_seed, type, $2, "");
                if(element == NULL) {
                  YYERROR;
                }
                if(type == DDST_STRING) {
                  dds_seed_string(element, NULL, var_size);
                }
              }
        | decl_type vname ';' desc
            {
                if($1 == DDST_CHAR) { /* Check about refining type */
                  if(var_size > 0) {
                    type = DDST_STRING;
                  } else if(var_size == 0) {
                    type = DDST_PTR;
                  }
                } else {
                  type = $1;
                }

                element = dds_add_element(Dds_seed, type, $2, $4);
                if(element == NULL) {
                  YYERROR;
                }
                if(type == DDST_STRING) {
                  dds_seed_string(element, NULL, var_size);
                }
            }
      ;
decl_type : INT
            { $$ = DDST_INT; }
          | FLOAT
            { $$ = DDST_FLOAT; }
          | DOUBLE
            { $$ = DDST_DOUBLE; }
          | CHAR
            { $$ = DDST_CHAR; }
      ;
```

(continued)

Listing 9.11 *(continued)*

```
vname : WORD
        {
                var_size = -1;
                $$ = var_name;
        }
      | '*' WORD
        {
                var_size = 0;
                $$ = var_name;
        }
      | WORD '[' NUMBER ']'
        {
                $$ = var_name;
                var_size = $2;
        }
        ;


desc : COMMENT
        {
            /* reference area between comment tokens */
            var_desc[strlen(var_desc) - 2] = '';
            $$ = &var_desc[2];
         }
        ;

%%
#include <stdio.h>
#include "lex_yy.c"

/* Pointer to the dynamic data structure which is being
   built */
int Dds_error;
#define DDS_ERR_SYNTAX 1
static DDS *Dds_seed;

void yyerror(s)
char *s;
{
  Dds_error = DDS_ERR_SYNTAX;
}


DDS *dds_compile_C(fptr)
FILE *fptr;
```

```
{
    DDS *dds;

    if((dds = dds_create()) != NULL) {
        dds_init_C_parser(fptr);
        Dds_seed = dds;
        yyparse();
    }
    return(dds);
}
```

It contains a function called dds_compile_C( ), which is called with one argument. This argument is a text string that contains the C-style specifications for a dynamic data structure. It returns a pointer to a dynamic data structure. If the pointer is NULL, then no dynamic data structure was created.

An example of a structural definition that will compile using dds_compile_C( ) is as follows:

```
struct {
    int i;      /* An integer value */
    float f;
}
```

This will create a dynamic data structure with two elements. The first has a type of int (integer), a name of "i" and a description of "An integer value." The second element has a type of float, a name of "f" and no description.

A limitation to dds_compile_C( ) is that it expects the source of what it will compile to be stored in a disk file. This means that if you had a variable in an application that contained a C-style description of a dynamic data structure, you would have to write this string to a file, invoke dds_compile_C( ), on the file and delete the file. There are two ways to solve this drawback. One is to write a new version of dds_compile_C( ) that has as its source an application variable, or to make it simpler, to do what was just described. A function that will do the later is given in Listing 9.12. The function dds_str_compile_C( ) accepts one argument, a pointer to a string of characters. It then creates a temporary file, places the string in it, invokes dds_compile_C( ), obtains the created dynamic data structure, and closes (and re-moves) the temporary file. It then returns a pointer to the new dynamic data structure.

Yet another function that can prove very useful when developing applications that use dynamic data structures is a function that can print a clear text description of a dynamic data structure. Listing 9.13 contains the source for such a function. This function, dds_desc_dds( ), accepts three arguments. The first is a pointer to a dynamic data structure. The second is a pointer to a buffer in which to place the descriptor text. If this pointer is NULL, the function then prints the description to the screen. The final argument is the count of the number of bytes that may be placed where the second

Listing 9.12   Source for the function dds_desc_dds( ), which produces a clear text description of a dynamic data structure.

```
/*----------------------------------------------------------
   Prints the contents of a dynamic data
   structure.
   ------------------------------------------------------*/
#include "dds.h"

/* This in-line macro is used in dds_desc_dds. It assumes
   the existance of 'cnt', which contains the count of the
   current number of characters in 'b', and 'max', which is the
   maximum number of characters 'b' can hold. A variable called
   'slen' must also exist and is used for temporary storage.
*/ #define add_str(b, s)                       \
       if(b == NULL) {                         \
         printf("%s", s);                      \
       } else {                                \
         slen = strlen(s);                     \
         if(cnt + slen >= max) return(0);      \
         strcat(b, s);                         \
         cnt += slen;                          \
       }

dds_desc_dds(dds, buffer, max)
DDS *dds;
char buffer[];
int max;
{
   DDS_ELEMENT *dds_element;
   char tmp_buffer[512];
   int cnt = 0;
   int slen;

   if(dds == NULL) {
     if(buffer == NULL) {
       printf("Nothing defined, DDS = NULL\n");
     }
     return(0);

   }

   if(buffer != NULL) {
     strcpy(buffer, "");
   }
```

```
      add_str(buffer, "struct {\n");
      dds_element = dds->first_element;
      while(dds_element != NULL) {
        add_str(buffer, "  ");
        add_str(buffer, dds_type_str(dds_element));
        add_str(buffer, " ");
        add_str(buffer, dds_element->name);
        if(dds_element->data.type == DDST_STRING) {
          sprintf(tmp_buffer, "[%d]", dds_element->data.value.s.len);
          add_str(buffer, tmp_buffer);
        }
        add_str(buffer, "; /* ");
        add_str(buffer, dds_element->desc);
        add_str(buffer, " */\n");
        dds_element = dds_element->right;
      }
      add_str(buffer, "}\n");

      return(1);
    }
/*-------------------------------------------------------
   Returns a pointer to a textual description
   of an elements type. The string that holds
   the text is reused with each call.
---------------------------------------------------------*/
char *dds_type_str(dds_element)
DDS_ELEMENT *dds_element;
{
   static char Temp_str[128];

   switch(dds_element->data.type) {
    case DDST_INT:
       strcpy(Temp_str, "int");
       break;
    case DDST_FLOAT:
       strcpy(Temp_str, "float");
       break;
    case DDST_DOUBLE:
       strcpy(Temp_str, "double");
       break;
    case DDST_CHAR:
    case DDST_STRING:
       strcpy(Temp_str, "char");
```

(continued)

Listing 9.12   *(continued)*

```
        break;
    case DDST_PTR:
        strcpy(Temp_str, "char *");
        break;
    case DDST_BIT:
        strcpy(Temp_str, "bit");
        break;
    case DDST_TIME:
        strcpy(Temp_str, "time");
        break;
    case DDST_DATE:
        strcpy(Temp_str, "date");
        break;
    case DDST_DDS:
        strcpy(Temp_str, "dds");
        break;
    case DDST_ELEMENT:
        strcpy(Temp_str, "dds_element");
        break;
    }
    return(Temp_str);
}
```

Listing 9.13   Source for the function dds_str_compile_C( ), which creates a dynamic data structure given a string containing a description of it.

```
#include "dds.h"
#include <stdio.h>
#include <dir.h>
/*_____

   Interface to the C style DDS compiler that allows
   for the DDS description to be a text string.
   _____*/
DDS *dds_str_compile_C(str)
char str[];
  {
  FILE *fptr;
  DDS *dds;
  char name[9];

  strcpy(name, "RPXXXXXX");
  mktemp(name);
```

```
if((fptr = fopen(name, "w+")) == NULL) {
  return(NULL);
}
fprintf(fptr, "%s", str);
fflush(fptr);
rewind(fptr);
dds = dds_compile_C(fptr);
fclose(fptr);
remove(name);

return(dds);
}
```

argument points. If the second argument is NULL, this can be any number, since the argument is ignored.

One more useful function is one that will compare two dynamic data structures and return a value that indicates whether the two dynamic data structures have the same structure. Listing 9.14 contains the source for a function, called dds_compare_dds( ), which will do this. This function accepts two arguments, both pointers to dynamic data structures. It returns true (1) if they have identical structure and false (0) if they do not.

A final function that can be useful in selected instances is one that will create a new instance of an existing element, especially if the new instance will be an exact copy of the existing element. The reason is that there are times where you might want to preserve a single value within a dynamic data structure, but there is no longer a need for the rest of the dynamic data structure. A function that will do this is in Listing 9.15. The function dds_clone_element( ) in Listing 9.15 expects one argument, a pointer to an existing dynamic data structure element. It returns a pointer to a new instance of this passed element or NULL if it was unable to create the new instance.

9.4 SUMMARY

Presented in this chapter is the foundation for the application of dynamic data structures in a variety of real-world situations. This foundation consists of several functions that provide basic dynamic data structure functions. This includes functions to create, manage, and destroy dynamic data structure. The chosen design approach was to use referential realization, explicit type declaration, and encapsulation configuration control.

In addition to the basic functions, a few general functions are presented. These include functions for value realization by either expression evaluation or by binding, functions for high-level definition of dynamic data structures using a C-style structure

Listing 9.14 Source for the function dds_compare_dds( ), which compares the structure of two dynamic data structures.

```
#include "dds.h"
/*_____

  Compares two DDS to and returns 0 if they do not match
  and 1 if they do.
                                                              */
_____
dds_compare_dds(this, that)
DDS *this;
 DDS *that;
{
  DDS_ELEMENT *this_element;
  DDS_ELEMENT *that_element;

  this_element = this->first_element;
  that_element = that->first_element;
  while(this_element != NULL) {
     if(that_element == NULL) { /* Mis-match */
      return(0);
     }
     if(this_element->data.type != that_element->data.type) { /* Mis-
  match */
       return(0);
     }
     this_element = this_element->right;
     that_element = that_element->right;
  }
  if(that_element != NULL) return(0);
  return(1);
}
```

Listing 9.15 Source for the function dds_clone_element( ), which makes an exact copy of an existing dynamic data structure element.

```
#include "dds.h"
/*_____

  Makes an exact copy of a given element.
  Returns a pointer to the copy.
                                                              */
_____
DDS_ELEMENT *dds_clone_element(element)
DDS_ELEMENT *element;
 {
   DDS_ELEMENT *dds_element;
   char *ptr;
```

```
    if(element == NULL) return(NULL);

    dds_element = (DDS_ELEMENT *)malloc(sizeof(DDS_ELEMENT));
    if(dds_element == NULL) return(NULL);
    memcpy(dds_element, element, sizeof(DDS_ELEMENT));

    /* If string type and malloced copy that too */
    if(dds_element->data.type == DDST_STRING &&
        dds_element->data.value.s.malloced) {
      ptr = (char *)malloc(dds_element->data.value.s.len);
      memcpy(ptr, dds_element->data.value.s.ptr,
                  dds_element->data.value.s.len);
      dds_element->data.value.s.ptr = ptr;
    }
    return(dds_element);
}
```

definition approach, and a function for printing a plain text description of a dynamic data structure.

POINTS TO PONDER

9.1 With only the basic functions, how would you realize the values maintained in a dynamic data structure.

9.2 Given the functions presented in this chapter, what would the typical calling sequence be in order to get the value of an element? Use expression evaluation to get the value, and assume that all you know is the name of the element and the dynamic data structure it is in.

9.3 Describe an alternate approach to implementing the type conversion portion of the value realization functions. The new approach should allow an application to provide one or more of the conversion functions without a need to rewrite or alter the function dds_do_bind( ).

Dynamically Linked **10**
Applications

It is quite common to build applications in separate and distinct parts. These parts are then brought together at some time to create a complete application. This process is referred to as the "link phase of compilation." In conventional systems all references to variables and functions in all components of the application where resolved during the link phase. The result being a stand alone application. Today this isn't necessarily true. In some systems you can maintain libraries (called "sharable libraries") as separate components and the link phase only partially resolves all references to these libraries. The final resolution is done at run-time. This is called "dynamic linking."

Some very common examples of dynamically linked libraries are the ROM (read-only memory) BIOS on PCs and the ROM Toolbox on Macs. References to executable portions of the ROMs can be placed in an application, but the process of locating the actual portion of the ROM to execute is done at run-time, commonly through a lookup table maintained at a fixed location in memory.

A compiled application that uses shared libraries isn't the only kind of application where dynamic linking is done. Interpreters are another class of dynamically linked applications. With an interpreter references to specific functions or procedures are made in a form that is not immediately executable. The interpreter then links the reference to the proper function in a step-by-step fashion. Normally the reference is made with clear text instructions, but tokenized instructions could also be used.

Using dynamic linking can be beneficial in several ways. The first is reduced storage requirements for applications. A real gain is achieved in this area only if more than one application can make use of a common component. Another benefit is that dynamic linking makes it is possible to change the way shared portions of an application operate without the need to relink the nonshared portion. This is especially useful when different groups (or companies) have autonomy over the different components of the application. Shared libraries from system vendors and in-house applications is a good example. Yet another benefit is that with dynamic linking the capabilities of an application may be augmented at run-time, without any recompilation or linking.

A major drawback to using dynamically linked applications is that startup and possibly execution time is increased. The amount of increase can range from miniscule to very apparent, depending on the implementation. There are other less important drawbacks, which we won't delve into. Instead let's concentrate on how dynamically linked applications can be implemented using dynamic data structures.

10.1 THE CHALLENGE

Develop a toolkit of functions that will allow the registration of a function so that it may be called by an application as the result of some external command; an interpreter is a good example. It should be possible to expand the list of registered functions at run-time. The returned value of a called function should be accessible. To demonstrate the viability of the implementation of this toolkit, write an interpreter that will read a clear text command that has a function syntax and execute the appropriate registered function.

10.2 THE SOLUTION

Since we must have a means to register and subsequently call a function, it's obvious that we will need a structure to maintain all pertinent information about a function. In order to call a function, we need three elements of information about the function. The first is its location in memory. In C this takes the form of a pointer to the function. The second element is the return value of the function. The third element is the entry requirements for the function.

For this implementation we'll manage the three elements of information with a dynamic data structure. Since we must be able to register functions at will, we will manage all registered functions with a single dynamic data structure. Using dynamic data structures makes this quite simple since a dynamic data structure can easily be expanded at run-time. We'll place a higher-level structure on this dynamic data structure by requiring elements to be added in groups of three. The first element will contain a pointer to the function, the second the return value, and the third will be a pointer to a dynamic data structure that contains all the entry arguments. Figure 10.1 depicts the layout of the dynamic data structure just described. The function that will be responsible for maintaining this high-level structure is the function which is used to add an application function to the list of registered functions. Listing 10.1 contains the source for such a function, called add_func( ). The function add_func( ) has five arguments. The first is a pointer to the dynamic data structure in which functions will be registered. By allowing the dynamic data structure that contains registered functions to originate in the calling application, it is possible to maintain multiple and separate lists of functions. The second argument is a text string, which is the name by which the function is referred to. The third argument is a pointer to the function. The fourth argument is the type code for the return value of the function. The fifth and final argument is a pointer to a dynamic data structure that describes the entry requirements.

The fifth argument of add_func( ) is a weak point since it requires that the de-

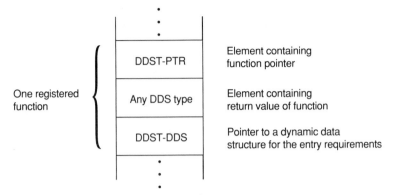

Figure 10.1 Layout of the dynamic data structure used to maintain information about registered functions.

veloper must construct dynamic data structures to match the calling arguments of the function. Even though specifying the entry requirements of a function cannot be avoided, it is possible to simplify how this is done. Listing 10.2 contains the source for a function called register_func( ), which provides a simpler interface to the add_func( ) function. The function register_func( ) is called with at least five arguments. The first four are identical to add_func( ). Following the fourth argument is a variable number of entry requirement specifications that consist of pairs of values. The first value in the pair is whether the argument is an input (read-only) argument or an output (read/write) argument. The second value in the pair is the dynamic data structure data type code for the data type of the argument. The entry requirement specifications are terminated by a zero-value argument. If a registered function has no arguments, then a zero must follow the fourth argument to register_func( ). I'll refer you to the application presented later in this chapter for examples.

What register_func( ) does with the variable arguments is construct the appropriate dynamic data structure and then calls add_func( ), which actually adds the function to the list of registered functions.

Once a function is registered, we need some way to call the function. Listing 10.3 contains the source for a function called call_func( ) that will do this. It has three arguments. The first is a pointer to the dynamic data structure containing the list of registered functions, the second is the reference name given to the function when it was registered, and the third function is a dynamic data structure containing the arguments for the function. The first thing call_func( ) does is search for the existence of a function that has the given reference name by calling find_func( ) (discussed next). If a matching function is found, then the passed arguments for the function are checked to make sure that they match what the function expects. If passed arguments match, then the values in the elements of the passed dynamic data structure are packed tightly into a block a memory. After this is completed, the desired function is called with the arguments passed to it. When the called function returns, the return

Listing 10.1 Source for add_func( ), which registers a function for possible dynamic calling.

```
/*-----------------------------------------------------------
   Adds a function to the list of registered functions.
   Builds a triple-element DDS. The first element is
   a pointer to a function, the second is the return;
   value, and the third is a pointer to a DDS that
   describes the expected arguments to the function.

   Returns 1 if successful, 0 otherwise.
   -----------------------------------------------------------*/
#include "dds.h"
add_func(func_list, func_ptr, func_name, ret_type, func_args)
DDS *func_list;
char (*func_ptr)();
char func_name[];
int ret_type;
DDS *func_args;
{
    DDS_ELEMENT *element;

    /* Add pointer to function */
    element = dds_add_element(func_list, DDST_PTR, func_name,
                            "Function pointer");
    if(element == NULL) return(0);
    element->data.value.ptr = (char *)func_ptr;

    /* Add return value */
    element = dds_add_element(func_list, ret_type, func_name,
                            "Return value");
    if(element == NULL) return(0);

  /* Add pointer to argument list */
    element = dds_add_element(func_list, DDST_DDS, func_name,
                            "Argument list");
    if(element == NULL) return(0);
    element->data.value.ptr = (char *)func_args;
    return(1);
}
```

Listing 10.2 Source for register_func( ), which is a simplified interface to add_func( ).

```c
#include <stdarg.h>
#include "dds.h"
#include "interp.h"


/*----------------------------------------------------
   Simplifies the adding of functions to a
   function list. It creates a dynamic data structure
   that matches the passed variable aguments.
--------------------------------------------------------*/
register_func(func_list, func_ptr, func_name, ret_type)
DDS *func_list;
int (*func_ptr)();
char func_name[];
int ret_type;
{
  DDS *dds;
  char arg_name[DDS_MAX_NAME + 1];
  char arg_desc[DDS_MAX_DESC + 1];
  int cnt;
  int type;
  int direction;
  va_list vargs;

  if((dds = dds_create()) == NULL) return(0);

  va_start(vargs, ret_type);
  direction = va_arg(vargs, int);
  cnt = 1;
  while(direction != 0) {
   type = va_arg(vargs, int);
   switch(direction) {
     case INPUT:
       sprintf(arg_name, "input: %d", cnt);
       break;
     case OUTPUT:
       sprintf(arg_name, "output: %d", cnt);
       break;
     default: /* Syntax problem */
       dds_destroy(dds);
       return(0);
   }
   sprintf(arg_desc, "for %s()", func_name);
```

```
  if(dds_add_element(dds, type, arg_name, arg_desc) == NULL) {
     dds_destroy(dds);
     return(0);
  }
  direction = va_arg(vargs, int);
  cnt++;
  }


  add_func(func_list, func_ptr, func_name, ret_type, dds);
  return(1);
}
```

Listing 10.3   Source for call_func( ), which is used to call any registered function.

```
/*------------------------------------------------
   Calls a function that has been registered as
   a callable DDS in a dynamic data structure.
-----------------------------------------------*/
#include "dds.h"
#include "interp.h"

#define MAX_ARG_STACK   128

DDS_ELEMENT *call_func(func_list, func_name, func_args)
DDS *func_list;
char func_name[];
DDS *func_args;
{
   DDS_ELEMENT *element;
   DDS_ELEMENT *e_ptr;
   DDS_ELEMENT *ret_value;
   DDS *expected_args;
   char (*c_func)();
   double (*d_func)();
   int (*i_func)();
   float (*f_func)();
   char * (*ptr_func)();
   char *ptr;
   int i;
   int cnt;
   int e_size;
   int nchar;
   struct {
```

(continued)

Listing 10.3 *(continued)*

```
    char stack[MAX_ARG_STACK];
} args;

element = find_func(func_list, func_name);
if(element == NULL) {
    fprintf(stderr,
      "There is no registered function by the name of %s\n",
func_name);
    return(NULL);
}


ret_value = element->right;
/* Check that passed arguments match expected arguments */
expected_args = (DDS *)ret_value->right->data.value.ptr;
if(!dds_compare_dds(func_args, expected_args)) {
    fprintf(stderr, "Argument mismatch calling function: %s\n",
        element->name);
    return(NULL);
}


/* Build up argument list */
e_ptr = func_args->first_element;
ptr = args.stack;
cnt = 0;
while(e_ptr != NULL) {
    if(e_ptr->data.type == DDST_STRING) {  /* special treatment */
       e_size = dds_sizeof(DDST_PTR);
    } else {
       e_size = dds_sizeof(e_ptr->data.type);
    }
    if(cnt + e_size >= MAX_ARG_STACK) {
        fprintf(stderr, "Argument stack exceed!\n");
        return(NULL);
    }
    if(e_ptr->data.type == DDST_STRING) {  /* special treatment */
        memcpy(ptr, (char *)&e_ptr->data.value.s.ptr, e_size);
    } else {
        memcpy(ptr, (char *)&e_ptr->data.value, e_size);
    }
    cnt += e_size;
    ptr += e_size;
    e_ptr = e_ptr->right;
}
```

```
/* Call function and store returned value */
switch(ret_value->data.type) {
    case DDST_INT:
        i_func = (int (*) ())element->data.value.ptr;
        ret_value->data.value.i = (*i_func)(args);
        break;
    case DDST_DOUBLE:
        d_func = (double (*) ())element->data.value.ptr;
        ret_value->data.value.d = (*d_func)(args);
        break;
    case DDST_FLOAT:
        f_func = (float (*) ())element->data.value.ptr;
        ret_value->data.value.f = (*f_func)(args);
        break;
    case DDST_CHAR:
        c_func = (char (*) ())element->data.value.ptr;
        ret_value->data.value.c = (*c_func)(args);
        break;
    case DDST_PTR:
        ptr_func = (char * (*) ())element->data.value.ptr;
        ret_value->data.value.ptr = (*ptr_func)(args);
        break;
}
/* Place returned results in proper arguments in DDS */
/* Output arguments have a name which begins with "output" */
e_ptr = func_args->first_element;
ptr = args.stack;
while(e_ptr != NULL) {
    e_size = dds_sizeof(e_ptr->data.type);
    if(strncmp("output", e_ptr->name, 6) == 0) {
        if(e_ptr->data.type == DDST_STRING) { /* special treatment */
            nchar = e_ptr->data.value.s.len;
            if(strlen(ptr) + 1 < nchar) nchar = strlen(ptr) + 1;
            strncpy(e_ptr->data.value.s.ptr, ptr, nchar);
        } else {
            memcpy((char *)&e_ptr->data.value, ptr, e_size);
        }
    }
    ptr += e_size;
    e_ptr = e_ptr->right;
}
return(element);    /* Success */
}
```

value is loaded into the element reserved for it in the list of registered functions. Then all values in the output arguments of the function are copied into the proper element in the argument list passed to the call_func( ) function.

There is one unique aspect of call_func( ) that deserves more discussion, and that is how arguments are actually passed to the called function. A feature of most C compilers is that when you pass a structure as an argument to a function, the entire contents of the structure are pushed on the function's argument stack. This is in strong contrast to when you pass an array of characters or an array of any other thing. When you pass an array a pointer to the array is passed. By taking advantage[1] of the way structures are dealt with, we can build up an argument stack that will match that desired by the function and pass this to the function as a single block of memory. Even though (in most cases) the passed block is larger than what the called function expects, the called function will ignore the excess. On return from the function, the call stack is always cleared up to the first argument.

In call_func( ) a reference is made to a function called find_func( ). Listing 10.4 contains the source for this function. It expects two arguments. The first[2] is a pointer to the dynamic data structure that contains the list of registered functions. The second is the reference name of the function to search for. It returns a pointer to the element in the list of registered functions at which the function definition begins. If it fails to find a function, a NULL pointer is returned.

10.3 EXAMPLE APPLICATION

To demonstrate the functions just presented, let's write a simple interpreter. This interpreter will read in clear text files that contain commands that are specified with a functional notation. A command will have the canonical form of

```
func_name([argument, argument . . . ])
```

where func_name is the name of the function, the parentheses are literal and between the parentheses can be any number of arguments separated by commas. To make things simple, there will be no variable declarations. This means that the parser must determine the data type of the passed arguments. One approach to do this could be to extract the function name and locate the description of the arguments it expects, and then coerce the passed arguments into the proper form. There is an easier way, and it is related to how values are specified. We'll use the following definitions on how arguments are to be defined:

- A string will consist of any number of characters between double quotes (").
- A floating-point number (double) is any series of digits that also contains a decimal point.
- An integer is any series of digits that do not contain a decimal point.

---

[1]Some would say abusing.
[2]You've heard this one before.

Listing 10.4   Source for find_func( ), which locates a registered function.

```
/*-------------------------------------------------
   Returns a pointer to the first element in a function
   definition block.
   -------------------------------------------------*/
#include "dds.h"

DDS_ELEMENT *find_func(func_list, func_name)
DDS *func_list;
char func_name[];
{
   DDS_ELEMENT *element;

   element = func_list->first_element;
   while(element != NULL) {
      if(strcmp(func_name, element->name) == 0) return(element);
      element = element->right;   /* Move to return value */
      element = element->right;   /* Move to arguments */
      element = element->right;   /* Move to function pointer */
   }
   return(NULL);
}
```

These three data types (character array, double, and int) should be sufficient for use with most functions.

Listing 10.5 contains the source for a function [called parse_func( )] that will parse the next line of text in a file. It expects two arguments. The first is a pointer to a preopened file, and the second is a pointer to a character array in which the name of the function will be placed. It returns a pointer to a dynamic data structure that contains the translated arguments specified in the text. It returns a NULL pointer if the end of file is reached or if there is any kind of syntax error.

There are two other functions in Listing 10.5. The first is called push_value( ), which requires two arguments. The first argument is a pointer to a dynamic data structure, and the second is a plain text value. What push_value( ) does is infer the data type of the plain text value using the rules detailed previously, create a dynamic data structure element of the proper type, and add it to the passed dynamic data structure. The other function in Listing 10.5 is clean_line( ). This function removes any leading and trailing white space from a string. This allows for more freedom in the visual structure of the text in the source file.

Now that we have a parser, all we need is an application that will glue the parse_func( ), register_func( ), and call_func( ) functions together in a reasonable fashion. Listing 10.6 contains the source for such an application, which we'll call "interp10." It expects a single argument on the command line which is the name of

Listing 10.5 Source for parse_func( ), push_value(), and clean_line( ), which are used to tokenize a textual description of a function call.

```c
#include <stdio.h>
#include <ctype.h>
#include "dds.h"
#include "interp.h"


/*------------------------------------------------------------
   Parses a string and extracts the function name portion
   and returns a pointer to a DDS that contains the
   arguments of the function. Returns a NULL pointer
   if the syntax is wrong.
-----------------------------------------------------------*/
DDS *parse_func(fptr, func_name)
FILE *fptr;
char func_name[];
{
   char *src;
   char *dest;
   char *ptr;
   char value[MAX_ARG_LENGTH];
   DDS *dds;
   char buffer[MAX_ARG_LENGTH + 1];
   int scanning;

   scanning = 1;
   while(scanning) {
      if(fgets(buffer, sizeof(buffer), fptr) == NULL) return(NULL);
      if(buffer[0] == '#') { continue;  }          /* A comment */
      clean_line(buffer);
      if(strlen(buffer) == 0) { continue;  }       /* Nothing to do */
      scanning = 0;
   }

   src = buffer;
   dest = func_name;

   while(*src != '(') {
     if(isspace(*src)) { src++;  continue;  }
     if(*src == '\0') return(NULL);
     *dest = *src;
     dest++;
     src++;
   }
```

```
   *dest = '\0';
   src++;

   dds = dds_create();
   dest = value;
   while(*src != ')') {
     if(*src == '\0') { dds_destroy(dds); return(NULL);   }
     if(*src == ',') { /* End of value */
      *dest = '\0';
      push_value(dds, value);
      dest = value;
     } else if(*src == '"') {   /* Skip to end of quoted string */
      do {
       *dest = *src;
       dest++;
       src++;
      } while(*src != '"' && *src != '\0');
      if(*src == '\0') { dds_destroy(dds); return(0);   } /* error */
     } else {   /* direct copy */
      *dest = *src;
      dest++;
     }
     src++;
   }
   *dest = '\0';
   if(strlen(value) > 0) {
     push_value(dds, value);
   }
   return(dds);
}


/*-------------------------------------------------
   Adds an element to a DDS. The value of the
   element is passed as a string. The type of
   of the element is determined by characteristics
   detected in the string.
-------------------------------------------------*/
push_value(dds, value)
DDS *dds;
char value[];
{
   double atof();
```

(continued)

Listing 10.5 *(continued)*

```
int i;
int end;
int type;
char *ptr;
char *head;
int ival;
double dval;
DDS_ELEMENT *element;

/* Determine type of value */
end = strlen(value);
for(i = 0;  i < end;  i++) {
  if(value[i] == '"') {
   type = (int)DDST_PTR;
   break;
  }
  if(value[i] == '.') {
   type = (int) DDST_DOUBLE;
   break;
  }
  if(isdigit(value[i])) {
   type = (int) DDST_INT;
  }
}

/* Now add the element to the DDS */
switch(type) {
  case DDST_PTR:
   ptr = value;
   while(*ptr != '"') ptr++;
   ptr++;
   head = ptr;        /* Point to character after first quote */
   while(*ptr != '"' && ptr != '\0') ptr++;
   *ptr = '\0';         /* End string at trailing quote */
   element = dds_add_element(dds, DDST_STRING, "", "argument");
   dds_seed_string(element, NULL, strlen(head) + 1);
   strcpy(element->data.value.s.ptr, head);
   if(element == NULL) return(0);
   element->data.value.ptr = malloc(strlen(head) + 1);
   strcpy(element->data.value.ptr, head);
   break;
  case DDST_DOUBLE:
```

```
        dval = atof(value);
        element = dds_add_element(dds, DDST_DOUBLE, "", "argument");
        if(element == NULL) return(0);
        dds_set_element_value(element, &dval, DDST_DOUBLE);
        break;
      case DDST_INT:
        ival = atoi(value);
        element = dds_add_element(dds, DDST_INT, "", "argument");
        if(element == NULL) return(0);
        dds_set_element_value(element, &ival, DDST_INT);
        break;
      default:
        break;
    }
    return(1);
}


/*------------------------------------------------------
   Cleans up an input line by removing all leading and
   trailing white space.
   ------------------------------------------------------*/
clean_line(buffer)
char buffer[];
{
    char *src;
    int i;

    src = buffer;

    while(*src != '\0' && isspace(*src)) { src++; }
    strcpy(buffer, src);
    for(i = strlen(buffer) - 1;  i >= 0;  i--) {
      if(!isspace(buffer[i])) { buffer[i + 1] = '\0';  break;  }
    }
    return(strlen(buffer));
}
```

Listing 10.6   Source for the interpreter example.

```
#include <stdio.h>
#include "dds.h"
#include "interp.h"


/*-------------------------------------------------
    An example application that demonstrates how
    dynamic data structures can be used to build
    an interpreter.
---------------------------------------------------*/
DDS *Func_list;

main(argc, argv) int argc;
char *argv[];
{

/* Functions which will be registered so that they can
    called by the interpreter.
*/
  int print();
  double add();
  double sin();
  int pop_print();

  FILE *fptr;
  char buffer[MAX_ARG_LENGTH];
  char func_name[MAX_ARG_LENGTH];
  char last_func[MAX_ARG_LENGTH];
  DDS *func_args;
  int ret_val;

  strcpy(last_func, "");

  if(argc < 2) {
   printf("Proper usage: interpl source_file\n");
   exit(0);
  }

 if((fptr = fopen(argv[1], "r")) == NULL) {
   perror(argv[1]);
   exit(0);
  }

  Func_list = dds_create();
```

```
  if(Func_list == NULL) {
  fprintf(stderr, "Unable to create dynamic data structure\n");
  exit(0);
  }


/* Add callable functions to the function list */
  register_func(Func_list, add, "add", DDST_DOUBLE,
          INPUT, DDST_DOUBLE,
          INPUT, DDST_DOUBLE,
          0);
  register_func(Func_list, print, "print", DDST_INT,
          INPUT, DDST_STRING,
          0);
  register_func(Func_list, pop_print, "pop_print", DDST_INT,
          INPUT, DDST_STRING,
          0);
  register_func(Func_list, sin, "sin", DDST_DOUBLE,
          INPUT, DDST_DOUBLE,
          0);

/* Interpret the file */
  while((func_args = parse_func(fptr, func_name)) != NULL) {
    if(call_func(Func_list, func_name, func_args) == NULL) {
        fprintf(stderr,
            "Function '%s' is not a registered function.\n",
  func_name);
    }
    dds_destroy(func_args);
  }
  exit(0);
}
```

the file that contains the text to be interpretered. After checking that a file name has been passed and that the file actually exists, it then creates a dynamic data structure that will hold the list of registered functions. It then registers the functions that can be called by the interpreter.

For this implementation four functions are registered: print( ), add( ), pop_print( ), and sin( ). The functions print( ), add( ), and pop_print( ) are presented in Listing 10.7, whereas sin( ) is the same one that is available in the standard C math library. Each function in Listing 10.7 is quite simple. The function print( ) expects a string and prints it to the screen. In the string you can embed standard C escape sequences. The interpretation of these characters must be done by print( ) because they are translated at compile time rather than by the printf( ) function. So in order for an interpreter to provide the same capability, it must translate the escape sequences.

Listing 10.7   Source for the functions print( ), add( ), and pop_print( ), which are used in the interpreter example.

```c
#include "dds.h"
#include "interp.h"


/*-------------------------------------------------
   Function to print a string to the screen.
------------------------------------------------*/
int print(string)
char *string;
{
  char *ptr;

  ptr = string;
  while(*ptr != '\0') {
   if(*ptr == '\\') {
      ptr++;
      switch(*ptr) {  /* Escape characters are translated at */
                      /* compilation so they need to be interpreted */
        case 'n':
            putchar('\n');
            break;
        case 'r':
            putchar('\r');
            break;
        case 't':
            putchar('\t');
            break;
        case 'b':
            putchar('\b');
            break;
        case 'v':
            putchar('\v');
            break;
        case 0:
            return(1);
        default:
            putchar(*ptr);
            break;
      }
    } else {
        putchar(*ptr);
    }
    ptr++;
```

```
  }
  return(1);
 }


/*-------------------------------------------------------
  Function to add two numbers and print the result.
-------------------------------------------------*/
double add(x, y)
double x, y;
{
  return(x + y);
}


/*-------------------------------------------------------
  Function to print the return value of a previously
  called function.
-------------------------------------------------*/
int pop_print(func_name)
char func_name[];
{
  extern DDS *Func_list;

  DDS_ELEMENT *element;
  double d_val;

  element = find_func(Func_list, func_name);
  if(element == NULL) { return(0);   }

  element = element->right;
  switch(element->data.type) {
   case DDST_INT:
      printf("%d", element->data.value.i);
      break;
   case DDST_DOUBLE:
      d_val = element->data.value.d;
      printf("%lf", d_val);
      break;
   case DDST_FLOAT:
      printf("%f", element->data.value.f);
      break;
   case DDST_CHAR:
      printf("%c", element->data.value.c);
      break;
```

(continued)

Listing 10.7 *(continued)*

```
  case DDST_PTR:
      printf("%s", element->data.value.ptr);
      break;
  }
  return(1);
}
```

The add( ) function expects two floating point arguments, adds them together, and returns the result.

The last function, pop_print( ), is probably the most interesting of the three since it demonstrates a unique feature that arises from the way in which the list of callable functions is maintained. As part of the definition of a function there is an element in the list in which the return value of the function is maintained. This is a persistent element, and so the return value of the most recent call to any function can be obtained. This is what pop_print( ) does; it expects one argument: the name of the function to print the most recent return value.

Referenced in Listings 10.5, 10.6, and 10.7 is an include file by the name of "interp.h." Listing 10.8 contains the source for this file. This file contains definitions of a few parameters and functions.

A series of commands that will call each registered function at least once is presented in Listing 10.9. In order for the interpreter to execute these commands, the

Listing 10.8 The include file interp.h used in the interpreter example.

```
/*---------------------------------------

    Definitions for use with the dynamic
      data structure implemetation of the
      interpreter functions.
    --------------------------------------*/
#ifndef _INTERP_
#define _INTERP_       1


#define MAX_ARG_LENGTH 512

/* Neither INPUT nor OUTPUT can be 0 */
#define INPUT  1
#define OUTPUT 2


DDS *parse_func();
DDS_ELEMENT *find_func();


#endif _INTERP_
```

Listing 10.9 Example commands for the interpreter.

```
print("Hello world!\n")

add(3.2, 1.5);
 print("3.2 + 1.5 = ")
pop_print("add");
 print("\n")

sin(3.0)
print("sin(3.0) = ")
pop_print("sin")
```

commands must be placed in a file and the name of that file should be passed as the first argument to interp10.

10.4 SUMMARY

In this chapter we looked at how dynamically linked applications could be implemented using dynamic data structures. This is an important area of implementation because dynamically linked applications are becoming increasingly prevalent. The drive behind this is that it allows for incremental changes of different portions of an application without the need for recombining all portions of the application. This could be costly in terms of human, computer, logistical, and other resources.

A topic of dynamically linked applications not discussed in much detail was that of dynamically linked libraries. The reason is that to address it properly is beyond the scope of this chapter. We can, however, discuss how it might be done. One possible approach would be to modify the linker so that a stub function is actually linked to the application for each function referenced in the application that exists in a shared library. The purpose of the stub function is to package its passed arguments into a dynamic data structure and invoke the proper registered function [with a call to call_func( )].

In addition to inserting a stub function, another function would have to be added to the application. This function would be called before the main function of the application. This function would attach the shared library to the application and initialize the list of callable functions in that library. Each shared library would have its own function list. There might be some naming convention for the function lists since each function stub will require access to the proper list in order to pass it on to call_func( ).

The actual mechanism of attaching a shared library to an application will depend on the environment in which it is implemented. On some systems it could be implemented by allocating more system memory and loading the library into this area. The location of functions in the shared library could be resolved by a lookup table contained in the sharable library that maps offsets to each function. This lookup table is read when the library is loaded, and the function pointers in the function list are updated so that they actually point to the proper function. Another possible implementation is that the sharable library is run as a separate process with arguments and results being exchanged by means of some interprocess protocol. There are other possibilities, but I think you get the idea.

As you can see, adding shared libraries to a system involves some very low-level changes to the linker. It also requires some means to create sharable libraries, which differs from the way ordinary libraries are created. These are topics better suited to a book on compiler and linker construction. Additional information on shared libraries can be found in [Gin89].

POINTS TO PONDER

10.1   A drawback to call_func( ) is that it does not allow support for variable argument functions [like printf( )]. Describe how call_func( ) can be altered so that it could also call variable argument functions.

10.2   Write a function that could be used to add to the interpreter example the ability to instantiate and assign values to variables. Use dynamic data structures in some way.

10.3   Describe how you would modify the parser in the interpreter example to recognize variable declarations and variables as arguments to functions.

Nth-Generation Languages | **11**

As time progresses people find more and more ways to use the computer to assist them in doing tasks and solving problems. Coupled with this is an evolution in the way we instruct a computer. Commonly this is called "programming," and we use programming languages to do it. A programming language is simply a symbolic description of how we would like a computer to perform a task. Early on in the history of the computers this was done with assembly languages. As the complexity of tasks increased, there was an accompanying need to instruct a computer at a higher level of abstraction. Each level of abstraction is referred to as a "generation" since it builds on and augments the abstractions that existed in the previous level. This evolution continues today and will continue in the future.

In this chapter we will explore how dynamic data structures can be used to build *N*th-generation languages, that is, generations that go beyond the level of abstraction in which dynamic data structures are implemented.

11.1 THE CHALLENGE

Show how dynamic data structures can be used to build or implement portions of programming languages that are a generation ahead of the language that the dynamic data structures are implemented in. To accomplish this, implement the signature specific function calling aspect of C++, a LISP interpreter, and the generic facility of the Ada[1] programming language.

11.2 THE SOLUTION

There are three separate tasks specified in the challenge, so we'll deal with them one at a time.

---

[1] Registered trademark of the U.S. Government, Ada Joint Program Office (and that's no joke.)

11.2.1 C++

The signature of a function consists of its name, its return value, and the number and type of each argument. In C++ [Str87] (unlike C) you can have functions with the same name, but with different signatures, and the compiler can distinguish which function to actually call. In Chapter 10 the registration and selective calling of functions was demonstrated. If we make minor modifications to the call_func( ) and find_func( ) functions presented in Chapter 10 we can implement a means to call a function based on its signature.

There will be one limitation to this implementation, and that is that the return value of the function will not be considered in determining which function to call. The reason for this is that the interpreter presented in Chapter 10 (which will be used in this implementation also) does not provide a means for determining the desired return type of a function call in the program text.

Listing 11.1 gives the source for a modified call_func( ) function called

Listing 11.1   Source for cpp_call_func( ), which calls a registered C++ function.

```
/*---------------------------------- -------------------------
    Calls a function that has been registered as
    a callable DDS in a dynamic data structure.
---------------------------------------------------------- */
#include "dds.h"
#include "interp.h"

#define MAX_ARG_STACK   128

DDS_ELEMENT *cpp_find_func();

DDS_ELEMENT *cpp_call_func(func_list, func_name, func_args)
DDS *func_list;
char func_name[];
DDS *func_args;
{
    DDS_ELEMENT *element;
    DDS_ELEMENT *e_ptr;
    DDS_ELEMENT *ret_value;
    DDS *expected_args;
    char (*c_func)();
    double (*d_func)();
    int (*i_func)();
    float (*f_func)();
    char * (*ptr_func)();
    char *ptr;
    int i;
```

```
int cnt;
int e_size;
int nchar;
struct {
   char stack[MAX_ARG_STACK];
} args;

element = cpp_find_func(func_list, func_name, func_args);
if(element == NULL) { return(NULL); }

ret_value = element->right;
/* Check that passed arguments match expected arguments */
expected_args = (DDS *)ret_value->right->data.value.ptr;
if(!dds_compare_dds(func_args, expected_args)) {
   fprintf(stderr, "Argument mismatch calling function: %s\n",
      element->name);
      return(NULL);
}

/* Build up argument list */
e_ptr = func_args->first_element;
ptr = args.stack;
cnt = 0;
while(e_ptr != NULL) {
   if(e_ptr->data.type == DDST_STRING) {  /* special treatment */
     e_size = dds_sizeof(DDST_PTR);
   } else {
     e_size = dds_sizeof(e_ptr->data.type);
   }
   if(cnt + e_size >= MAX_ARG_STACK) {
      fprintf(stderr, "Argument stack exceed!n");
      return(NULL);
   }
   if(e_ptr->data.type == DDST_STRING) {  /* special treatment */
     memcpy(ptr, (char *)&e_ptr->data.value.s.ptr, e_size);
   } else {
     memcpy(ptr, (char *)&e_ptr->data.value, e_size);
   }
   cnt += e_size;
   ptr += e_size;
   e_ptr = e_ptr->right;
}
```

(continued)

Listing 11.1 *(continued)*

```
/* Call function and store returned value */
switch(ret_value->data.type) {
    case DDST_INT:
        i_func = (int (*) ())element->data.value.ptr;
        ret_value->data.value.i = (*i_func)(args);
        break;
    case DDST_DOUBLE:
        d_func = (double (*) ())element->data.value.ptr;
        ret_value->data.value.d = (*d_func)(args);
        break;
    case DDST_FLOAT:
        f_func = (float (*) ())element->data.value.ptr;
        ret_value->data.value.f = (*f_func)(args);
        break;
    case DDST_CHAR:
        c_func = (char (*) ())element->data.value.ptr;
        ret_value->data.value.c = (*c_func)(args);
        break;
    case DDST_PTR:
        ptr_func = (char * (*) ())element->data.value.ptr;
        ret_value->data.value.ptr = (*ptr_func)(args);
        break;
}


/* Place returned results in proper arguments in DDS */
/* Output arguments have a name which begins with "output" */
e_ptr = func_args->first_element;
ptr = args.stack;
while(e_ptr != NULL) {
    e_size = dds_sizeof(e_ptr->data.type);
    if(strncmp("output", e_ptr->name, 6) == 0) {
        if(e_ptr->data.type == DDST_STRING) { /* special treatment */
            nchar = e_ptr->data.value.s.len;
            if(strlen(ptr) + 1 < nchar) nchar = strlen(ptr) + 1;
            strncpy(e_ptr->data.value.s.ptr, ptr, nchar);
        } else {
            memcpy((char *)&e_ptr->data.value, ptr, e_size);
        }
    }
    ptr += e_size;
    e_ptr = e_ptr->right;
}
return(element);  /* Success */
}
```

cpp_call_func( ). The function cpp_call_func( ) differs from call_func( ) in only one way: it calls cpp_find_func( ) rather than find_func( ). In all other aspects it functions identically to call_func( ); this includes the entry requirements. So the first argument is a pointer to the list of registered functions, the second is the name of the function to call, and the third is a dynamic data structure containing the arguments for the function. If a function that matches the given signature is found, then it is called.

Listing 11.2 presents the source for the modified find_func( ) called cpp_find_func( ). The major difference between cpp_find_find( ) and find_func( ) is that in cpp_find_func( ), once a function with the given name is found, the passed arguments are checked to see if they match those expected by the function. If they do, then it is considered a match; otherwise it is not. Like find_func( ), cpp_find_func( ) expects three arguments. The first is the list of registered functions,

Listing 11.2   Source for cpp_find_func( ), which locates a registered C++ function.

```
/*-------------------------------------------------------------
   Returns a pointer to the first element in a function
   definition block that meets the name and entry
   requirements.
   -------------------------------------------------------- */
#include "dds.h"

DDS_ELEMENT *cpp_find_func(func_list, func_name, arg_list)
DDS *func_list;
char func_name[];
DDS *arg_list;
{
  DDS_ELEMENT *element;
  DDS_ELEMENT *tmp_element;

  element = func_list->first_element;
  while(element != NULL) {
    if(strcmp(func_name, element->name) == 0) { /* Check arguments */
      tmp_element = element->right;       /* Move to return value */
      tmp_element = tmp_element->right; /* Move to arguments */
      if(dds_compare_dds(arg_list, (DDS *)tmp_element->data.value.ptr)) {
        return(element);
      }
    }
    element = element->right; /* Move to return value */
    element = element->right; /* Move to arguments */
    element = element->right; /* Move to function pointer */
  }
  return(NULL);
}
```

the second is the name of the function to search for, and the third consists of the entry arguments. If no match is found, cpp_find_func( ) returns a NULL pointer; otherwise a pointer to the first element in the function definition is returned.

To demonstrate that cpp_call_func( ) and cpp_find_func( ) do in fact do what is claimed, we'll implement two versions of an add( ) function. The first add( ) function, which we'll call add_double_double( ), will sum two double numbers and return the result. The second, which we'll call add_string_string( ), will concatenate (sum) two strings and return a pointer to the result. Listing 11.3 contains the source for these two add functions. Also included in Listing 11.3 is a function called return_print( ). This will print the return value of the most recently called function. It does this by passing

Listing 11.3 Source for add_double_double( ), add_string_string( ), and return_print( ), which are C++ functions used to demonstrate signature-specific calling.

```
#include "dds.h"


/*-----------------------------------------------------
   Function to add two numbers and return the result.
-----------------------------------------------------*/
double add_double_double(x, y)
double x, y;
{
  return(x + y);
}


/*-----------------------------------------------------
Function to add one string to the end of another.
-----------------------------------------------------*/
char *add_string_string(s1, s2)
char s1[];
char s2[];
{
    static char add_ss_buffer[1028];

    int n;

    strncpy(add_ss_buffer, s1, sizeof(add_ss_buffer) - 1);
    add_ss_buffer[sizeof(add_ss_buffer) - 1] = '\0';
    n = sizeof(add_ss_buffer) - strlen(add_ss_buffer) - 1;

    strncat(add_ss_buffer, s2, n);
    return(add_ss_buffer);
}
```

```
/*-------------------------------------------------------
   Function to print the return value of a previously
   called function.
   -----------------------------------------------------*/
int return_print()
{
   extern DDS *Func_list;
   extern DDS_ELEMENT *Last_call;

   DDS_ELEMENT *element;

   if(Last_call == NULL) { return(0); }

   print_element(Last_call->right);
}
```

to print_element( ) the pointer to the element that is associated with the return value of the most recently called function. This pointer is obtained from the global variable Last_call, which should point to the first element in the list of registered functions that was most recently called.

The function print_element( ), presented in Listing 11.4, prints the value associated with a given element. The format used is the default C format for the value's data type. Only one argument is passed to print_element( ), a pointer to a dynamic data structure element.

To demonstrate the use of cpp_call_func( ), cpp_find_func( ), add_double_double( ), add_string_string( ), print_return( ), and print_element( ), we'll write a variation of the interpreter presented in Chapter 10. This new interpreter, which we'll call scpp (for "simple cpp"), is presented in Listing 11.5. This differs from the one presented in Chapter 10 in three ways. The first difference is that the function cpp_call_func( ), rather than call_func( ), is called. The second difference is that a global variable Last_call is defined. This variable is assigned the pointer that cpp_call_func( ) returns. This pointer refers to the first element for the called function in the list of registered functions, if the call was successful. As discussed previously, this variable (Last_call) is used by return_print( ) to print the return value of the most recently called function. The final difference is which functions are registered. The functions that are registered include the new functions just presented as well as print( ) from Chapter 10.

A sample source of instructions that will test each registered function is presented in Listing 11.6. When the name[2] to the file that contains these instructions is passed

---

[2]You can pick any name you like. I prefer "delme.pls."

on the command line to scpp, you should see something like

```
1.23 + 2.34 = 3.57000
'this' + 'and that' = this and that
```

printed on the screen.

11.2.2 LISP Data Items

LISP [Ber85] is a list-oriented processor that is typically implemented as an interpreter. LISP has one superdata type, and that data type is the list (naturally). In LISP a list is defined as a collection of items, where items can be atoms, lists (also called

Listing 11.4   Source for print_element( ), which prints the contents of a dynamic data structure element.

```
#include "dds.h"


/*----------------------------------------------------
   Function to print the value of a dynamic data
   structure element.
   ------------------------------------------------*/
print_element(element)
DDS_ELEMENT *element;
 {
  switch(element->data.type) {
   case DDST_INT:
      printf("%d", element->data.value.i);
      break;
   case DDST_DOUBLE:
      printf("%lf", element->data.value.d);
      break;
   case DDST_FLOAT:
      printf("%f", element->data.value.f);
      break;
   case DDST_CHAR:
      printf("%c", element->data.value.c);
      break;
   case DDST_PTR:
      printf("%s", element->data.value.ptr);
      break;
   case DDST_STRING:
      printf("%s", element->data.value.s.ptr);
      break;
  }
  return(1);
}
```

"sublists"), and identifiers. A list begins with an opening parenthesis and ends with a closing parenthesis. Dynamic data structures can be used to maintain LISP lists (also called "s-expressions") in a very effective manor. To demonstrate this we'll implement the eval( ) function of LISP. This function [eval( )] is central to all LISP interpreters.

Listing 11.7 contains the source for the eval( ) function. This requires two arguments. The first is a string that should contain a list, and the second is a pointer to

Listing 11.5   Source for a simple C++ interpreter called scpp.

```
#include <stdio.h>
#include "dds.h"
#include "interp.h"


/*----------------------------------------------------

   An example application that demonstrates how
   dynamic data structures can be used to build
   C++ style type specific function caller.
----------------------------------------------------*/
DDS *Func_list;
DDS_ELEMENT *Last_call = NULL;


DDS_ELEMENT *cpp_call_func( );

main(argc, argv)
int argc;
char *argv[ ];
{

/* Functions which will be registered so that they can
   called by the interpreter.
*/
   double add_double_double( );
   char *add_string_string( );
   int return_print( );
   int print( );
   FILE *fptr;
   char buffer[MAX_ARG_LENGTH];
   char func_name[MAX_ARG_LENGTH];
   char last_func[MAX_ARG_LENGTH];
   DDS *func_args;
   int ret_val;
```

(continued)

Listing 11.5 *(continued)*

```
strcpy(last_func, "");

if(argc < 2) {
  printf("Proper usage: scpp source_file\n");
  exit(0);
}

if((fptr = fopen(argv[1], "r")) == NULL) {
  perror(argv[1]);
  exit(0);
}

Func_list = dds_create();
if(Func_list == NULL) {
  fprintf(stderr, "Unable to create dynamic data structure\n");
  exit(0);
}

/* Add callable functions to the function list */
register_func(Func_list, add_double_double, "add", DDST_DOUBLE,
    INPUT, DDST_DOUBLE,
    INPUT, DDST_DOUBLE,
    0);
register_func(Func_list, add_string_string, "add", DDST_PTR,
    INPUT, DDST_STRING,
    INPUT, DDST_STRING,
    0);
register_func(Func_list, return_print, "return_print", DDST_INT,
    0);
register_func(Func_list, print, "print", DDST_INT,
    INPUT, DDST_STRING,
    0);

/* Interpret the file */
while((func_args = parse_func(fptr, func_name)) != NULL) {
  if((Last_call = cpp_call_func(Func_list, func_name, func_args)) ==
  NULL) {
      fprintf(stderr,
          "Function '%s' is not a registered function.\n", func_name);
  }
  dds_destroy(func_args);
}
exit(0);
}
```

Listing 11.6 Example commands for use with scpp.

```
print("1.23 + 2.34 = ");
add(1.23, 2.34);
return_print();
print("\n");

print("'this ' + ' that' = ");
add("this ", "and that");
return_print();
print("\n");
```

an integer in which is returned the count of the number of bytes to the closing parenthesis in the passed list. The return value of eval( ) is a pointer to a dynamic data structure element. In this element is the value returned by the last list that was executed.

The eval( ) function is a single-line LISP interpreter. It both parses a list and calls the proper function. It does this by building a dynamic data structure that contains the evaluated items in a list. The first item in a list is always considered the name of the function to execute, with one exception, quoted strings. In this implementation quoted strings are designated by preceding a list with an apostrophe. In LISP a list may contain sublists; this implementation can handle this since care was taken to make it possible to call eval( ) recursively.

To demonstrate the use of eval( ), let's write an interactive interpreter. Listing 11.8 contains the source for such an interpreter; let's call it "lisp" to reflect its purpose. When you run this application, all the functions that can be called by the interpreter are registered using the functions developed in Chapter 8. In this implementation only the add( ) function of Chapter 8 is registered.

When you start lisp, it checks the command line for arguments. If no arguments appear on the command line, you are prompted to input an s-expression. What you enter is evaluated, and the return value is printed on the screen by the function

Listing 11.7 Source for LISP eval( ), the heart of a LISP interpreter.

```
#include   "dds.h"
#include "interp.h"


/*----------------------------------------------------------------
Evaluates a LISP expression.
---------------------------------------------------------------*/
#define advance() *src++;  (*cnt)++

DDS_ELEMENT *eval(buffer, cnt)
char buffer[];
```

(continued)

Listing 11.7   *(continued)*

```
int *cnt;
{
  extern DDS *Func_list;

  char value[MAX_ARG_LENGTH];
  char func_name[MAX_ARG_LENGTH];
  int first;
  int skip;
  int list;
  char *src;
  char *dest;
  DDS *dds;
  DDS_ELEMENT *dds_element;

  src = buffer;
  dest = func_name;
  first = 1;
  list = 0;
  *cnt = 0;

  dds = dds_create();
  if(dds == NULL) {
      fprintf(stderr,
        "System error, unable to create dynamic data structure.\n");
      return(NULL);
  }

  if(*src == '(') {        /* This is a list */
        list = 1;
        advance();
  }
  while(*src != '\0') {
        switch(*src) {
          case '(': /* Evaluate sub-list */
            skip = 0;
            dds_element = eval(src, &skip);
            if(dds_element == NULL) {
              printf("Error evaluating: %s\n", src);
              return(NULL);
            }
            dds_append_element(dds, dds_element);
            src += skip;
            *cnt += skip;
```

```
          break;
      case ')':          /* Execute if list */
        advance();
        if(!list) {
          fprintf(stderr, "Syntax error, extra parenthesis.n");
          return(NULL);
        }
        *dest = '\0';
        if(first) {
          if(strlen(func_name) == 0) { /* Just an atom */
          dds_element = dds_clone_element(dds->last_element);
          return(dds_element);
        }
        first = 0;
      } else {
        push_value(dds, value);
      }
      if((dds_element = call_func(Func_list, func_name, dds)) ==
        NULL) { return(NULL);
      }
      dds_element = dds_clone_element(dds_element->right);
      dds_destroy(dds);
    return(dds_element);
  case '\128':          /* take literal (quoted) */
    advance();
    dest = value;
    *dest = '"';
    *dest++;
    switch(*src) {
      case '(': /* Scan to ending closing parenthesis */
        advance();
        while(*src != ')') {
          *dest = *src;
          *dest++;
          advance();
      }
        advance();
        break;
    default: /* Scan to non-alpha */
      while(isalnum(*src)) {
        *dest = *src;
        *dest++;
```

(continued)

Listing 11.7 *(continued)*

```
              advance();
          }
          break;
      }
      *dest = '"';
      *dest++;
      *dest = '\0';
      push_value(dds, value);
      dest = value;
      break;
    default:
      if(!list) {
        fprintf(stderr, "Syntax error, indentfiers not allowed\n");
        return(NULL);
      }
      if(isspace(*src)) { /* Save value */
        *dest = '\0';
        if(first) {
          first = 0;
        } else {
            push_value(dds, value);
        }
        dest = value;
        advance();
    } else {
      *dest = *src;
      dest++;
      advance();
    }
    break;
  }
}

if(list) {
  fprintf(stderr, "Syntax error, missing ending parenthesis.\n");
  return(NULL);
} else {
  dds_element = dds_clone_element(dds->last_element);
  dds_destroy(dds);
  return(dds_element);
}
}
```

Listing 11.8   Source for a LISP interpreter.

```
/*---------------------------------------------------
   Example application: LISP interpreter.
---------------------------------------------------*/
#include <stdio.h>
#include <ctype.h>
#include "dds.h"
#include "interp.h"

DDS *Func_list;
DDS_ELEMENT *eval();

main(argc, argv)
int argc;
char *argv[];
{
   double add();

   int bogus;
   FILE *fptr;
   char buffer[1024];
   char prompt[80];
   DDS_ELEMENT *dds_element;

   strcpy(prompt, "eval: ");
   if(argc < 2) {
     fptr = stdin;
   } else {
     fptr = fopen(argv[1], "r");
       if(fptr == NULL) {
         perror(argv[2]);
         exit(0);
       }
   }

   Func_list = dds_create();
   if(Func_list == NULL) {
      printf("Unable to create function list dynamic data structure!\n");
      exit(0);
   }

   /* Register callable functions */
   register_func(Func_list, add, "add", DDST_DOUBLE,
```

(continued)

Listing 11.8   *(continued)*

```
      INPUT, DDST_DOUBLE,
      INPUT, DDST_DOUBLE,
      0);

   if(fptr == stdin) {
      printf("\n%s", prompt);
   }
   while(fgets(buffer, sizeof(buffer), fptr) != NULL) {
      clean_line(buffer);
      if(strlen(buffer) == 0) { continue; }      /* Nothing to do */
      if((dds_element = eval(buffer, &bogus)) == NULL) {
        fprintf(stderr, "Unable to execute command.\n");
        } else {
          lisp_print(dds_element);
          dds_free_element(dds_element);
        }
        if(fptr == stdin) {
          printf("\n%s", prompt);
        }
   }
}


/*-------------------------------------------------------------
  Prints the value of a dynamic data structure element
  in LISP format.
  -----------------------------------------------------------*/
lisp_print(dds_element)
DDS_ELEMENT *dds_element;

{
  print_element(dds_element);
}
```

Listing 11.9   Example commands for the LISP interpreter.

```
'(1.2 + 1.2 + 1.2 = )
(add 1.2 (add 1.2 1.2))
```

lisp_print( ), which requires one argument a pointer to a dynamic data structure element. You are then prompted again for some input. If any arguments appear on the command line, they are considered the name of the file in which LISP s-expressions exist. This file is opened and the interpreter executes all the commands in the file. An example file is given in Listing 11.9. When this file is given to the LISP interpreter, it will print the string "1.2 + 1.2 + 1.2 =" to the screen. The reason is that this is considered an atom by the interpreter and results in the text between the parentheses being printed out to the screen. Printed immediately after that will be the answer "3.6," which results from the list evaluating the second line of the file.

This implementation of a LISP interpreter is in no way complete. It lacks all but one LISP library function [add( )], and it does not support variables of any kind. Even so, it does demonstrate how useful dynamic data structures can be in providing support for programming languages that differ strongly in concept from the language that the dynamic data structures are implemented with.

11.2.3 Ada's Generic Facility

As part of the Ada language [GH80] there is a construct called a "generic facility." A generic facility is a subprogram or package that is not fully defined. It's more like a template since some portions of the facility are defined only when the generic subprogram or procedure is instantiated.[3] At the time of instantiation the unspecified portions of the facility are defined.

Since the implementation of an Ada compiler is beyond the scope of this book, we will demonstrate how dynamic data structures can be used to implement the generic facility of Ada by describing two components of an Ada compiler. The first component will be a means to register the template for a generic facility, and the second component will be a function that can be used to instantiate a generic subprogram of a package (which will be referred to collectively as a "generic unit").

We'll begin with how you might register the template for a generic unit. The functions required to do this already exist; they are the functions dds_create( ) and dds_add_element( ), presented in Chapter 9. You should be familiar with how these functions operate, so all we need is a description of how these functions could be used in an Ada compiler. The dds_create( ) function would be used whenever the declaration of a generic subprogram or package is encountered. The dynamic data structure that is returned will be used to hold definitions of the parameters that are required to complete the definition of the subprogram or package. As the declaration of the generic units is parsed, place holders will be encountered. Place holders are indicated by type declarations such as private, limited private, or the box construct (<>). Collectively the place holders define the required parameters when the generic unit is instantiated. All that is associated with these place holders is a name.

Once a generic unit is defined, it can be instantiated. On instantiation, a list of parameters must be supplied. There are two ways in which parameters may be

---

[3]To those of us who speak C, we call it "declared."

specified in Ada. One is positional, where the instantiation parameters are matched one to one to those required and in the order in which the parameters were declared in the generic unit. This is the same method used in calling functions in C. The other way in which parameters can be specified is by name. In this case the name of the parameter and the value it is to have are given. In either case a dynamic data structure can be created that will hold the parameters. When the compiler encounters the end of the instantiation of the generic unit, it must then fill in the place holders in the template. When this is done, the information in the dynamic data structure for the template and the dynamic data structure for the parameters are merged to become a single fully defined dynamic data structure that includes name and type information. This merged dynamic data structure is then associated in some way with the particular instantiation of the generic unit that created it.

11.3 SUMMARY

When we speak of Nth-generation language, it is implied that there is some sort of progenitor language. Typically the Nth-generation language enhances, simplifies, or refines one or more aspects of the progenitor language. In many cases the progenitor language is used to implement the Nth-generation language. One of the purest examples of this is the C++ programming language.

In this chapter we looked at how C and the concept of dynamic data structures could be used to build a foundation for three Nth-generation languages (C++, LISP, and Ada). For the C++ language, selective function calling based on the function's signature was implemented; for LISP, the eval( ) function was implemented; and for Ada, a method for implementing support for the generic facility was described.

Additional information on Ada can be found in [Geh83], and for LISP in [Wil84].

POINTS TO PONDER

11.1   Describe how you might maintain C++ objects. Note: An object consists of data and functions to operate on that data.

11.2   Write a LISP callable interface to the eval( ) function. In LISP eval( ) has one argument and that is an s-expression.

11.3   Describe how you might implement variables in the LISP interpreter.

Database Applications | **12**

Database applications come in a lot of shapes and sizes. To some, a database must be relational; to others, flatness is all that's important. Databases can also be hierarchical or graphical in structure. Regardless of the specific form a database takes, you can use dynamic data structures to provide clean and highly adaptive application interfaces to them.

12.1 THE CHALLENGE

In order to demonstrate how dynamic data structures can be used to solve database challenges, we will have to focus on a specific database paradigm. The specific paradigm we will study are those that are based on files with homogeneous record structures (flatfiles). This particular paradigm is used in most relational database management systems, as well as simpler data storage systems. Without choosing a paradigm, a specific challenge could not be presented.

Now for the challenge. We want an application that can provide the following:

- Access to flatfiles with any number of fields, any mixer of types for the fields, and any number of records
- A tabular listing of the contents of the flatfile
- A clear text method of choosing which fields to display

In essence this describes the basic functions of a data browser that can work on any flatfile. Without the use of dynamic data structures, this could be a huge project, but with the use of dynamic data structures, the solution can be presented in this chapter.

12.2 THE SOLUTION

The statement of the challenge implies that the following exists:

1. There is an external description of the structure of the flatfile. This description cannot be included with the data in the flatfile because this would violate the definition of a flatfile.
2. At a minimum, the description contains type information for each field in

the flatfile. Without this information, we could not accurately determine the structure of the flatfile.

3. The description contains plain text names for each field in the flatfile. Without this, we could not select fields by specifying a plain text name.

Presented in Chapter 9 was a set of functions for describing dynamic data structures using a C-style syntax. Since these functions provide the necessary support, we will require that the description of the flatfile structure be specified in a C-style syntax. This will also make the creation of a dynamic data structure to hold a record from the flatfile straightforward.

The foundation for the functions we'll need to work with flatfiles is presented in Listing 12.1. In Listing 12.1 there is a definition for a structure that describes a flatfile file. This structure (FLATFILE) contains two file pointers. One is for referencing the file that contains the data portion of the flatfile. The other is for referencing the file that contains a description of the structure of the data. The FLATFILE structure also contains a dynamic data structure variable (dds) that will serve as the storage point

Listing 12.1   Source for flatfile.h, which contains declarations for creating and using flatfile.

```
/*---------------------------------------------
   Definitions for use with flatfile functions.
   ---------------------------------------------*/
#ifndef _FLATFILE_
#define _FLATFILE_ 1

#include "dds.h"
#include <dir.h>

#define FF_MAX_EXT        MAXEXT
#define FF_MAX_NAME       MAXPATH

  typedef struct {
   FILE *data;
   FILE *desc;
   DDS *dds;
   char basename[FF_MAX_NAME + 1];
   int reclen;
} FLATFILE;

FLATFILE *flatfile_open();
void flatfile_close();
DDS_ELEMENT *flatfile_element_by_index();

#endif _FLATFILE_
```

for one record of flatfile data. The final element, reclen, is assigned the length (in bytes) of a single record. This can be used for record-level positioning in the flatfile and calculating the total number of records in the flatfile. The other items in Listing 12.1 are declarations for various flatfile functions.

The first of these flatfile functions is one that will open the flatfile. Listing 12.2 contains the source for a function, called flatfile_open( ), which will do just that. This function accepts two arguments. The first is the name of the flatfile. Physically a flatfile is stored as two files that have a common basename and a standard extension for each flatfile component. The standard extensions are ".DAT" for the data portion of the flatfile and ".DES" for the descriptive portion. When you supply the name of a flatfile, you use only the common basename, you never include either extension. The second argument to flatfile_open( ) is the mode to use when the flatfile is opened. If the second argument is an 'r', then the flatfile is opened for reading. If the second argument is 'w', then the flatfile is opened for writing. Flatfile_open( ) returns a pointer to a flatfile. If the pointer is NULL, the flatfile could not be opened.

In Listing 12.2 there is a second function called flatfile_load_dds( ). This function is called whenever a flatfile is opened for reading or when a new flatfile is created. It reads a C-style description of the structure of the flatfile and creates a dynamic data structure that matches the description. This is accomplished by reading the contents of the description file and compiling this into a dynamic data structure by calling dds_compile_C( ). Flatfile_load_dds( ) also calculates the record length by summing the size of each element in the dynamic data structure.

A complimentary function to flatfile_open is one that will perform an orderly closing of the flatfile. This involves flushing file buffers and removing any memory allocated on behalf of the flatfile. Listing 12.3 contains the source for such a function, called flatfile_close( ). Flatfile_close( ) requires just one argument, a pointer to a flatfile.

Listing 12.2   Source for flatfile_open( ), which opens a flatfile.

```
#include "flatfile.h"


/*------------------------------------------------------

   Opens a flatfile for either reading (r) or writing (w).
   If opened for reading the description of the structure
   of the flatfile is read and compiled.
   Returns a pointer to a FLATFILE structure.
---------------------------------------------------------*/
FLATFILE *flatfile_open(fname, mode)
char fname[];
char mode;
{
   FLATFILE *ffptr;
```

(continued)

Listing 12.2   *(continued)*

```
DDS_ELEMENT *element;
char tmpname[FF_MAX_NAME + 1];
char fmode[4];

  if(mode != 'r' && mode != 'w') {
    fprintf(stderr, "flatfile_open: mode must be either 'r' or 'w'n");
    return(NULL);
}


fmode[0] = mode;
fmode[1] = '\0';
if(mode == 'w') {          /* Open for updating */
 strcat(fmode, "+");
}

if((ffptr = (FLATFILE *)malloc(sizeof(FLATFILE))) == NULL) {
 perror("flatfile_open");
} else {  /* Everything O.K. */
 strcpy(ffptr->basename, fname, FF_MAX_NAME - FF_MAX_EXT);
 strncpy(tmpname, ffptr->basename, sizeof(tmpname) - FF_MAX_EXT);
 strcat(tmpname, ".des");
 if((ffptr->desc = fopen(tmpname, fmode)) == NULL) {
    perror(tmpname);
    free(ffptr);
    return(NULL);
}

 strcat(fmode, "b");    /* open in binary mode */
 strncpy(tmpname, ffptr->basename, sizeof(tmpname) - FF_MAX_EXT);
 strcat(tmpname, ".dat");
 if((ffptr->data = fopen(tmpname, fmode)) == NULL) {
    perror(tmpname);
    free(ffptr);
    return(NULL);
}

 if(mode == 'r') {
    flatfile_load_dds(ffptr);
 } else {
    ffptr->dds = NULL;
 }


}
```

```
   return(ffptr);
}


/*-------------------------------------------------
   Reads in and compiles the dynamic data structure
   definition that is in the descriptor file of
   flatfile.
   ------------------------------------------------*/
flatfile_load_dds(ffptr)
FLATFILE *ffptr;
{
   DDS_ELEMENT *element;

   ffptr->dds = dds_compile_C(ffptr->desc);
   if(ffptr->dds == NULL) {
     fprintf(stderr, "flatfile_load_dds: Unable to read data
       description.\n");
     return(NULL);
   }

   /* Calculate the length of a record */

   element = ffptr->dds->first_element;
   ffptr->reclen = 0;
   while(element != NULL) {
     ffptr->reclen += dds_sizeof(element->data.type);
     element = element->right;
   }
}
```

Listing 12.3 Source for flatfile_close( ), which performs operations related to closing a flatfile, and flatfile_delete( ), which closes and removes a flatfile.

```
#include "flatfile.h"


/*-------------------------------------------------
   Closes a flatfile and performs garbage collection.
   ------------------------------------------------*/
void
flatfile_close(ffptr)
FLATFILE *ffptr;
{
   if(ffptr == NULL) return;
```

(continued)

Listing 12.3   *(continued)*

```
ta);
   fclose(ffptr->desc);
   dds_destroy(ffptr->dds);
   free(ffptr);
   return;
}


/*---------------------------------------------
   Closes a flatfile and deletes the actual
   file.
---------------------------------------------*/
void
flatfile_delete(ffptr)
FLATFILE *ffptr;
{
   char ptr[FF_MAX_NAME + 1];
   if(ffptr == NULL) return;
   fclose(ffptr->data);
   fclose(ffptr->desc);
   strcpy(ptr, ffptr->basename);
   strcat(ptr, ".dat");
   remove(ptr);
   strcpy(ptr, ffptr->basename);
   strcat(ptr, ".des");
   remove(ptr);
   dds_destroy(ffptr->dds);
   free(ffptr);
   return;
}
```

Even though flatfile_open( ) allows you to create the basic components for a new flatfile (i.e., the properly named files), it does not provide a means for describing the structure of the newly created flatfile. Listing 12.4 contains the source for a function, called flatfile_define( ) which provides a simple means to do this. Flatfile_define( ) requires two arguments, the first is a pointer to a preopened flatfile (opened for writing), and the second is an array of character pointers; the end of the array is indicated by a NULL pointer. The character pointers should point to strings that contain a description of the desired structure for the flatfile. These strings are then written to the descriptive portion of the flatfile. The descriptions are then compiled by a call to flatfile_load_dds( ) so that an internal description of the structure of flatfile is obtained and the other flatfile related calls can be used on the newly created files.

Listing 12.4 Source for flatfile_define( ), which defines the structure of flatfile.

```
#include "flatfile.h"


/*----------------------------------------------
  Defines the structure for a flatfile.
----------------------------------------------*/
flatfile_define(ffptr, desc)
FLATFILE *ffptr;
char *desc[];
{
   char **dptr;

   dptr = desc;
   while(*dptr != NULL) {
     if(fputs(*dptr, ffptr->desc) == EOF) { return(0);  }
     fputs("\n", ffptr->desc);
     dptr++;
   }

   fflush(ffptr->desc);
   rewind(ffptr->desc);
   flatfile_load_dds(ffptr);

   return(1);
}
```

The ability to open a preexisting flatfile or create a new one certainly isn't very useful.[1] What is needed is a way to access the value of each field in a flatfile record. In Chapter 9 we developed a set of routines that allow you to either get or set the value of an element in a dynamic data structure. One way this can be done is by expression evaluation; the other is by binding. We will use these same functions [specifically dds_get_element_value( ), dds_set_element_value( ), and dds_bind( )] to provide access to the fields in the flatfile record. Each of these functions requires a pointer to a dynamic data structure element, so we need a function that will return a pointer to the dynamic data structure element that corresponds to a field in the flatfile. Listing 12.5 contains the source for two functions that can be used to do this. The first function in Listing 12.5, called flatfile_element_by_index( ), accepts two arguments. The first is a pointer to a flatfile, and the other is the index of the field in question. A field is identified by a zero-based number. This function returns a pointer to the element in the dynamic data structure that corresponds to the field index. It returns NULL if no element with the given index exists. The other function, flatfile_in-

---

[1]For most people it also lacks any amusement value whatsoever.

Listing 12.5 Source for flatfile_element_by_name( ) and flatfile_element_by_index( ), which returns
a pointer to the dds element that corresponds to a specific field in the flatfile.

```c
#include "flatfile.h"
#include <stdio.h>


/*-----------------------------------------------
   Returns the DDS_ELEMENT pointer to a field
   in a flatfile structure that has a specific
   index.
------------------------------------------------*/
DDS_ELEMENT *
flatfile_element_by_index(ffptr, idx)
FLATFILE *ffptr;
int idx;
{
  DDS_ELEMENT *element;
  int cnt = 0;

  if(ffptr == NULL) return(NULL);

  element = ffptr->dds->first_element;
  while(element != NULL) {
   if(cnt == idx) return(element);
   cnt++;
   element = element->right;
 }

  return(NULL);
}


/*-----------------------------------------------
   Returns the index of the field in a flatfile
   structure that has a specific name.
------------------------------------------------*/
flatfile_index_by_name(ffptr, name)
FLATFILE *ffptr;
char name[];
{
  DDS_ELEMENT *element;
  int cnt = 0;

  if(ffptr == NULL) return(NULL);

  element = ffptr->dds->first_element;
```

```
  while(element != NULL) {
    if(strcmp(element->name, name) == 0) return(cnt);
    cnt++;
    element = element->right;
  }

  return(-1);
}
```

dex_by_name( ), returns the index for the field that has a specific textual name. It returns −1 if no field with the given name exists. The number returned by flatfile_index_by_name( ) can be used with flatfile_element_by_index( ) to retrieve a pointer to the dynamic data structure element.

There remain just two other functions we need to complete a set of routines for dealing with flatfile files. The first of these is a function to write a record to a flatfile. Listing 12.6 contains the source for a function, called flatfile_write_rec( ), to do just this. The first thing that flatfile_write_rec( ) does is call dds_do_bind( ). This copies the contents of any application variable into the dynamic data structure element to which they are bound. This ensures that the element contains the most recently defined value and makes flatfile_write_rec( ) a trigger function for the write-oriented bind operation (as discussed in Chapter 6). After performing the bind, flatfile_write_rec( ) writes the contents of the data values maintained in the dynamic data structure to the flatfile. The data values are written so that the resulting record is packed as tightly as possible.

The last remaining function is the complement to the write function and is called flatfile_read_rec( ). This function reads a record from the flatfile and then performs a dds_do_bind( ) to update the values in all bound application variables. This makes flatfile_read_rec( ) a trigger function for read oriented binding. The source for flatfile_read_rec( ) is given in Listing 12.7.

12.3 EXAMPLE APPLICATIONS

Now things start to get fun because we have a collection of functions that we can use to create and work with flatfile. To demonstrate how to use these functions, we'll develop two applications. The first will read a description of the desired structure for a flatfile and create a flatfile to match the description and populate the flatfile with any number of records. The second application will read the contents of a flatfile and print formatted versions of the values for desired fields on the screen.

Listing 12.8 contains the source for an application (call it make_ff) that will create a flatfile. It expects two command-line arguments. The first is the name of the file that contains a C-style description for the desired structure of the resulting flatfile. The second argument is the desired number of records to seed the flatfile with. You could

Listing 12.6   Source for flatfile_write_rec( ), which creates a record in a flatfile. The contents of the record is taken from all bound application variables.

```
#include "flatfile.h"


/*------------------------------------------------
   Writes the contents of the dynamic data structure
   associated with the passed flatfile pointer to
   the flatfile data file. The contents are packed
   tightly as they are written.
------------------------------------------------*/
flatfile_write_rec(ffptr)
FLATFILE *ffptr;
{
  DDS_ELEMENT *element;

  if(ffptr == NULL) return(0);

  dds_do_bind(ffptr->dds, DDS_WRITE);
  element = ffptr->dds->first_element;
  while(element != NULL) {
   if(fwrite((char *)&element->data.value, dds_sizeof(element-
>data.type),
       1, ffptr->data) == 0) return(0);
   element = element->right;
  }

  return(1);
}
```

use the source of make_ff as a prototype for creating applications that can generate flatfiles specific to your needs. For now make_ff serves our immediate needs because we can use it to generate a flatfile that can be viewed with the application presented in Listing 12.9.

The application in Listing 12.9 (call it disp_ff) expects at least one command-line argument that is the name of the flatfile to display. You may optionally supply any number of subsequent arguments. These arguments are interpreted as the name of the fields in the flatfile to display. If you do specify these extra arguments, the fields are displayed in the order they appear on the command line. When disp_ff is run, it prints the selected portions of every record in the flatfile to the screen. It does not stop until the end of the flatfile is reached. If you would like to page through the output, you could redirect it into a utility like "more" or into a file and view the contents of the file with an editor.

Listing 12.7   Source for flatfile_read_rec( ), which loads the contents of the current record into all bound application variables.

```
#include "flatfile.h"


/*-----------------------------------------------
 Reads the next record in a flatfile and loads
  the contents into the dynamic data structure
  associated with the passed flatfile pointer.
---------------------------------------------/
flatfile_read_rec(ffptr)
FLATFILE *ffptr;
{
  DDS_ELEMENT *element;

  if(ffptr == NULL) return(0);
  if(feof(ffptr->data)) return(0);

  element = ffptr->dds->first_element;
  while(element != NULL) {
   if(fread((char *)&element->data.value, dds_sizeof(element->data.type),
       1, ffptr->data) == 0) return(0);
   element = element->right;
  }

  dds_do_bind(ffptr->dds, DDS_READ);
  return(1);
}
```

Listing 12.8   Source for an application to create a flatfile and generate data for it.

```
#include <stdio.h>
#include "flatfile.h"

char *Usage[] = {
   "Creates a flatfile given just a C style description",
   "in an external file.",
   "",
   " Proper usage: makeff <dds_desc> <nrecs>",
   "",
   "where <dds_desc> is the name of a file which contains",
   "a C style description of the structure for the flatfile",
   "and <nrecs> is the number of records the flat file is to have.",
   NULL
```

(continued)

Listing 12.8 *(continued)*

```
};

main(argc, argv) int argc;
 char *argv[];
 {
   FILE *fptr;
   FLATFILE *ffptr;
   double dval[128];
   char buffer[1024];
   char *desc[2];
   char **cptr;
   int nfields;
   int nrecs;
   int i,n;
   int cnt;

/* Check command line arguments */

   if(argc < 3) {
     cptr = Usage;

     while(*cptr != NULL) {
       puts(*cptr);

       cptr++;

     }
     exit(0);
   }

/* Process command line arguments */
   nrecs = atoi(argv[2]);
   if(nrecs < 1) {
      printf("There should be at least one record in the flat
  file.\n");
        exit(0);
   }

   fptr = fopen(argv[1], "r");
   if(fptr == NULL) {
      perror(argv[1]);
      exit(0);
   }
```

```
     i = fread(buffer, 1, sizeof(buffer) - 1, fptr);
     buffer[i] = '\0';   /* Insure proper termination */
     desc[0] = buffer;
     desc[1] = NULL;
     fclose(fptr);

/* Now create the flatfile */

     if((ffptr = flatfile_open("ff", 'w')) == NULL) {
       exit(0);
     }

     flatfile_define(ffptr, desc);

     dds_desc_dds(ffptr->dds, NULL, 0);
     nfields = ffptr->dds->e_count;
     printf("Nfields: %d\n", nfields);
     printf("Record length: %d\n", ffptr->reclen);

/* bind application variables to elements in DDS */
     for(i = 0; i < nfields; i++) {
       dds_bind(ffptr->dds, flatfile_element_by_index(ffptr, i),
         &dval[i], DDST_DOUBLE);
     }

/* Assign values to variables */
     printf("\n");
     printf("Creating %d records ...", nrecs);
     fflush(stdout);

     for(n = 0; n < nrecs; n++) {
       for(i = 0; i < nfields; i++) {
        dval[i] = i * n;

       }
       flatfile_write_rec(ffptr);
     }

     flatfile_close(ffptr);

     printf("done.\n");

     exit(0);
}
```

Listing 12.9 Source for an application to format and display the contents of a flatfile.

```c
#include "flatfile.h"

#define MAX_WIDTH        80
#define MAX_COLS         128

char *Usage[] = {
  "Displays the contents of a flatfile.",
  "",
  " Proper usage: dispff <ff_name> [<field name> ...]",
  "",
  "where <ff_name> is the name of the flatfile to display and",
  "<field name> is the name of the field in the flatfile to display.",
  NULL
};

main(argc, argv)
int argc;
char *argv[];
{
FLATFILE *ffptr;
  DDS_ELEMENT *dds_element;
  char **cptr;
  char cval[MAX_COLS][MAX_WIDTH];
  char headline[MAX_COLS * MAX_WIDTH];
  char ctmp[MAX_WIDTH];
  unsigned more;
  int nfields;
  int i;
  int cnt;
  int idx;

  if(argc < 2) {
    cptr = Usage;
    while(*cptr != NULL) {
     printf("%s\n", *cptr);
     cptr++;
    }
    exit(0);
  }

  /* Open flatfile */
  if((ffptr = flatfile_open(argv[1], 'r')) == NULL) {
    exit(0);
```

```
        }

    strcpy(headline, "| # ");
    nfields = 0;
    more = 1;
    if(argc > 2) {
        i = 2;
    } else {
        i = 0;
    }
    while(more) {
        if(argc > 2) {          /* Precess command line argument */
            if(i == argc) break;        /* done */
            idx = flatfile_index_by_name(ffptr, argv[i]);
            i++;
            if(idx == -1) {  /* Name doesn't exist */
                printf("A field with the name '%s' does not exist.\n", argv[i]);
                exit(0);
            }
        } else {                    /* Process all elements */
            if(i == ffptr->dds->e_count) break;         /* done */
            idx = i;
            i++;
        }
        dds_element = flatfile_element_by_index(ffptr, idx);
        strcpy(cval[nfields], "");
        if(dds_element == NULL) {
            fprintf(stderr, "Element %d does not exist\n", idx);
        } else {
            dds_bind(ffptr->dds, dds_element, cval[nfields], DDST_STRING);
            dds_seed_string(dds_element, cval[nfields], MAX_WIDTH);
        }
        sprintf(ctmp, "|%15s", dds_element->name);
        strcat(headline, ctmp);
        nfields++;
    }
    strcat(headline, "|");

/* For each record in the flatfile */
    cnt = 0;
    while(flatfile_read_rec(ffptr)) {
        if((cnt % 24) == 0) { /* Print header */
            print_hline(nfields);
```

(continued)

Listing 12.9   *(continued)*

```
    printf("%s\n", headline);
    print_hline(nfields);
    }
    cnt++;
    printf("|%3d ", cnt);
    for(i = 0;  i < nfields;  i++) {
       printf("|%15s", cval[i]);
    }
    printf("|\n");
  }
  print_hline(nfields);
  printf("\n");
  printf("Number of records: %d\n", cnt);

  flatfile_close(ffptr);
}


/*----------------------------------------------
  Prints a horizontal line that spans the entire
  listing.
-----------------------------------------------*/
print_hline(nfields)
int nfields;
 {
    int i;

    printf("------");
    for(i = 0;  i < nfields;  i++) {
       printf("---------------");
    }
    printf("\n");
}
```

A sample of the output produced by disp_ff for a flatfile that contains three columns, for the integers *i*, *j*, and *k*, is given in Figure 12.1.

12.4 SUMMARY

Presented in this chapter were a set of basic functions for manipulating flatfiles and two example applications that use these functions. Even though the example applications presented in this chapter are somewhat trivial, you should be able to extrapolate

```
 _____
|  # |                     i |            j |               k |
|----|-----------------------|--------------|-----------------|
|  1 |                     0 |     0.000000 |        0.000000 |
|  2 |                     0 |     1.000000 |        2.000000 |
|  3 |                     0 |     2.000000 |        4.000000 |
|  4 |                     0 |     3.000000 |        6.000000 |
|  5 |                     0 |     4.000000 |        8.000000 |
|  6 |                     0 |     5.000000 |       10.000000 |
|  7 |                     0 |     6.000000 |       12.000000 |
|  8 |                     0 |     7.000000 |       14.000000 |
|  9 |                     0 |     8.000000 |       16.000000 |
| 10 |                     0 |     9.000000 |       18.000000 |
 -------------------------------------------------------------
Number of records: 10
```

Figure 12.1 Example output from the application disp_ff.

the effectiveness of the solution and make a judgment as to how well dynamic data structures can solve other database challenges.

One thing you'll find out when you develop systems to deal with data is that if you limit the variety of structures to just a few choices, you will ultimately encounter someone who needs something you don't provide. Accommodating these requests can add a great deal to the cost of maintaining the data system. With a data system that is based on a dynamic data structure approach, there's no need for an application programmer to constantly modify the system to accommodate new structures. The ability to do this is inherently in the system.

Additional information on the design of database systems can be found in [Bra87] and [Dat75].

POINTS TO PONDER

12.1 Write a snippet of C code that will define a new data type called RECORD that has the same structure as is described in the description portion of a flatfile called "ff." This snippet should (without modification) generate an accurate structure for RECORD each time it is compiled.

12.2 Write a function that will position the pointer to the data portion of a flatfile to the beginning of on any record in the flatfile.

Information Transfer | **13**

Information transfer involves the exchange of information between two or more systems. Typically this exchange of information is accomplished by means of communicating processes, but it can also be accomplished with intermediated files in a store-and-forward type of implementation.

Information-transfer systems have many similarities to database systems in that any type of information can be transferred. Where they differ is that the source of the information can be either static or dynamic in an information-transfer system. For instance, one system may request information about the current load on another system. Since this is a dynamic aspect of a system, the exact information that is returned will depend on when the question is poised. This is in strong contrast to what you would expect from a static database where a specific question should always yield the same result, regardless of when you ask the question (provided, of course, the database has not been changed).

In most implementations of information-transfer systems a client–server model is used. Such a model consists of an originator of a request, called a "client," and the recipient and respondent to the request, called the "server." This model applies regardless of whether the client and server reside on the same machine. There are many systems that use this model; the most notable in the UNIX world is the Network File System (NFS from Sun Microsystems, Inc.) and the X-window system (from MIT).

13.1 THE CHALLENGE

Demonstrate the use of dynamic data structures in an information-transfer system. The specific system to develop is one that will allow the "calling" of functions that are external to an application. These functions should be implemented as a server application, whereas the calling application is a client. Make the system general enough so that the server functions can reside on any machine and can be accessed through whatever network capability might exist.

As a specific example, develop a set of server functions that will return

1. A list of files that match a given pattern. (Wildcards should be allowed in the pattern.)
2. The various resources available on a machine.

Also develop an application (client) that will demonstrate how each of these functions can be called.

13.2 THE SOLUTION

Various approaches can be taken in the implementation of a solution. Whatever approach we take, it's clear that there must exist some sort of protocol for invoking server function and for communicating between the client and the server. This very same issue has been dealt with by previous developers since the need to communicate between systems has existed.[1] While each solution has its merits, there is one that suits our requirements perfectly: the remote procedure call (RPC) specification. This specification details the application interface for a set of functions that implement the calling of remote functions (or procedures). It also specifies the protocol for the communication between the application (client) and the remote procedure (server).

In its entirety an RPC system consists of approximately 30 function calls. The purpose of these calls ranges from security functions like encrypting and decrypting information during an exchange, to authenticating the rights of a user to call specific functions, to establishing connections to remote procedures. Consequently, the task of implementing every aspect of an RPC system is beyond the scope of this chapter. What can be done is an implementation of the most basic components of an RPC system.

Let's start with the details of the RPC protocol. Basically the communication between the application and the remote procedure is accomplished by passing messages. The structure of the message depends on whether it originates from the application or from the remote procedure. An application message (request) has at least five elements, each of which is described in Table 13.1. These five elements constitute the call header. The call header is followed by the input arguments that are passed to the remote procedure.

A reply message, one originating from a remote procedure, has a header with at least two arguments. These are described in Table 13.2. Following the reply header is the output from the remote procedure, which can be any number or values.

In some implementations of RPC (e.g., Sun Microsystems'), there are mechanisms for secure message passing and authentication of the rights of the calling program. When this functionality is added to RPC, corresponding changes must be made to the message structures. It's sufficient for our immediate purposes to omit these features.

When these requirements are converted into C code, you get something like Listing

---

[1]That's before some of us were born.

Table 13.1   Description of Elements in the Message Header Required for Calling Remote Procedures

C data type	Common name	Description
Unsigned	xid	Contains a transaction identifier; this is a number assigned by the client and is used by the server to identify which request a response is for
Unsigned	rpcvers	The version number of the RPC protocol
Unsigned	prog	The number of the program to invoke
Unsigned	vers	The version of the program procedure to use
Unsigned	proc	The procedure to call

13.1. Listing 13.1 also has a few other items that will be used by the RPC functions. Listing 13.1 is referred to as "rpc.h" in subsequent listings.

There remains one other important component of the RPC specification. That something is how the program, version, and procedure numbers are translated into physical applications that contain the procedure. This is accomplished by use of a simple, clear text database file that contains an association between a program number and a specific application. The format of an entry in this file is

```
program_name    program_number    aliases
```

Each item can be separated by any number of tabs or spaces, and a line that begins with a hash (#) is a comment and everything to the end of the line is ignored.

As mentioned previously, the plan is to implement only the most basic functionality of an RPC system. To do this we need one thing: an application callable function that will in turn call a remote procedure, pass parameters to it, and wait for the results. RPC defines one such function: callrpc( ). This function has eight arguments, which are described (in argument order) in Table 13.3.

Aside from the fixed arguments detailed by the RPC specification, there is no restriction on how a message is passed to and from a remote procedure. This means that there are a variety of ways to do that task. You could use an intermediate file, a network protocol, command-line arguments, or shared memory. For the purpose of the presentation in this chapter we will use an area of shared memory as the conduit for message passing. This restricts the application and the process that contains the remote procedure to a single machine. However, we can still simulate a network-type RPC system by requiring callrpc( ) to invoke a dispatcher application that will determine which application contains the remote procedure. The dispatcher will then

Table 13.2   Description of Elements in Reply Header Required for Returning Results from a Remote Procedure

C data type	Common name	Description
Unsigned	xid	Contains the identifier for the transaction this reply corresponds to; this is the number that appeared in the call message
Unsigned	perror	The number of the RPC error which has occurred, if any

Listing 13.1 Source for the include file rpc.h, which contains descriptions for use with creating and using remote procedure calls.

```
----------------------------------------------
Definitions for use with the RPC functions.
----------------------------------------------*/
#ifndef _RPC_
#define _RPC_   1

typedef struct {
  unsigned xid;
  unsigned rpcvers;
  unsigned prog;
  unsigned vers;
  unsigned proc;
} RPC_CALL_HEADER;

typedef struct {
  unsigned xid;
  unsigned errno;
} RPC_REPLY_HEADER;

#define RPC_FIXED_XID  1
#define RPC_VERSION        1

/* Error codes */
#define RPC_SUCCESS        0
#define RPC_FAILURE        1

/* Keys for allocating shared memory */
#define RPC_CALL_KEY    1
#define RPC_REPLY_KEY   2

#define RPC_FILE          "rpc"
#define RPC_MAX_DDS_DESC          1024

int rpc_dds_to_shm();
int rpc_dds_from_shm();

/* Error codes and messages */
#define RPC_SUCCESS                0
#define RPC_FAILURE                1
#define ERR_RPC_BAD_PROTO          2
#define ERR_RPC_BAD_PROG           3
```

(continued)

Listing 13.1 *(continued)*

```
#define ERR_RPC_BAD_VERSION      4
#define ERR_RPC_BAD_PROC         5
#define ERR_RPC_CALL_MISMATCH    6
#define ERR_RPC_REPLY_MISMATCH   7
#define ERR_RPC_NO_DISP          9
#define ERR_RPC_NO_MEMORY        10
#define ERR_RPC_NO_RPC_FILE      11
#define RPC_NERRORS              12

#ifdef RPC_PERROR
int Rpc_errno;
#else
extern int Rpc_errno;
#endif

#endif _RPC_
```

mutate into this application, which in turn completes the communication with the calling application.

Before we depart too far from the aspects of callrpc( ), we need to take a closer look at what the arguments inproc and outproc are used for. Both inproc and outproc refer to functions. It is the responsibility of inproc to supply the parameter portion of the call message. The actual parameters are referred to by "in." The function referred to by outproc is called after receiving a reply message. Its purpose is to extract the returned values that follow the reply message header and place the results in location referred to by "out."

Since we are exploring how dynamic data structures can be used in this situation, we will require that "in" and "out" refer to dynamic data structures. This in turn requires that the functions inproc and outproc must operate on dynamic data structures. Each of these functions must have three arguments. The first argument is a pointer to the area of shared memory to operate on, the second argument is the dynamic data structure to use, and the final argument is a byte offset from the beginning of the first argument at which the dynamic data structure is to be placed. The function inproc( ) is expected to place a C-style description of the dynamic data structure beginning at the byte offset indicated by the third argument. The description is to be terminated by a zero byte. Following the description is to be placed the value for each element in the dynamic data structure. The function outproc expects a C-style description of a dynamic data structure, followed by the data for each element.

The functions inproc and outproc also play a very crucial role when messages are passed between machines of differing architectures. The reason is that a specific value may be represented differently on different machines. So it's typical in network-based implementations of RPC that inproc also normalizes all values into a machine-

Table 13.3 Description of the Arguments for the Function callrpc( )

Type	Name	Description
char *	host	The name of the host on which to invoke the remote procedure call
u_long	prognum	The number of the program that contains the procedure call
u_long	versnum	The version number of the procedure to call
u_long	procnum	The number of the procedure to call
char *	inproc	Local function to encode the arguments to the remote procedure
char *	in	The address of the arguments to supply the remote procedure
char *	outproc	Local function to decode the results returned from the remote procedure
char *	out	The address to place the results of returned from the remote procedure

Note: u_long is an unsigned long.

independent form prior to transport and that outproc denormalizes (converts to machine-dependent form) the returned values. The most common method for accomplishing this is to use eXternal Data Representation (XDR). The constraints on our design limit us to the same the host, so we don't have to worry about normalizing and denormalizing the values. We'll just pass them directly through.

Now let's look at an implementation that meets the design issues just discussed. Listing 13.2 contains the source for an implementation of callrpc( ). The arguments callrpc( ) expects were detailed previously in the chapter. As mentioned previously, the arguments in and out are expected to be dynamic data structures.

There are several things to note in this implementation of callrpc( ). First, the host name is considered the path to the dispatcher. Ordinarily this is treated as an actual host name, but this version of callrpc( ) was designed to work on PC DOS machines (it's not limited to this operating system; it will also work under other operating systems). If you think of a path as a network host ID, then it can simulate a network. The next noteworthy aspect is that callrpc( ) expects an application called "rpc_disp" to exist. This application dispatches any RPC requests to the proper RPC application. Finally, since callrpc( ) is not truly networked based,[2] it utilizes shared memory for communicating to rpc_disp and subsequently other RPC applications. In more typical implementations (like those under UNIX) the dispatcher resides at a well-known network port address.

The use of shared memory is not too different from using sockets or data streams for transporting data from one application to another. How shared memory is used in this version of an RPC system is that the application that is calling the RPC procedure creates two segments of shared memory. The first segment is used to pass the calling arguments to the procedure, and the second segment is used to return the results in. Both segments are of the appropriate size to contain all the necessary information. Since we will use dynamic data structures to hold our arguments (both calling and

---

[2]So that it can run under wimpy operating systems like PC DOS.

Listing 13.2   Source for callrpc( ), which calls a remote procedure.

```
#include <dos.h>
#include "dds.h"
#include "shm.h"
#include "rpc.h"

#define SIZEOF_SEGMENT 16
typedef unsigned long u_long;


/*-----------------------------------------------
   Calls a remote procedure, passing the given
   arguments and returning with the results.
   Returns 0 on success, -1 on failure.
-----------------------------------------------*/
callrpc(host, prognum, versnum, procnum, inproc, in , outproc, out)
char host[];
u_long prognum;
u_long versnum;
u_long procnum;
int (*inproc());
char *in;
int (*outproc());
char *out;
{

    char command[256];
    int ret_val;
    unsigned need;
    u_long in_memloc;
    u_long out_memloc;
    struct SREGS segment;
    char far *call_buffer;
    char far *reply_buffer;
    int id;
    RPC_CALL_HEADER *rpc_call;
    RPC_REPLY_HEADER *rpc_reply;
    char dir_sep[3];

    strcpy(dir_sep, "");

/* Build a message buffer area for both the call and reply buffers */
    need = sizeof(RPC_CALL_HEADER) + rpc_dds_size(in);
    id = shmget(RPC_CALL_KEY, need, IPC_CREATE);
    call_buffer = shmat(id, NULL, 0);
```

```
  if(call_buffer == NULL) {
    Rpc_errno = ERR_RPC_NO_MEMORY;
    return(Rpc_errno);
  }
  rpc_call = (RPC_CALL_HEADER *)call_buffer;

  need = sizeof(RPC_REPLY_HEADER) + rpc_dds_size(out);
  id = shmget(RPC_REPLY_KEY, need, IPC_CREATE);
  reply_buffer = shmat(id, NULL, 0);
  if(reply_buffer == NULL) {
    Rpc_errno = ERR_RPC_NO_MEMORY;
    return(Rpc_errno);
  }
  rpc_reply = (RPC_REPLY_HEADER *)reply_buffer;

/* Set values in call header */
  rpc_call->xid = RPC_FIXED_XID;
  rpc_call->rpcvers = RPC_VERSION;
  rpc_call->prog = prognum;
  rpc_call->vers = versnum;
  rpc_call->proc = procnum;
  inproc(call_buffer, in, sizeof(RPC_CALL_HEADER));
  rpc_dds_to_shm(reply_buffer, out, sizeof(RPC_REPLY_HEADER));

/* build up command to invoke the RPC dispatcher
   In this example 'host' is interpreted as the
   name of the dispatcher.
*/

  if(strlen(host) > 0) {
   if(host[strlen(host) - 1] != '\\') {
      strcpy(dir_sep, "\\");
   }
  }

/* Look out, this is VERY Turboc dependent!! */
  sprintf(command, "%s%srpc_disp %d %u:%u %d %u:%u\n", host, dir_sep,
     RPC_CALL_KEY, FP_SEG(call_buffer), FP_OFF(call_buffer),
     RPC_REPLY_KEY, FP_SEG(reply_buffer), FP_OFF(reply_buffer));

  if(system(command) == -1) {
   Rpc_errno = ERR_RPC_NO_DISP;
```

(continued)

Listing 13.2 *(continued)*

```
  return(Rpc_errno);
}
  Rpc_errno = rpc_reply->errno;

/* Check return status of call */

  if(rpc_reply->xid != RPC_FIXED_XID) { return(RPC_FAILURE); }

  outproc(reply_buffer, out, sizeof(RPC_REPLY_HEADER));

  return(Rpc_errno);
}
```

return), we need a function that will determine just how large a segment of memory is required in order to hold a specific dynamic data structure. In Listing 13.3 there is a function called rpc_dds_size( ), which will return the count of the number of bytes required to hold a C-style description of the passed dynamic data structure and the data associated with the dynamic data structure. The function callrpc( ) uses this function to determine how much shared memory to allocate. To perform the actual allocation of each shared memory segment, calls to shmget( ), and shmat( ) are made. The allocation of shared memory is done in two steps. The first is a call to shmget( ), which creates or locates an area of shared memory and then a call to shmat( ), which maps a piece of shared memory into the local address space of the application.

There are three arguments to shmget( ). The first is a key. This key is a number that distinguishes one segment of shared memory from another, and it must be the same in all applications that will share the segment. The second argument designates the amount of desired shared memory, and the third argument is a composite of flags that modify the function's operation. One flag is IPC_CREATE, which requests that the segment of shared memory be created. This must be done by at least one application that uses the shared memory. For this implementation callrpc( ) will have this responsibility. If the flag is 0 (zero), then shmget( ) searches the systems for the shared-memory segment; if one exists, the return value from shmget( ) is an identifier for the segment of shared memory. This identifier is used by shmat( ) (and other shared-memory calls) to manipulate the segment.

The function shmat( ) also has three arguments. The first of these is the identifier of the shared-memory segment to operate on [returned by shmget( )]. The second argument is the address in the current application to attach the segment at. If this argument is 0, shmat( ) will attach the segment at a location of its choosing. The third argument is a composite flag that can be used to qualify the types of operations that can be performed on the segment (i.e., read or read/write).

You might wonder why I'm going into such detail about these two functions. The

Listing 13.3 Source for rpc_dds_size( ), which determines the memory needs for a dynamic data structure.

```
#include "rpc.h"
#include "dds.h"


/*-----------------------------------------------------
   Returns the count of the number of bytes required
   for the storage of a DDS in an RPC message.
   -----------------------------------------------------*/
rpc_dds_size(dds)
DDS *dds;
{
  char buffer[RPC_MAX_DDS_DESC];
  DDS_ELEMENT *dds_element;
  int need = 0;

  if(dds == NULL) {        /* Nothing defined */
    return(need);
  }

  if(dds_desc_dds(dds, buffer, RPC_MAX_DDS_DESC) == 0) { /* desc too
    big */
   return(need);
  }

  need = strlen(buffer) + 1;  /* Need to include zero byte */
  dds_element = dds->first_element;
  while(dds_element != NULL) {
    if(dds_element->data.type == DDST_STRING) {
      need += dds_element->data.value.s.len;
    } else {
      need += dds_sizeof(dds_element->data.type);
    }
    dds_element = dds_element->right;
  }
  return(need);
}
```

reason is quite simple, even though these functions are available in most UNIX releases;[3] they are lacking from many other environments, for example, most C compilers on an IBM PC or compatible running DOS. So that this implementation can be run in these environments, Listing 13.4 contains the source for a version of shmget( ) and shmat( ) that will work in a TurboC environment. Listing 13.4 also contains a function called init_shm( ), which does not have a UNIX counterpart, which takes two arguments. The first argument is the count of the number of arguments passed on the command line to the application, and the second is an array of pointers to the arguments. These are commonly called argc and argv, respectively, in the main( ) function. What init_shm( ) expects in argv are pairs of values. The first value in the pair is a key (or identifier) for the shared-memory segment, and the second argument in the pair is the address of the start of the memory segment. The address is formatted as a segment and offset address separated by a colon (i.e., 8000:1440). There can be any number of pairs.

Since this implementation is tailored for the PC DOS environment, every application that will use shared memory must make a call to init_shm( ). Also the application that creates a shared-memory segment and wishes another application to use it must communicate the address to the other application. For our little RPC system, we'll do this with command-line arguments. The function callrpc( ) does just this when it calls rpc_disp.

Listing 13.5 contains the source for the include file "shm.h" referenced in Listing 13.4. In this file are definitions of IPC_CREATE and related variables required by the TurboC versions of shmget( ) and shmat( ).

The actual operation of filling the data area of the shared memory involves extracting the value of each element of the dynamic data structure and packing it into the data area of the shared-memory segment. Listing 13.6 contains the source for two functions that can be used to do this. The function rpc_dds_to_shm( ) packs the data in a dynamic data structure into an area of memory, while rpc_dds_from_shm( ) loads the data in an area of memory into a dynamic data structure. Each of these calls has three arguments. The first is a pointer to the area of memory to operate on, the second is a pointer to a dynamic data structure, and the third is the offset from the beginning of the memory to the C-style description. This allows the functions to operate directly on shared memory that has been created for communicating to remote procedures. While these functions are used internally in the RPC functions presented in this chapter, they can also be used as the arguments inproc and outproc.

Now let's turn to the RPC dispatcher application required by callrpc( ). In Listing 13.7 is one implementation of a dispatcher. The first action of this application is to attach to the shared-memory segment created by callrpc( ). This is accomplished with a call to shmget( ) and shmat( ). After attaching the shared memory the dispatcher reads the call header and extracts the program number. It then opens the file "rpc," which should contain a table of program numbers and application names in the format detailed previously. If the dispatcher found a match, it then mutates into the proper

---

[3]UNIX system V, release 4, and SunOS, release 4.0, are two examples.

Listing 13.4   Source for the shared-memory functions init_shm( ), shmget( ), and shmat( ).

```
#include "shm.h"


static char *Shm_ptr[SHM_MAX_SEGMENTS];
static int Shm_cnt = 0;
static char **Shm_argv;
static int Shm_argc;


/*------------------------------------------------
   Initializes the shared memory lookup table.
---------------------------------------------- */
init_shm(argc, argv)
int argc;
char *argv[];
{
  int i;

  Shm_argc = argc;
  Shm_argv = argv;
  for(i = 0; i < SHM_MAX_SEGMENTS; i++) {
    Shm_ptr[i] = NULL;
  }
}


/* ------------------------------------------------
   Returns a pointer to an area of shared memory.
   Tailored for TurboC. Must be compiled with either
   the compact, large, or huge model.
-------------------------------------------------------- */
char *shmat(shmid, shmaddr, shmflag)
int shmid;
char far *shmaddr;
int shmflag;
{
  unsigned int ds;
  unsigned int off;
  int tmp_id;

  if(shmaddr != NULL) { /* Not supported */
    return(NULL);
  }
```

(continued)

Listing 13.4 *(continued)*

```
if(shmid > 1 && shmid < Shm_argc) {  /* Its an internal region */
  sscanf(Shm_argv[shmid], "%u:%u", &ds, &off);
  return(MK_FP(ds, off));
}

/* Its an internal segment */
tmp_id = -shmid;
tmp_id-;
if(tmp_id < Shm_cnt) {
  return(Shm_ptr[tmp_id]);
}
/* Its not valid */
return(NULL);
}


/*-------------------------------------------------------
   Gets the id for a piece of shared memory. It also can
   create a new segment. This is specific to Turboc.
   Must be compiled with either the compact, large, or huge
   model.
-------------------------------------------------------*/
shmget(key, size, shmflag)
int key;
int size;
int shmflag;
{
   int i;

   if(shmflag & IPC_CREATE) {  /* Create the segment */
     if(Shm_cnt >= SHM_MAX_SEGMENTS) { return(0); }
     Shm_ptr[Shm_cnt] = (char *)malloc(size);
     Shm_cnt++;
     return(-Shm_cnt);
   }

/* Search external map for a match to "key" */
   for(i = 1; i < Shm_argc; i+=2) {
     if(key == atoi(Shm_argv[i])) { return(i + 1); }
   }

   return(0);
}
```

Listing 13.5 Source for the include file shm.h, which is required by the shared-memory functions.

```
/*----------------------------------------------
   Definitions for the use of shared memory.
----------------------------------------------*/
#ifndef _SHM_
#define _SHM_   1

#include <stdio.h>
#include <dos.h>
#include <alloc.h>

#define IPC_CREATE        1

#define SHM_MAX_SEGMENTS          16

char *shmat();

#endif _SHM_
```

Listing 13.6 Source for the functions rpc_dds_to_shm( ) and rpc_dds_from_shm( ), which perform the necessary operations for moving information to and from a dynamic data structure and a segment of shared memory.

```
#include "rpc.h"
#include "dds.h"

/*----------------------------------------------
   Function to copy the contents of a dynamic
   data structure into the proper area of
   shared memory for an RPC call.
------- -------------------------------------*/
rpc_dds_to_shm(shm_ptr, dds, offset)
char *shm_ptr;
DDS *dds;
int offset;
{
  char *dest;
  char *source;
  char buffer[RPC_MAX_DDS_DESC];
```

(continued)

Listing 13.6   *(continued)*

```
DDS_ELEMENT *dds_element;
int size;

if(dds == NULL) {        /* Nothing defined */
  return(0);
}

dest = shm_ptr + offset;

/* Load description */
if(dds_desc_dds(dds, dest, RPC_MAX_DDS_DESC) == 0) { /* desc too
  big */
 return(0);
}
dest += strlen(dest) + 1;

/* load data values */
dds_element = dds->first_element;
while(dds_element != NULL) {
 if(dds_element->data.type == DDST_STRING) {
    size = dds_element->data.value.s.len;
    source = dds_element->data.value.s.ptr;
  } else {
    size = dds_sizeof(dds_element->data.type);
    source = (char *)&dds_element->data.value;
  }
 memcpy(dest, source, size);
 dest += size;
 dds_element = dds_element->right;
 }
 return(1);
}


/*-----------------------------------------------
  Function to copy the contents of a dynamic
  data structure in a shared memory message into
  an application's DDS.
  -----------------------------------------------*/
rpc_dds_from_shm(shm_ptr, dds, offset)
char *shm_ptr;
DDS *dds;
int offset;
{
```

```
char *source;
char *dest;
char buffer[RPC_MAX_DDS_DESC];
DDS_ELEMENT *dds_element;
int size;

if(dds == NULL) {          /* Nothing defined */
 return(0);
}


source = shm_ptr + offset;

/* skip description - an error check could be made here */
source += strlen(source) + 1;

/* load data values */
dds_element = dds->first_element;
while(dds_element != NULL) {
  if(dds_element->data.type == DDST_STRING) {
    size = dds_element->data.value.s.len;
    dest = dds_element->data.value.s.ptr;
  } else {
    size = dds_sizeof(dds_element->data.type);
    dest = (char *)&dds_element->data.value;
  }
  memcpy(dest, source, size);
  source += size;
  dds_element = dds_element->right;
}
 return(1);
}
```

application by calling execve( ). If it doesn't find a match, it returns with an error ERR_RPC_BAD_PROC message. If it doesn't find the file "rpc," it returns ERR_RPC_NO_FILE.

Errors such as these, as well as failures of the remote procedure calls, can be difficult to report back to the user of an application that uses an RPC. The reason is that the dispatcher and the remote procedures are, for the most part, disallowed access to the user's screen. To help with the dilemma of reporting errors, there is a function called rpc_perror( ), which can be used to report RPC-related errors in the fashion that perror( ) is used to report errors of local functions. Listing 13.8 contains the source for an implementation of rpc_perror( ).

Listing 13.7   Source for a remote procedure call (RPC) dispatcher (rpc_disp.)

```
/*-------------------------------------------------------
    RPC_DISP: RPC call dispatcher. Designed for use with
    TurboC, compile with the compact or large model.
-------------------------------  -------  --------------*/
#include <stdio.h>
#include <dos.h>
#include "shm.h"
#include "rpc.h"

main(argc, argv., envp)
int argc;
char *argv[];
char *envp[];
{
    int ds;
    int off;
    unsigned int found;
    unsigned int prog_num;
    char prog_name[256];
    char buffer[1024];
    struct SREGS segment;
    FILE *fptr;
    int id;
    RPC_CALL_HEADER *rpc_call;
    RPC_REPLY_HEADER *rpc_reply;

    if(argc < 5) exit(-1);   /* Not enough arguments */
    init_shm(argc, argv);

    /* Attach shared memory */
    id = shmget(RPC_CALL_KEY, 0, 0);
    rpc_call = (RPC_CALL_HEADER *)shmat(id, NULL, 0);
    id = shmget(RPC_REPLY_KEY, 0, 0);
    rpc_reply = (RPC_REPLY_HEADER *)shmat(id, NULL, 0);

    if((fptr = fopen(RPC_FILE, "r")) == NULL) {
     rpc_reply->errno = ERR_RPC_NO_RPC_FILE;
     exit(-1);
    }

/* Search for name of program, given the program's RPC number */
    found = 0;
    while(fgets(buffer, sizeof(buffer), fptr) != NULL) {
```

```
    if(buffer[0] == '#') continue;        /* a comment */
    sscanf(buffer, "%s %u", prog_name, &prog_num);
    if(prog_num == rpc_call->prog) {
        found = 1;
         break;
    }
  }

  if(!found) {
   rpc_reply->errno = ERR_RPC_BAD_PROG;
   exit(-1);
   }

  argv[0] = prog_name;
  execve(prog_name, argv, envp); /* If this returns program not run */
  rpc_reply->errno = ERR_RPC_BAD_PROG;
  exit(-1);
}
```

Listing 13.8   Source for rpc_perror( ), which is used to report errors related to remote procedure calls.

```
#include <stdio.h>
#define RPC_PERROR 1
#include "rpc.h"

/*------------------------------------------------------------
   Prints an error message that corresponds to the
   the current definition in Rpc_errno. Note: this function
   expects RPC_FAILURE to be the first error code and
   RPC_NERRORS to contain the count of the number of possible
   errors.
   ----------------------------------------------------------*/
rpc_perror(filler)
char filler[];
{
    char *errmsg[RPC_NERRORS];

    errmsg[RPC_FAILURE] =
        "Unclassigied failured.";
    errmsg[ERR_RPC_BAD_PROTO] =
        "Unsuppoted RPC protocol version.";
```

(continued)

Listing 13.8 *(continued)*

```
  errmsg[ERR_RPC_BAD_PROG] =
    "Requested program number is not valid.";
  errmsg[ERR_RPC_BAD_VERSION] =
    "Requested version number is not supported.";
  errmsg[ERR_RPC_BAD_PROC] =
    "Requested procedure is not available.";
  errmsg[ERR_RPC_CALL_MISMATCH] =
    "Calling arguments do not match required arguments.";
  errmsg[ERR_RPC_REPLY_MISMATCH] =
    "Return arguments do not match required structure.";
  errmsg[ERR_RPC_NO_DISP] =
    "Unable to contact RPC dispatcher.";
  errmsg[ERR_RPC_NO_MEMORY] =
    "Unable to allocate required memory.";
  errmsg[ERR_RPC_NO_RPC_FILE] =
    "Can not open RPC index table.";

  fprintf(stderr, "%s: ", filler);
  if(Rpc_errno < RPC_FAILURE || Rpc_errno >= RPC_NERRORS) {
    fprintf(stderr, "Error number %d\n", Rpc_errno);
  } else {
    fprintf(stderr, "%s\n", errmsg[Rpc_errno]);
  }
}
```

13.2.1 Remote Procedures

As stated in the challenge at the beginning of this chapter, we were to implement an RPC system that would support two remote procedures. The first procedure was to return a list of file names that matched a given mask, and the second was to return resource information about the host system. Both of these operations are very system-specific because both file systems and architectures can vary from machine to machine.

Listing 13.9 presents the source for an application, call it fsglob, which contains a function that can be called as a remote procedure. The function will return a list of file names that match a given mask. It expects one calling argument, the mask, and returns a string filled with the file names. The source in Listing 13.9 is specific to the PC DOS environment and must be compiled with TurboC.

Listing 13.9 has merit even if you don't use a PC since the important aspects of the application are independent of the file-system-dependent portions (those portions

Listing 13.9 Source for the remote procedure fsglob, which returns file names that match a given mask.

```
/*-----------------------------------------------
 A file system GLOB remote remote procedure call.
 ----------------------------------------------*/
#include <stdio.h>
#include "dir.h"
#include "rpc.h"
#include "shm.h"
#include "dds.h"
#include "rpc_xpl.h"

char *Glob_1_retval = " \n\
  struct {                                                        \n\
     int count;           /* Number of matching files */          \n\
     char names[2];       /* Names of files which match mask */ \n\
  }     \
";


/*-----------------------------------------------
  An application containing procedures
  (functions) that can be called as remotely.
  ----------------------------------------------*/
main(argc, argv)
int argc;
char *argv[];
{
  RPC_CALL_HEADER *call_header;
  RPC_REPLY_HEADER *reply_header;
  char *call_args;
  char *reply_args;
  char *call_ptr;
  char *reply_ptr;
  int id;
  char *shm_ptr;
  int i;

  init_shm(argc, argv);

  /* Attach all the shared memory to process */
  id = shmget(RPC_CALL_KEY, 0, 0);
  call_ptr = shmat(id, NULL, 0);
```

(continued)

Listing 13.9 *(continued)*

```
if(call_ptr == NULL) {          /* failed to get shared memory */
 exit(0);
}

id = shmget(RPC_REPLY_KEY, 0, 0);
reply_ptr = shmat(id, NULL, 0);
if(reply_ptr == NULL) {         /* failed to get shared memory */
 exit(0);
}

call_header = (RPC_CALL_HEADER *)call_ptr;
call_args = call_ptr + sizeof(RPC_CALL_HEADER);
reply_header = (RPC_REPLY_HEADER *)reply_ptr;
reply_args = reply_ptr + sizeof(RPC_REPLY_HEADER);
reply_header->xid = call_header->xid;
if(call_header->rpcvers != RPC_VERSION) {        /* Don't support */
  reply_header->errno = ERR_RPC_BAD_PROTO;
  exit(0);
}

/* Now run the desired procedure (function) */
switch(call_header->proc) {
 case 1:
    reply_header->errno = glob(call_header->vers, call_args,
      reply_arg
    break;
  default:
    reply_header->errno = ERR_RPC_BAD_PROC;
    break;
}
 exit(0);
}


/*--------------------------------------------------------
 Finds all files that match a given mask.
 Returns with the reply_args filled with the results.
 --------------------------------------------------------*/
glob(version, call_args, reply_args)
unsigned int version;
char *call_args;
char *reply_args;
{
  DDS *call_dds;
```

```
    DDS *reply_dds;
    DDS *return_dds;
    DDS_ELEMENT *element;
    struct ffblk ffblk;
    char *ptr;
    int max;
    int done;
    int slen;
    int cnt =0;
    int nfiles = 0;

/* Build up DDS for passed arguments */
    call_dds = dds_str_compile_C(call_args);
    rpc_dds_from_shm(call_args, call_dds, 0);

    reply_dds = dds_str_compile_C(reply_args);

    /* Check arguments for both call and reply DDS */
    switch(version) {
     case 1:
        if(call_dds->e_count ! = 1) return(RPC_FAILURE);
        if(call_dds->first_element->data.type ! = DDST_STRING) {
         return(ERR_RPC_CALL_MISMATCH);
        }
         return_dds = dds_str_compile_C(Glob_1_retval);
         break;
     default: /* Not supported */
        return(ERR_RPC_BAD_VERSION);
    }

    if(!dds_compare_dds(return_dds, reply_dds)) {
      dds_destroy(reply_dds);
      dds_destroy(return_dds);
      return(ERR_RPC_REPLY_MISMATCH_);
    }

    switch(version) {
      case 1:
        dds_destroy(return_dds); /* no need for this anymore */
        nfiles = 0;
        cnt = 0;
        element = reply_dds->first_element->right;
        ptr = element->data.value.s.ptr;
```

(continued)

Listing 13.9 *(continued)*

```
    max = element->data.value.s.len;
    done = findfirst(call_dds->first_element->data.value.s.ptr,
        &ffbl
    while(!done) {
      nfiles++;
      slen = strlen(ffblk.ff_name) + 1;     /* include 0 byte */
      if(cnt + slen > max) {
        return(RPC_FAILURE);
      } else {
        memcpy(ptr, ffblk.ff_name, slen);
        cnt += slen;
        ptr += slen;
      }
      done = findnext(&ffblk);
    }
    dds_set_element_value(reply_dds->first_element,
        &nfiles, reply_dds->first_element->data.type);
    break;
  }
  rpc_dds_to_shm(reply_args, return_dds, 0);
  dds_destroy(return_dds);
  dds_destroy(call_dds);
  return(RPC_SUCCESS);
}
```

that are tied to the operating system and compiler). The important aspects of the application are that any number of remote procedures can be in a single remote procedure and that there may be any number of versions of a single application. This is true of any application that contains remote procedure calls and is required by the nature of the RPC protocols. How the application determines which internal function will service a call to a remote procedure is by a set of **switch** and **case** statements.[4] After attaching to the shared memory used to communicate to the remote procedure call, the application switches on the procedure number to route the request to the proper function in the application. This moves closer to the exact remote procedure. The second switch occurs in the function. This switch is done on the requested version of the remote procedure. This then results in the desired remote procedure being executed.

In Listing 13.10 is the source for an application, call it resource, which contains

---

[4]You could also use **if . . . then,** but that's too much like FORTRAN to be palatable.

a function that can be called as a remote procedure. The function will return a structure filled with the various capabilities and devices on the host system. It requires no calling arguments. It, too, is written for the PC DOS environment and must be compiled by TurboC. In both fsglob and resource the use of dynamic data structures contributes significantly to the simplicity of the application and the quality assurance of argument matching. In a typical implementation of the RPC protocol the data portion is simply a stream of bytes with no descriptive information associated with it. Hence, it is expected that the calling program passes the proper arguments and that the value or values returned from the remote procedure are of the same type expected by the calling application. If the remote procedure were a local function, the matching of arguments and the returned values could be guaranteed during compilation, but because a remote procedure is not part of an application, this cannot be done. With a dynamic data structure approach to interprocess communication, the types of each argument can be checked to ensure quality and compatibility, because structure information is passed with the data.

A noteworthy aspect of fsglob and resource is that the main( ) functions are

Listing 13.10 Source for the remote procedure resource that returns information of system resources.

```
/*-----------------------------------------------
  System resources remote procedure call.
-----------------------------------------------*/
#include <stdio.h>
#include "rpc.h"
#include "shm.h"
#include "dds.h"

/* Definition of the resource, version 1 return value */
 char *Resource_1_retval = " \n\
  struct {                                          \n\
      int n_printers;    /* Number of printers */   \n\
      int game_io;       /* Is Game I/O attached */ \n\
      int n_serial;      /* Number of serial */     \n\
      int dma;           /* Is DMA is possible */   \n\
      int n_disk;        /* Number of floppy disks */ \n\
      int has_fp;        /* Does it have a FP chip */ \n\
      int bootable;      /* Is system bootable */   \n\
      int memory;        /* Memory size in Kbytes */ \n\
  }    \
  ";
```

(continued)

Listing 13.10   *(continued)*

```
/*----------------------------------------------
   A application that contains procedures
   (functions) that can be called as remotely.
   ----------------------------------------------*/
main(argc, argv)
int argc;
char *argv[];
{
  RPC_CALL_HEADER *call_header;
  RPC_REPLY_HEADER *reply_header;
  char *call_args;
  char *reply_args;
  char *call_ptr;
  char *reply_ptr;
  int id;
  char *shm_ptr;

  init_shm(argc, argv);

  /* Attach all the shared memory to process */
  id = shmget(RPC_CALL_KEY, 0, 0);
  call_ptr = shmat(id, NULL, 0);

  id = shmget(RPC_REPLY_KEY, 0, 0);
  reply_ptr = shmat(id, NULL, 0);
  if(reply_ptr == NULL) {        /* Unable to get shared memory */
    exit(0);
  }

  call_header = (RPC_CALL_HEADER *)call_ptr;
  call_args = call_ptr + sizeof(RPC_CALL_HEADER);
  reply_header = (RPC_REPLY_HEADER *)reply_ptr;
  reply_args = reply_ptr + sizeof(RPC_REPLY_HEADER);
  reply_header->xid = call_header->xid;
  if(call_header->rpcvers != 1) {        /* Don't support */
    reply_header->errno = ERR_RPC_BAD_PROTO;
    exit(-1);
  }

  /* Now run the desired procedure (function) */
  switch(call_header->proc) {
   case 1:
      reply_header->errno =
```

```
                resource(call_header->vers, call_args, reply_args);
      break;
    default:
      reply_header->errno = ERR_RPC_BAD_PROC;
      break;
  }
  exit(0);
}


/*-------------------------------------------------------
  Determines the resources available on the system.
  Returns with the reply_args filled with the results.
---------------------------------------------------------*/
resource(version, call_args, reply_args)
unsigned int version;
char *call_args;
char *reply_args;
{
  DDS *call_dds;
  DDS *reply_dds;
  DDS *return_dds;
  int i;
  char *name;
  FILE *fptr;
  int itmp;
  union {
    unsigned int value;
    struct {
      unsigned int bootable:1;  /* on a PC bit fields are LSB to
        MSB */
      unsigned int has_fp:1;
        unsigned int ram_size:2;
        unsigned int video_mode:2;
        unsigned int n_disk:2;
        unsigned int dma:1;
        unsigned int n_serial:3;
        unsigned int game_io:1;
        unsigned int serial_ptr:1;
        unsigned int n_printers:2;
    } item;
  } equip;

  struct {
```

(continued)

Listing 13.10   *(continued)*

```
  int arg[8];
} ret_val;

/* Build up DDS for passed arguments - note no call arguments */
  reply_dds = dds_str_compile_C(reply_args);

  /* Check arguments for both call and reply DDS */
  switch(version) {
  case 1:
      return_dds = dds_str_compile_C(Resource_1_retval);
      break;
   default: /* Not supported */
      return(ERR_RPC_BAD_VERSION);
  }

  if(!dds_compare_dds(return_dds, reply_dds)) {
   dds_destroy(reply_dds);
   dds_destroy(return_dds);
   return(ERR_RPC_REPLY_MISMATCH);
  }

/* Now perform the requested operation */
dds_destroy(reply_dds);        /* No need for this anymore */
switch(version) {
   case 1:
      equip.value = biosequip();
      equip.item.dma = (equip.item.dma + 1) % 2;        /* Invert */
      equip.item.n_disk++;
      itmp = equip.item.n_printers;
      dds_set_element_value(dds_get_element(return_dds, "n_printers"),
          &itmp, DDST_INT);
      itmp = equip.item.game_io;
      dds_set_element_value(dds_get_element(return_dds, "game_io"),
          &itmp, DDST_INT);
      itmp = equip.item.n_serial;
      dds_set_element_value(dds_get_element(return_dds, "n_serial"),
          &itmp, DDST_INT);
      itmp = equip.item.dma;
      dds_set_element_value(dds_get_element(return_dds, "dma"),
          &itmp, DDST_INT);
      itmp = equip.item.n_disk;
      dds_set_element_value(dds_get_element(return_dds, "n_disk"),
```

```
            &itmp, DDST_INT);
        itmp = equip.item.has_fp;
        dds_set_element_value(dds_get_element(return_dds, "has_fp"),
            &itmp, DDST_INT);
        itmp = equip.item.bootable;
        dds_set_element_value(dds_get_element(return_dds, "bootable"),
            &itmp, DDST_INT);
        itmp = biosmemory();
        dds_set_element_value(dds_get_element(return_dds, "memory"),
            &itmp, DDST_INT);
        rpc_dds_to_shm(reply_args, return_dds, 0);
        dds_destroy(return_dds);
        return(RPC_SUCCESS);
    }
}
```

extremely similar. In fact, the main( ) functions can be used as a template for creating other applications that support remote procedure calling. This is also true in full-scale implementation and because of this some companies offer tools that create the templates by using high-level specification languages.[5]

A lookup table that maps the remote procedures to the proper application is given in Listing 13.11 This is used by rpc_disp to determine which RPC application to run in order to respond to RPC requests.

13.3 EXAMPLE APPLICATIONS

An application that will call each remote procedure is presented in Listing 13.12. The tokens EX_RESOURCE and EX_FSGLOB used in the application in Listing 13.12 are in the include file rpc_xpl.h. Listing 13.13 contains the source for rpc_xpl.h. When the application in Listing 13.12 is run, it one-by-one calls resource and fsglob, and displays the returned results. Since dynamic data structures are used for the in and out arguments to each call to callrpc( ), the inproc and outproc arguments are the functions rpc_dds_to_shm( ) and rpc_dds_from_shm( ), respectively. This is true whether the remote procedure is fsglob or resource. In fact, this would be true for any call to any remote procedure. The reason is that a dynamic data structure contains sufficient information so that functions like rpc_dds_to_shm( ) and

---

[5]Sun Microsystem's rpcgen is one example.

Listing 13.11   Listing of a lookup table of remote procedures that can be used by rpc_disp.

```
# This is an RPC look up table. The format of the file is
# name   RPC reference number
resource        1
fsglob          2
```

rpc_dds_from_rpc( ) can be constructed in such a way that they can apply to any dynamic data structure.

In ordinary implementations of callrpc( ) the inproc and outproc function must be tailored to the specific arguments that are required. This means that a change in the structure of the expected arguments results in a change to in or out and a corresponding change in the function. While changes in the structure of in or out cannot be avoided, by using dynamic data structures you can avoid any need for changing inproc or outproc.

Listing 13.12   Source for an example application that calls fsglob and resource.

```
#include <stdio.h>
#include "dds.h"
#include "rpc.h"
#include "rpc_xpl.h"


/*-----------------------------------------------
    Example of how to call Remote Procedures.
---------------------------------------------*/
main()
{  DDS *in;
   DDS *out;
   DDS_ELEMENT *element;
   char glob_call[256];
   char glob_ret[2048];
   char buffer[80];
   char *ptr;
   int i;
   int ival;
   int ret;
   int count;
```

```
/* Set up for calling resource function */
out = dds_create();
dds_add_element(out, DDST_INT, "n_printers",  "Number of printers    :");
dds_add_element(out, DDST_INT, "game_io",     "Is Game I/O attached  ?");
dds_add_element(out, DDST_INT, "n_serial",    "Number of serial      :");
dds_add_element(out, DDST_INT, "dma",         "Is DMA is possible    ?");
dds_add_element(out, DDST_INT, "n_disk",      "Number of floppy disks:");
dds_add_element(out, DDST_INT, "has_fp",      "Does it have a FP chip?");
dds_add_element(out, DDST_INT, "bootable",    "Is system bootable    ?");
dds_add_element(out, DDST_INT, "memory",      "Memory size in Kbytes :");

init_shm(0, NULL);

printf("Calling the resource RPC ... ");
/* Call the resource function */
ret = callrpc("", EX_RESOURCE, 1L, 1L,
                rpc_dds_to_shm, NULL, rpc_dds_from_shm, out);
printf("done\n");
if(ret != 0) {
 printf("RPC call failed\n");
 rpc_perror("because");
} else {
/* Print out results */
 printf("Press <ENTER> for the results ...");
 gets(buffer);
 printf("For questions: 0 => NO, 1 => YES\n\n");
 element = out->first_element;
 while(element != NULL) {
    dds_get_element_value(element, &ival, DDST_INT);
    printf("%s %d\n", element->desc, ival);
      element = element->right;
 }
}

/* Clean up */
dds_destroy(out);

/* Set up for calling glob function */
in = dds_create();
out = dds_create();

element = dds_add_element(in, DDST_STRING, "mask", "File name mask");
dds_seed_string(element, glob_call, sizeof(glob_call));
```

(continued)

Listing 13.12 *(continued)*

```
dds_add_element(out, DDST_INT, "count", "Number of names");
element = dds_add_element(out, DDST_STRING, "names", "List of
names");
dds_seed_string(element, glob_ret, sizeof(glob_ret));

/* Call the glob function */
strcpy(glob_call, "*.*");
printf("Calling the FSGLOB RPC ...");
ret = callrpc("", EX_FSGLOB, 1L, 1L,
                rpc_dds_to_shm, in, rpc_dds_from_shm, out);
printf("done\n");
if(ret != 0) {
  printf("RPC call failed\n");
  rpc_perror("because");
} else {
  printf("Press <ENTER> for the results ...");
  gets(buffer);
  element = dds_get_element(out, "count");
  dds_get_element_value(element, &count, DDST_INT);
  printf("Number of matching files: %d\n", count);
  ptr = glob_ret;
  for(i = 0;  i < count;  i++) {
      printf("%s\n", ptr);
        ptr += strlen(ptr) + 1;
  }
}
/* Clean up */
dds_destroy(in);
dds_destroy(out);

exit(0);
}
```

13.4 SUMMARY

The use of dynamic data structures for information transfer can be beneficial in many different instances. One instance is in the assurance of the quality of the passed information. Since dynamic data structures contain descriptive information of the structure of the data, it is possible to check or adapt to the structure of passed information. In applications where the structure is important (like remote procedure calls), you can ensure that the data that it received has the proper structure.

Listing 13.13 Source for the include file rpc_xpl.h, which defines the tokens that are used to call specific remote procedures.

```
/*-----------------------------------------------------------
   Definitions for procedure numbers for
   the example routines.
   -------------------------------------------------------*/
#ifndef _RPC_EXAMPLE_
#define _RPC_EXAMPLE_ 1

#define EX_RESOURCE     1L
#define EX_FSGLOB       2L


#endif _RPC_EXAMPLE_
```

Another instance where dynamic data structures are beneficial is in reducing the complexity of an application without sacrificing functionality. In fact, as we've seen throughout this book, functionality is often increased without added complexity.

Yet another instance is in the reduction of work related to upgrades or enhancements. The example application in Listing 13.12 is a case in point. Only one function is required for encoding arguments and one for decoding, regardless of the structure of the calling and returned arguments.

POINTS TO PONDER

13.1 Describe how a remote procedure differs from an internal function and a function in a shared library.

13.2 Rewrite shm_dds_to_shm( ) so that it would write to a network port rather than to shared memory. Assume that a port is referenced by an integer value.

Distributed Information | **14**

Since the development of networks to connect computer systems there has been a steady trend to decentralize[1] all aspects of computer systems. This includes hardware, software, and (most recently) the information that these systems use. This has resulted in a growing need to deal with distributed information. In Chapter 13, we explored techniques for transferring information, and those techniques are used in distributed information systems. What we explore in this chapter is not how information can be transferred, but what we do with that information once we obtain it from various sources.

There are many motivations for storing information in a distributed fashion. One primary reason is that specific information can be located in close proximity to those who are responsible for it. For example, in a large corporation you might have regional offices. Each office is then responsible for maintaining information about its region, but at corporate headquarters there is a need to collect information from each regional office so that the entire corporation can be monitored. One approach to achieving this might be to copy the information from each regional office and store it at the corporate headquarters. A drawback to this approach is that the information at the corporate headquarters is out of date as soon as the information at any of the regional offices is altered. An alternative approach is to leave the information at each regional office and when a question needs to be answered a query is sent to each regional office and the results are combined into a single answer. This is a decomposable searching problem, and dynamic data structures can be used in the implementation of such a distributed information system.

14.1 THE CHALLENGE

Use dynamic data structures and the concept of decomposable searching to develop a method of obtaining a single answer from one or more distinct sets of information.

---

[1]We are now in the age of Copernican computing. The computer is no longer the center of the universe; the network is.

This is the same as the "large corporation" example mentioned previously. The results are to be displayed on the screen.

14.2 THE SOLUTION

To confine the scope of the solution we will limit our implementation to using one or more local sets of information. This is analogous to having one or more distributed sets of information (for example, at regional offices). What distinguishes the distributed problem from the local one is the method of accessing the data. By using multiple local sets we avoid the complications of distributed access while still solving the decomposable searching problem.

In Chapter 12 we developed a means to access data within flatfiles. We will use that same method for accessing the different information sets. So what remains to be implemented is a means to query an information set (flatfile in this case) and a way to combine the results of a query against two separate sets of information into a single result. That is, we need to develop a binary operator that will combine two sets of information. Since we are combining information sets, the binary operator that we will need is an "addition" operator that will add two sets of results and generate a new set. Since we are allowing any number of separate information sets, this "addition" operation will need to be performed repeatedly in a way that is analogous to a summation.

For our query function we want to supply a textual description of the query. We will limit the syntax of the query to one of the following three forms (just to make things simple):

    column>value
    column<value
    column=value

where "column" is the name of a column in the flatfile and "value" is the constraint value for the operator. We will limit ourselves to only numeric values. The results of the query should be returned to the application in the form of a dynamic data structure. The results from each information set will be stored separately and combined when all results have been collected.

The nature of this type of problem is not implemented well using the linked list dynamic data structure developed and used in previous chapters. So we need an alternate form of dynamic data structure. Since this is a decomposable searching problem, we will use a decomposable data structure. Choosing a decomposable data structure imposes one more constraint on us, namely, we need to be able to maintain arrays of data structures. For our example we'll use a static data structure with the three elements x, y, and z. Listing 14.1 contains the definition for such a structure, which is called ELEMENT. The constant "ELEMENT_NFIELDS" is defined to be the number of elements in the ELEMENT structure. This is used by the query

Listing 14.1 Source for the include file element.h, which contains the definition of the ELEMENT structure.

```
/*-----------------------------------------
    Includes file "element.h".
    Definition of the ELEMENT structure.
-------------------------------------------*/
#ifndef _element.h_
#define _element.h_      1

typedef struct {
    double x, y, z;
} ELEMENT;

#define ELEMENT_NFIELDS 3

#endif _element.h_
```

function (defined in Listing 14.8) to determine how many fields in the flatfiles to which to bind. It is also used in the function that prints results to the screen (in Listing 14.9) to determine header information for the display. Other uses of ELEMENT_NFIELDS will be discussed in more detail where appropriate.

Now let's define a data structure for managing a decomposable data structure. What we need to accomplish is a coherent way to maintain a collection of arrays that may be partially filled. A data structure that accomplishes this is given in Listing 14.2 and is called DECOMP. DECOMP is actually a simple link list structure consisting of DECOMP_ARRAY structures. The DECOMP_ARRAY structure contains information about individual arrays and a pointer that is to point to the next DECOMP_ARRAY. Also contained in Listing 14.2 is a structure, called QUERY, for holding the information about the query that is to be applied to the flatfiles. In addition, Listing 14.2 has the type declarations for all functions.

The structure definitions in Listing 14.2 are very generic. They do not need to know anything specific about the ELEMENT structure. Since the structures are not concerned, the functions that use them (for the most part) do not need to be concerned as well. This means that the functions that we will now implement can be used to construct a variety of decomposable data structures.

Listing 14.3 contains a function called decomp_make( ). This function creates and initializes an instance of the DECOMP structure and returns a pointer to it. It returns NULL if it is unable to create an instance. Remember that an instance of a DECOMP structure is simply a linked list of DECOMP_ARRAY structures. So we need a function that will create and initialize instances for a DECOMP_ARRAY structure. Listing 14.4 contains such a function, called decomp_array_make( ). As part of initialization of a DECOMP_ARRAY structure, an array of elements must be created. The number of elements in the array is passed as the only argument to decomp_ar-

Listing 14.2 Source for the include file decomp.h, which contains declarations for creating and using decomposable data structures.

```
/*----------------------------------------------------
   Includes file "decomp.h" for decomposable set example.
   ----------------------------------------------------*/
#ifndef _decomp.h_
#define _decomp.h_        1

#include <stdio.h>        /* For definition of NULL */
#include "dds.h"          /* For definition of DDS_MAX_NAME */
#include "element.h"      /* For definition of ELEMENT */

#ifdef __BORLANDC__
/* A bug exists in Borland C++ 2.0, so we can't use free() */
#define free(x)
#endif __BORLANDC__

typedef struct {
   char element[DDS_MAX_NAME + 1];
   char op;
   double constraint;
} QUERY;

typedef struct DECOMP_BLOCK {
   int nels;
   int max_els;
   ELEMENT *data;
   struct DECOMP_BLOCK *next;
} DECOMP_ARRAY;

typedef struct {
   DECOMP_ARRAY *array_list;
   DECOMP_ARRAY *last_array;
} DECOMP;

int decomp_add_elem();
int decomp_binary_add();
ELEMENT *make_array();
DECOMP *decomp_make();
DECOMP_ARRAY *decomp_array_make();
void decomp_dump();
QUERY *decomp_parse_query();

#define PLURAL(x)        x == 1 ? "" : "s"

#endif _decomp.h_
```

Listing 14.3 Source for the function decomp_make( ), which creates an instance of a DECOMP structure.

```
#include "decomp.h"
/*------------------------------------------------------

    Creates an instance of a structure for maintaining
    a decomposable structure.
    ----------------------------------------------------*/
DECOMP *
decomp_make()
{
    DECOMP *ptr;

    ptr = (DECOMP *)malloc(sizeof(DECOMP));
    if(ptr != NULL) {
        ptr->array_list = NULL;
        ptr->last_array = NULL;
    }
    return(ptr);
}
```

ray_make( ). The static function make_array( ) creates the actual array. The function make_array( ) works no matter what the definition of the ELEMENT structure is.

Now we need a function to add elements to a decomposable structure. At this point we need to decide on the transformation to use. For our example let's minimize the storage requirements. This means that we need to use the binary transform. Listing 14.5 contains the source for a function called decomp_add_element( ), which adds elements to a decomposable data structure. The function decomp_add_element( ) expects two arguments. The first is a pointer to a DECOMP structure, and the second is a pointer to an ELEMENT. If the DECOMP structure does not contain any elements, an instance of a DECOMP_ARRAY is created that contains one element (The first nonzero number in the binary sequence.) The decomposable data structure is then augmented by the new element. This may require a consolidation of all existing elements into a single, larger array, or it may require the simple act of adding one element array to the existing decomposable data structure. The maximum number of elements in any DECOMP_ARRAY is always a power of 2 (in accordance with the binary counting scheme).

The functions decomp_make( ), decomp_array_make( ), and decomp_add_element( ) are all that is needed to create and maintain a decomposable data structure. The most complicated function is decomp_add_element( ), and even that is rather straightforward. However, there are times when it is useful to look at the details of a decomposable data structure. The function decomp_dump( ), in Listing 14.6, provides the means to easily print a system-level description of a decomposable data structure. The function decomp_dump( ) expects one argument, a pointer to a

Listing 14.4   Source for the functions decomp_array_make( ) and make_array( ), which create instances of a DECOMP_ARRY structure.

```c
#include "decomp.h"


/*-------------------------------------------------
   Creates a DECOMP_ARRAY structure that is
   used to maintain an array of ELEMENTS. Also
   calls make_array() to create the array ELEMENTS.
   'max_els' is the number of elements the array
   is to have.
--------------------------------------------------*/
DECOMP_ARRAY *
decomp_array_make(max_els)
int max_els;
{
   DECOMP_ARRAY *ptr;

   ptr = (DECOMP_ARRAY *)malloc(sizeof(DECOMP_ARRAY));
   if(ptr != NULL) {
      ptr->nels = 0;
      ptr->max_els = max_els;
      ptr->next = NULL;
      ptr->data = make_array(max_els);
      if(ptr->data == NULL) {
         free(ptr);
         ptr = NULL;
      }
   }
   return(ptr);
}


/*-------------------------------------------------
   Creates an array of ELEMENT structures.
--------------------------------------------------*/
static ELEMENT *
make_array(nels)
int nels;
{
   ELEMENT *ptr;

   ptr = (ELEMENT *)malloc(sizeof(ELEMENT) * nels);
   return(ptr);
}
```

Listing 14.5 Source for the function decomp_add_element( ), which adds elements to a decomposable data structure.

```c
#include "decomp.h"


/*-------------------------------------------------
   Adds elements to a decomposable structure using
   a binary transform algorithm.
-------------------------------------------------*/
decomp_add_element(decomp, elem)
DECOMP *decomp;
ELEMENT *elem;
{
   DECOMP_ARRAY *dptr;
   DECOMP_ARRAY *ptr;
   DECOMP_ARRAY *next_ptr;
   int i;

   if(decomp == NULL) return(0);

   if(decomp->array_list == NULL) { /* First time ever */
      dptr = decomp_array_make(1);
      if(dptr == NULL) return(0);
      decomp->array_list = dptr;
      decomp->last_array = dptr;
   } else if(decomp->array_list->max_els != 1) { /* special case */
      dptr = decomp_array_make(1);
      if(dptr == NULL) return(0);
      dptr->next = decomp->array_list;
      decomp->array_list = dptr;
   } else {
      ptr = decomp->array_list;
      while(ptr->next != NULL) {
         if(ptr->next->max_els > 2 * ptr->max_els) {
            break;
         }
         ptr = ptr->next;
       }
      dptr = decomp_array_make(ptr->max_els * 2);
      if(dptr == NULL) return(0);
      ptr = decomp->array_list;
      while(ptr != NULL) {
         if(ptr->max_els > dptr->max_els) break;
         for(i = 0; i < ptr->max_els; i++) {
```

```
            memcpy(&dptr->data[dptr->nels], &ptr->data[i],
                sizeof(ELEMENT)));
            dptr->nels++;
        }
        free(ptr->data);
        next_ptr = ptr->next;
        free(ptr);
        ptr = next_ptr;
    }
    dptr->next = ptr;
    decomp->array_list = dptr;
    if(ptr == NULL) {
        decomp->last_array = dptr;
    }
}
memcpy(&dptr->data[dptr->nels], elem, sizeof(ELEMENT));
dptr->nels++;
return(1);
}
```

DECOMP structure. It then prints out a description for each instance of a DECOMP_ARRAY in the linked list described by the DECOMP pointer.

Now let's direct our attention to what we need in order to parse a textual query into usable information. In Listing 14.7 is a function called decomp_parse_query( ). This function expects one argument, a pointer to a string containing the textual query. It then divides the query into three components: the flatfile field name, the operator, and the constraint value. This information is then placed in an instance of a QUERY structure that is created in the function. A pointer to a QUERY structure is returned if the parsing was successfully; otherwise a NULL is returned.

We now have all the components we need to query a flatfile and return the results as a decomposable data structure. The function decomp_query( ) in Listing 14.8 does just that. The function decomp_query( ) expects three arguments. The first is a pointer to a preopened flatfile, the second is a pointer to a QUERY structure that contains a parsed query, and the third is a pointer to a DECOMP structure into which the results from the query will be placed. Decomp_query( ) begins searching the flatfile for matches to the query by binding a local variable to the field in the flatfile that matches the field name in the query. If the field name is not found, then the query fails. Next, the first ELEMENT_NFIELDS in the flatfile are bound to local variables. These are used to assign values to the elements within the ELEMENT structure. After this the flatfile is scanned from beginning to end for records that match the constraint of the query. If a matching record is found, a local instance of the ELEMENT structure is populated with the values from bound variables and the ELEMENT

Listing 14.6 Source for the function decomp_dump( ), which produces a system-level description of a decomposable data structure.

```c
#include "decomp.h"

#ifdef __BORLANDC__
#include <dos.h>
#else
#define FP_SEG(x)      x
#define FP_OFF(x)      0
#endif __BORLANDC__
/*-----------------------------------------------
  Prints a system-level description of a DECOMP
  structure.
-----------------------------------------------*/
void
decomp_dump(decomp)
DECOMP *decomp;
{
    DECOMP_ARRAY *dptr;
    int cnt = 0;

    if(decomp == NULL) {
        printf("decomp: NULL\n");
        return;
    }
    dptr = decomp->array_list;
    while(dptr != NULL) {
        cnt++;
        printf("Block: %d\n", cnt);
        printf("  max_els: %d\n", dptr->max_els);
        printf("  nels   : %d\n", dptr->nels);
        printf("  data   : %x:%x\n", FP_SEG(dptr->data),
            FP_OFF(dptr->data));
        printf("\n");
        dptr = dptr->next;
    }
}
```

structure is added to the decomposable data structure. The number of matching records is returned.

Once we obtain the results from applying the query to all the flatfiles, we want to display the results. How this is accomplished is highly dependent on the definition of the ELEMENT data structure. A function, called print_results( ), which will print the contents of a decomposable data structure that contains elements with a

Listing 14.7 Source for the function decomp_parse_query( ), which parses a query into its various components.

```c
#include <string.h>
#include <math.h>
#include "decomp.h"


/*-------------------------------------------
    Parses a string containing a query into
    a query structure.
--------------------------------------------*/
QUERY *
decomp_parse_query(query_str)
char query_str[];
{
    QUERY *query;
    char *ptr = NULL;
    int itmp;

    if(strlen(query_str) < 3) return(NULL);

    query = (QUERY *)malloc(sizeof(QUERY));
    if(query != NULL) {
       ptr = strchr(query_str, '>');
       if(ptr == NULL) {
          ptr = strchr(query_str, '<');
          if(ptr == NULL) {
             ptr = strchr(query_str, '=');
          }
       }
       if(ptr != NULL) {
          query->op = *ptr;
          *ptr = '\0';
          strncpy(query->element, query_str, DDS_MAX_NAME);
          query->element[DDS_MAX_NAME] = '\0';
          query->constraint = atof(ptr + 1);
          *ptr = query->op;
       } else {
          free(query);
          query = NULL;
       }
    }
    return(query);
}
```

Listing 14.8 Source for the function decomp_query( ), which applies a query to a flatfile and returns the results in a decomposable data structure.

```c
#include "decomp.h"
#include "flatfile.h"


/*----------------------------------------------
  Applies a query against a flatfile and returns
  the results in the decomposable structure.
----------------------------------------------*/
decomp_query(ffptr, query, decomp)
FLATFILE *ffptr;
QUERY *query;
DECOMP *decomp;
{
   DDS_ELEMENT *dds_element;
   double dval[ELEMENT_NFIELDS];
   double conval;
   int nrecs = 0;
   FLATFILE *tmp_fptr;
   char tmp_fname[9];
   char buffer[1024];
   ELEMENT element;
   int add_rec;
   int idx;
   int i;

   if(ffptr == NULL || query == NULL) return(NULL);

/* Map constraint field into application variable */
   idx = flatfile_index_by_name(ffptr, query->element);
   if(idx < 0) {
      fprintf(stderr, "Element %s does not exist\n", query->element);
      return(NULL);
   }

   dds_element = flatfile_element_by_index(ffptr, idx);
   if(dds_element != NULL) {
      dds_bind(ffptr->dds, dds_element, &conval, DDST_DOUBLE);
   }
   /* Map first ELEMENT_NFIELDS fields into application variables */

   for(i = 0; i < ELEMENT_NFIELDS; i++) {
```

```
        dds_element = flatfile_element_by_index(ffptr, i);
        if(dds_element != NULL) {
           dds_bind(ffptr->dds, dds_element, &dval[i], DDST_DOUBLE);
        }
    }


/* Scan for matching records */

    while(flatfile_read_rec(ffptr)) {
        add_rec = 0;
        switch(query->op) {
           case '>':
               if(conval > query->constraint) {
                   add_rec = 1;
               }
               break;
           case '<':
               if(conval < query->constraint) {
                   add_rec = 1;
               }
               break;
           case '=':
               if(conval == query->constraint) {
                   add_rec = 1;
               }
               break;
        }

        if(add_rec) {        /* Very dependent on the definition
               of ELEMENT */
           element.x = dval[0];
           element.y = dval[1];
           element.z = dval[2];
           decomp_add_element(decomp, &element);
           nrecs++;
        }
    }

/* All done */
  return(nrecs);
}
```

specific structure, is presented in Listing 14.9. The contents of the decomposable data structure are printed in a tabular form with the value of the ELEMENT_NFIELD constant used to determine the exact format of the header and footer of the table.

Up until now the functions we have developed work with a single decomposable data structure. Since our goal is to be able to obtain results for applying a query to more than one flatfile, we need a function that can combine multiple results into a single coherent result. This can be done with a binary operator that performs an "addition" of two decomposable structures. In this case the "addition" is achieved by appending one decomposable data structure to another. Listing 14.10 contains the source for a function, called decomp_binop_add( ), which will do this. The function decomp_binop_add( ) requires two arguments, both pointers to DECOMP structures. The second DECOMP structure is added to the first by appending the elements in the second to the first. So, on return the first DECOMP structure contains all the elements it had on entry plus all the elements in the second.

Listing 14.9   Source for the function print_results( ), which displays the contents of a decomposable data structure.

```
#include "decomp.h"


/*------------------------------------------
   Prints the contents of the decomposable
   structure in a tabular form.
---------------------------------------------*/
void
print_results(decomp)
DECOMP *decomp;
{
   DECOMP_ARRAY *dptr;
   int i;
   int cnt;

   void print_element();

   /* Print out header for table */

   printf("| Instance |");
   for(i = 0; i < ELEMENT_NFIELDS;i++) {
      printf(" Element %2d |", i);
   }
   printf("\n");
   printf("+----------+");
```

```
    for(i = 0; i < ELEMENT_NFIELDS; i++) {
        printf("------------+");
    }
     printf("\n");

    /* Now print out the element information */

    cnt = 1;
    dptr = decomp->array_list;
    while(dptr != NULL) {
        for(i = 0; i < dptr->nels; i++) {
            printf("| %8d |", cnt);
            print_element(&dptr->data[i]);
            printf("\n");
            cnt++;
        }
        dptr = dptr->next;
    }

    /* Finish up */
    printf("+----------+");
    for(i = 0; i < ELEMENT_NFIELDS; i++) {
        printf("------------+");
    }
    printf("\n");
}


/*-------------------------------------------------
    Prints the contents of an ELEMENT structure.
    Specific to a particular declaration of ELEMENT.
-----------------------------------------------------*/
static void
print_element(element)
ELEMENT *element;
{
    char *fmt;

    fmt = "%11.5lf |";

    printf(fmt, element->x);
    printf(fmt, element->y);
    printf(fmt, element->z);
}
```

Listing 14.10   Source for the function decomp_binop_add( ), which adds to decomposable data structures together.

```c
#include "decomp.h"
/*-----------------------------------------------------

    Adds (combines) one decomposable structure to
    another. This would be analogous to "decomp1 += decomp2;"
    ----------------------------------------------------*/
decomp_binop_add(decomp1, decomp2)
DECOMP *decomp1;
DECOMP *decomp2;
{
    DECOMP_ARRAY *dptr;
    int i;

    if(decomp1 == NULL || decomp2 == NULL) return(0);

    dptr = decomp2->array_list;
    while(dptr != NULL) {
        for(i = 0; i < dptr->nels; i++) {
            if(!decomp_add_element(decomp1, &dptr->data[i])) return(0);
        }
        dptr = dptr->next;
    }

    return(1);
}
```

14.3 AN EXAMPLE APPLICATION

To demonstrate how a distributed information application might be implemented, let's build an application that will accept a query and any number of flatfiles (which in our model represent distributed information sets). The query will be applied against each flatfile, and the results will be combined with a binary operator. The final results will be displayed on the screen.

Listing 14.11 contains the source for such an application. The application in Listing 14.11, which we'll call "14_11," expects at least two command-line arguments. The first is a query, and the second and subsequent arguments are the names of flatfiles. It searches each passed flatfile for any record that matches the specified query. The results for each flatfile are maintained in separate DECOMP structures. After searching all the flatfiles, the results are combined into a single DECOMP structure. System-level information about the combined results is printed to the screen, followed by a tabular listing of the results.

Listing 14.11   Source for the distributed information application.

```
#include "decomp.h"
#include "flatfile.h"

#define MAX_INFO_SETS  25

char *Usage[] = {
   "Create a decomposable structure. Proper usage:",
   "",
   "   decomp {qeury} {flatfile} [{flatfile} ...]",
   "",
   "where {query} is a query to apply to each {flatfile}.",
   "A query must be in the form",
   "",
   "   {field_name}{rel_op}{value}",
   "",
   "where {field_name} is the name of a field common to all",
   "{flatfile}, {rel_op} is one of: > (greater than), < (less than)",
   " or = (equal to). {value} must be a numeric value.",
   NULL
};

main(argc, argv)
int argc;
char *argv[];
{
   DECOMP *decomp[MAX_INFO_SETS];
   ELEMENT element;
   FLATFILE *ffptr;
   QUERY *query;
   int nels;
   int i;
   char **cptr;
   int matches = 0;

   void print_results();

   if(argc < 3) {
      cptr = Usage;
      while(*cptr != NULL) {
         printf("%s\n", *cptr);
         cptr++;
      }
      exit(0);
   }
```

(continued)

Listing 14.10   *(continued)*

```
    query = decomp_parse_query(argv[1]);
    if(query == NULL) {
       printf("Improperly constructed query.\n");
       exit(0);
    }


    if(argc > MAX_INFO_SETS) {
       printf("Too many flatfiles were specified (maximum = %d).\n",
          MAX_INFO_SETS - 1);
       exit(0);
    }


    for(i = 2; i < argc; i++) {
       decomp[i] = decomp_make();
       if(decomp[i] == NULL) {
          printf("Unable to create decomp structure %d\n", i);
          exit(0);
       }
       ffptr = flatfile_open(argv[i], 'r');
       if(ffptr == NULL) {
          printf("Unable to open flatfile '%s', skipping.\n", argv[i]);
       } else {
          matches += decomp_query(ffptr, query, decomp[i]);
       }
       flatfile_close(ffptr);
    }

/* Now combine all results will binary operator */
    decomp[0] = decomp_make();
    if(decomp[0] == NULL) {
       printf("Unable to create decomp structure 0\n");
       exit(0);
    }


    for(i = 2; i < argc; i++) {
       if(!decomp_binop_add(decomp[0], decomp[i])) {
          printf("Binary operator failed at decomp %d\n", i);
          exit(0);
       }
    }

    printf("Dump of resulting decomposable structure:\n");
    decomp_dump(decomp[0]);
```

```
printf("Results:\n");
printf("%d matche%s\n", matches, PLURAL(matches));
if(matches > 0) {
   print_results(decomp[0]);
}

exit(0);
return(0);
}
```

If we have flatfiles called "ff1" and "ff2," each with identical structure, and there exists a column called "*j*" in both flatfiles, then the command

`14_11 "j<4.0" ff1 ff2`

will return all records for which the value in the *j* column is less than 4.0. The query is enclosed in quotes so that the command interpreter does not interpret the "less than" (<) sign as I/O redirection. Also, in MS DOS spaces take precedence over quotes, so no spaces are allowed within the quoted string.

Suppose that when you run the command

`14_11 "j<4.0" ff1`

the flatfile ff1 contains 10 records and that the value of the *j* column goes from 0.0 to 9.0 in steps of 1.0. Even though the records in the flatfile are in ascending order according to the value in the *j* column, the results returned are not. The order of the records in the resulting decomposable data structure is 1.0, 2.0, 0.0, 3.0. The reason for this is a combination of how new arrays of ELEMENT structures are created and populated and contributions from the decomp_binop_add( ) function.

Figure 14.1 depicts the history of the decomposable data structure that results from applying the query to the flatfile and then what occurs when the resulting decomposable data structure is operated on by decomp_binop_add( ). In some situations the order of the returned records is not important, but in those situations where it is, some form of postprocessing must be done in order to reorder the results according to some desired criteria.

14.4 SUMMARY

A drawback to the implementation presented here is that the elements in the ELEMENT structure are static. This is in accordance with the definition of a decomposable data structure as discussed in the chapter on designing dynamic data structures (Chapter 3). However, it should be possible to make the ELEMENT structure a dynamic data structure that can adapt to whatever structure the flatfiles have. If this is done, then the functions presented in this chapter would be very generic and have

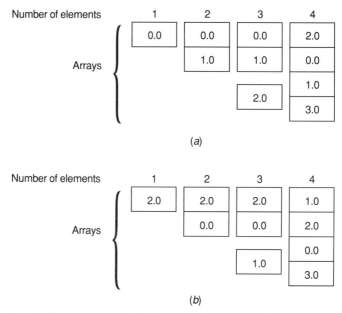

Figure 14.1 A pictorial representation of the history of a decomposable data structure. Part (*a*) depicts the history of the decomposable structure that occurs as the query is applied to the flatfile. Part (*b*) depicts what occurs as the function decomp_binop_add( ) operates on the decomposable data structure.

a more universal application. The only limitations that a dynamic data structure approach would impose is that the structure of the dynamic data structure be fixed before the creation of the decomposable data structure. This is so that the function make_array( ) could function properly. In general, this would be a minor limitation.

Another possible approach would be to make the decomposable data structure more object-oriented. In this case the ELEMENT structure could be a derived class and portions of the presented functions that are dependent on the actual declaration of the ELEMENT structure could be made virtual member functions of the class.

POINTS TO PONDER

14.1   Consider the situation where ELEMENT is converted into an object-oriented data type. Which portions of the source code presented in this chapter would become virtual member functions of an ELEMENT class?

14.2   Describe how you might implement a version of the example application that returns only unique records (no duplicates).

14.3   Describe how you might correct the reordering of records that occurs as records are added to the decomposable data structure and subsequently processed by decomp_binop_add( ).

Object-Oriented Systems | 15

Any change, especially in computer science, is propelled by necessity. Even today we are still exploring the extent to which computers can be used. In conjunction with this we are also exploring new programming methods, styles, and languages, all with the ultimate goal of making programming easier and more natural. One method that is now moving into prominence is that of object-oriented programming.

Even in the area of object-oriented programming, dynamic data structures can play a role. In this chapter we'll explore why this is true by looking at how dynamic data structures can be created, managed, and used in object-oriented applications. Since object-oriented languages offer capabilities not found in ordinary languages (like C), we'll build our dynamic data structure management routines from scratch. You might think this would take a very large chapter to do that. Actually we can develop all necessary routines and present an example in a modest-sized chapter.

15.1 THE CHALLENGE

As we adopt object-oriented methods and techniques, we begin to think in the sense of data objects. This leads to the next requirement that developers, programmers, and users will demand: object-oriented database management systems. So, this is the challenge: create an object-oriented database system. This system should demonstrate object retrieval and storage and have the properties of inheritance, and heterogeneous object linkage and allow for the definition of new objects by the developer.

15.2 THE SOLUTION

When designing an object-oriented database system the first thing you need to decide is just how closely associated each of the properties of an object should be tied. Such properties are public and private data, operator overloads, methods, and inheritance. The central question is: Which ones should reside in the data set, and which should reside in the database management system (DBMS)? The number of possible choices increases with the number of distinct, separable properties. For the purposes of this chapter we'll follow one simple rule in deciding what goes into the data set: simplicity of implementation.

In order to keep the implementation simple, we'll use whatever I/O support is available in the implementation language. Since all the presentations in this book are written in C, we'll use C++ as the implementation language. In C++ the simplest way to store and retrieve structured information from a file is to use the **fread( )** and **fwrite( )** functions, so we'll use them as our basis for retrieving and storing objects. This decision sets the answer to which portion of the object is stored in the data set, that is, just the data (public and private) portion. All active portions of the object (methods and so on) remain in the DBMS. The reason is that **fread( )** and **fwrite( )** functions in C++ deal only with the data portion of the object. At first this might seem strange, but it makes sense when you consider that in C++ the data portion for each object is unique for each object, but the methods of the object are shared.

The next step is to decide on the characteristics that a generic dynamic data structure object is to have. In the C implementation, dynamic data structures were required to define a union of all possible data types. In C++ there is no need to do this. In fact, we can define a generic dynamic data structure element that is so generic that new data types can be added to it with a minimum of effort. This is possible because of the existence of virtual functions and derived classes.

Since we are looking at object-oriented database applications, we will require only that a method exists for getting an object from a file (or stdin) and that there be a method for putting an object to a file (or stdout). In a more complete database management implementation you may also want to add methods for relational operations. Listing 15.1 (oodds.cpp) contains the definitions for an object class that meets these requirements. In Listing 15.1 there is a class called OODDS; this is the generic dynamic data structure object class. All database objects are derived from this class, including the database manager class OODB. The OODDS consists of a data portion that is a pointer to an object of class OODDS and three virtual member functions: set( ), get( ), and put( ). The set( ) method is used to define the value of each data element in the object based on a textual description. Hence it requires on argument that is a string. The get( ) method reads an object from a database file, and the put( ) method writes an object to a database file. Both get( ) and put( ) expect one argument that is a file pointer.

When you use virtual functions there must be at least one method defined for each virtual function. This method should be a member of the base class that contains the declaration of the virtual function. This is so that the method is global to all derived classes and will provide a definition for any virtual functions not defined in the derived class. Listing 15.1 also contains definitions for all virtual functions. Since it is expected that each derived class will override these functions, each method serves only as a place holder and prints a message that nothing is defined if called.

There are two unique aspects of this C++ implementation of dynamic data structures. The first is that all the information necessary for the management and use of

Listing 15.1 Source for the object-oriented dynamic data structure class called OODDS.

```
/*-------------------------------------------------------
   All classes of data used by the object-oriented DBMS.
   ----------------------------------------------------*/


#ifndef _OODDS_
#define _OODDS_ 1

#include <stdio.h>
#include <string.h>

#define OODDS_NAME_LEN 128
#define OODDS_DESC_LEN 256
#define OODDS_TYPE_LEN 64

class OODDS {
  public:
    OODDS *next;
    char name[OODDS_NAME_LEN + 1];
    char desc[OODDS_DESC_LEN + 1];
    char type[OODDS_TYPE_LEN + 1];
    void set_desc(char * str = "");
    void set_name(char * str = "");
    void set_type(char * str = "");
    virtual int set(char * str = "");
    virtual void get(FILE * fptr = stdin);
    virtual void put(FILE * fptr = stdout);
};


/*-------------------------------------------------------
   Functions that should be common to all derived classes.
   There should not be a need to override these functions.
   ----------------------------------------------------*/
void OODDS::set_desc(char * str) {
  strncpy(desc, str, OODDS_DESC_LEN);
  desc[OODDS_DESC_LEN] = '\0';
}

void OODDS::set_name(char * str) {
  strncpy(name, str, OODDS_DESC_LEN);
  name[OODDS_DESC_LEN] = '\0';
}

void OODDS::set_type(char * str) {
```

(continued)

Listing 15.1   *(continued)*

```
strncpy(type, str, OODDS_TYPE_LEN);
type[OODDS_TYPE_LEN] = '\0';
}


/*------------------------------------------------------------

   Do nothing member functions for the Object-Oriented
   Dynamic Data Structure (OODDS).
   These are virtual functions that can be replaced by
   specific functions in a derived class.
------------------------------------------------------------*/
int OODDS::set(char * str) {
  fprintf(stderr, "Nothing defined\n");
  return(0);
}

void OODDS::put(FILE * fptr) {
  fprintf(stderr, "Nothing defined\n");
}

void OODDS::get(FILE * fptr) {
  fprintf(stderr, "Nothing defined\n");
}


#endif _OODDS_
```

dynamic data structures is incorporated into the very simple OODDS object class and any classes that are derived from it. The second unique aspect is that the definition of supported data types is incremental. That is, new types may be added at any time. The process of creating a new data type is really quite simple and straightforward. The first step is to define a new class derived from the OODDS class. In this derived class you define the data portion required to hold the values for the new type and the two functions get( ) and put( ), which will respectively read and write the data for an object of the newly defined type.

While each set( ), get( ), and put( ) methods and the data structure for holding the value of an object will be unique for each derived class, there is one element of every derived class that is common. This is the OODDS pointer, which is used to form a link list of objects that constitute a record. This is a database management operation, so we will need a new class (with associated methods) for performing this. So we'll define an object-oriented database management class. Listing 15.2 (oodb.cpp) contains the source for one such class.

The object-oriented database management class (OODB) in Listing 15.2 contains several methods. The comments in the source in Listing 15.2 should be sufficient to

Listing 15.2 Source for the object-oriented database class called OODB.

```
/*-------------------------------------------
   Definition of the OODB class.
-------------------------------------------*/
#ifndef _OODB_
#define _OODB_   1
#include "oodds.cpp"
#include "const.h"

class OODB {
  FILE * fptr;
  unsigned int rcnt;
  OODDS * first;
  OODDS * next;
public:
  OODB();
  put();
  get();
  create(char * string);
  open(char * string);
  close();
  field(OODDS * mptr, char * name, char * desc);
  OODDS * get_object(char * name);
  dump();
  message();
};


/*-----------------------------------------------
   Opens a database.
-----------------------------------------------*/
OODB::open(char * string) {
  if(strcmp(string, "-") == 0) {
    fptr = stdin;
  } else {
    if((fptr = fopen(string, "r")) == NULL) return(FAILURE);
  }
  rcnt = 0;
}


/*-----------------------------------------------
   Creates a database.
-----------------------------------------------*/
OODB::create(char * string) {
```

(continued)

Listing 15.2   *(continued)*

```
  if(strcmp(string, "-") == 0) {
    fptr = stdout;
  } else {
    if((fptr = fopen(string, "w")) == NULL) return(FAILURE);
  }
  rcnt = 0;
}


/*----------------------------------------------
  Closes a database.
----------------------------------------------*/
OODB::close() {
  return(fclose(fptr));
}


/*----------------------------------------------
  Puts all fields in a object record into the
  opened database file.
----------------------------------------------*/
OODB::put() {
  OODDS *mptr;

  rcnt++;
  for(mptr = first; mptr != NULL; mptr = mptr->next)
  {
    if(fptr == stdout) printf(" | ");
    mptr->put(fptr);
  }
  if(fptr == stdout) printf(" |\n");
  return(1);
}


/*----------------------------------------------
  Gets all objects in an opened database.
----------------------------------------------*/
OODB::get() {
  OODDS *mptr;

  if(fptr == stdout) printf("Tuple %d\n", rcnt);
  for(mptr = first;mptr != NULL; mptr = mptr->next)
  {
    mptr->get(fptr);
  }
```

```
  rcnt++;
  return(rcnt);
}


/*----------------------------------------------
  The constructor for the OODB class.
------------------------------------------------*/
OODB::OODB() {
  first = NULL;
  next = NULL;
}


/*----------------------------------------------
  Defines a field in an object record.
------------------------------------------------*/
OODB::field(OODDS * mptr, char * name, char * desc) {
  if(first == NULL) {
     first = mptr;
     next = mptr;
  } else {
    next->next = mptr;
    next = mptr;
  }
  mptr->next = NULL;
  mptr->set_name(name);
  mptr->set_desc(desc);
  return(1);
}


/*----------------------------------------------
  Returns a pointer to the object that has a
  given name.
------------------------------------------------*/
OODDS *OODB::get_object(char * name) {
  OODDS *mptr;

  mptr = first;
  while(mptr != NULL) {
    if(strcmp(name, mptr->name) == 0) {
       break;
    }
  }
  return(mptr);
}
```

(continued)

Listing 15.2 *(continued)*

```
/*-----------------------------------------------
   Prints a description of the currently defined
   object record.
   ----------------------------------------------*/
OODB::dump() {
  OODDS *mptr;
  int cnt = 0;

  mptr = first;
  while(mptr != NULL) {
    printf("\n");
    printf("Object: %d\n", cnt);
    printf("   name: %s\n", mptr->name);
    printf("   desc: %s\n", mptr->desc);
    printf("   type: %s\n", mptr->type);
    cnt++;
  }
  return(cnt);
}


/*-----------------------------------------------
   Prints a message related to operations on
   an object-oriented database.
   ----------------------------------------------*/
OODB::message() {
  if(fptr == stdin) {
    printf("You are exected to enter %d record%c\n", DB_NRECS,
      DB_NRECS == 1? ' ': 's');
  }
  return(1);
}
#endif _OODB_
```

explain the purpose of the methods. However, there is a lot of hidden information about C++ in these methods that deserves some explanation.

The method OODB::field( ) is used to define elements in an object record. With each call to OODB::field( ), a new element is attached to the end of the link list. The OODDS pointer in the OODDS base class from which OODB is derived points to the beginning of the link list. The aspect of C++ subtly at work here is that in order to preserve all the class information about an object (like the member functions and the structure of its data), all nodes in the link list must be of the same base class. Hence the reason all supported object types must be derived from the OODDS class.

Once you have a link list of objects, it's a rather trivial operation to read or write the contents of the link list to a file. In the OODB class the member functions get( ) and put( ) are used for this. These are actually declared in the OODDS base class. These methods simply execute a **for**( ) loop, which calls the get( ) or put( ) for each field in the object record. The end of the object record is marked by a NULL pointer. The aspect of C++ subtly at work here is that even though the pointer in the **for**( ) loop is of class OODDS, information about attributes of the derived class for each element in the link list is preserved and the class-specific method is called.

In other chapters in this book the examples were built using the code presented in Chapter 12. By now you should have a good understanding of what each function described in Chapter 12 does. To help understand what each component of the OODB class is used for, let's look at what the Chapter 12 counterpart of each member function is. Table 15.1 contains the relationship between OODB member functions and Chapter 12 functions. Missing from the list in Table 15.1 are the ffget_element_value( ) and bind functions. There is actually no need for the counterpart of these function since application objects can be inserted directly into a dynamic data structure. In such case all data values in the objects are readily and directly accessible.

15.3 SOME OBJECTS

For this implementation of the object-oriented dynamic data structure we'll support three elementary classes: DATE, XYZ, and DATE_TIME. Listing 15.3 (date.cpp) contains the source for the DATE class. This class reads and writes dates in the format YYYY/MM/DD, where YYYY is the year (0 to 9999), MM is the month (1 to 12), and DD is that day of the month (1 to 31). For simplicity, no range checking is done on the values.

Listing 15.4 (xyz.cpp) contains the source for the object XYZ. This class reads three-dimensional vectors in the form X, Y, Z. where X is the value in the X direction; Y, in the Y direction; and Z, in the Z direction (naturally).

Table 15.1 OODDS Class Member Functions and Their Chapter 12 Counterparts

Class member function	Chapter 12 "flatfile" counterpart
OODB::field	flatfile_add_element( )
OODB::open( )	flatfile_open( )
OODB::close( )	flatfile_close( )
OODB::set( )	flatfile_write_rec( )
OODB::get( )	flatfile_read_rec( )
OODB::get_object( )	flatfile_get_element_by_name( )
<derived class>::set( )	flatfile_set_element_value( )
<derived class>::set_desc( )	flatfile_set_element_desc( )
<derived class>::set_name( )	flatfile_set_element_name( )

Listing 15.3 Source for the class DATE.

```
/*-----------------------------------------------
   Definition of the DATE object.
-----------------------------------------------*/
#ifndef _DATE_
#define _DATE_ 1

#include "oodds.cpp"
#include <time.h>
#include <stdlib.h>

class DATE : public OODDS {
   int year, month, day;
public:  DATE();
   set();
   int set(char * string);
   void put(FILE * fptr);
   void get(FILE * fptr);
};


/*-----------------------------------------------
   Constructor for DATE object. Initializes.
-----------------------------------------------*/
DATE::DATE() {
   DATE::set_type("DATE");
}


/*-----------------------------------------------
   Sets the date portion of the object according
   to the system time.
-----------------------------------------------*/
DATE::set() {
   struct tm *t;
   time_t ltime;

   time(&ltime);
   t = localtime(&ltime);
   year = t->tm_year;
   month = t->tm_mon+1;
   day = t->tm_mday;
   return(1);
}
```

```
/*------------------------------------------------
   Sets the date portion of the object according
   to contents of a string.
   -----------------------------------------------*/
int DATE::set(char * string) {
  char * dt = string;

  if(strlen(dt) == 0) {
    DATE::set();
  } else {
    year = atoi(dt);
    while(*dt != '/') dt++;
    dt++;
    month = atoi(dt);
    while(*dt != '/') dt++;
    dt++;
    day = atoi(dt);
    while(*dt != ' ' && *dt != '\0') dt++;
  }
  return ((int)(dt - string));
}


/*------------------------------------------------
   Puts the contents of the object to a file.
   -----------------------------------------------*/
void DATE::put(FILE * fptr) {
  if(fptr == stdout)
  {
    fprintf(fptr, "%04d/%02d/%02d", year, month, day);
  } else {
    fwrite((char *)&year, sizeof(int), 1, fptr);
    fwrite((char *)&month, sizeof(int), 1, fptr);
    fwrite((char *)&day, sizeof(int), 1, fptr);
  }
}


/*------------------------------------------------
   Loads the object from the contents of a file.
   -----------------------------------------------*/
void DATE::get(FILE * fptr) {
  char buffer[128];

  if(fptr == stdin)
  {
```

(continued)

Listing 15.3   *(continued)*

```
    printf("%s (yr/month/day): ", desc);
    fgets(buffer, sizeof(buffer), fptr);
    buffer[strlen(buffer) - 1] = '\0';
    DATE::set(buffer);
  } else {
    fread((char *)&year, sizeof(int), 1, fptr);
    fread((char *)&month, sizeof(int), 1, fptr);
    fread((char *)&day, sizeof(int), 1, fptr);
  }
}


#endif _DATE_
```

Listing 15.4   Source for the class XYZ.

```
/*------------------------------------------------
   Definition of the XYZ class.
------------------------------------------------*/
#ifndef _XYZ_
#define _XYZ 1

#include "oodds.cpp"
#include <time.h>
#include <stdlib.h>

class XYZ : public OODDS {
   double x;
   double y;
   double z;
public:
  XYZ();
  set(double v);
  set(char * string);
  XYZ operator=(XYZ &);
  void put(FILE *fptr);
  void get(FILE *fptr);
};


/*------------------------------------------------
   Constructor for XYZ object. Initializes.
------------------------------------------------*/
```

```
XYZ::XYZ() {
  XYZ::set_type("XYZ");
}


/*-----------------------------------------------
   Sets the value of the x, y, and z components
   to the same value.
-------------------------------------------------*/
XYZ::set(double v) {
  x = v;
  y = v;
  z = v;
  return(1);
}


/*-----------------------------------------------
   Sets the value of the x, y, and z components
   given a textual description of the value.
-------------------------------------------------*/
XYZ::set(char * string) {
  char * dt = string;

  if(strlen(dt) == 0) {
    XYZ::set(0.0);
  } else {
    x = atof(dt);
    while(*dt != ',' && *dt != ' ') dt++;
    dt++;
    y = atof(dt);
    while(*dt != ',' && *dt != ' ') dt++;
    dt++;
    z = atof(dt);
  }
  return(strlen(string));
}


/*-----------------------------------------------
   Puts the contents of the object to a file.
-------------------------------------------------*/
void XYZ::put(FILE *fptr) {
  if(fptr == stdout)
  {
    fprintf(fptr, "[%lf, %lf, %lf]", x, y, z);
```

(continued)

Listing 15.4   *(continued)*

```
  } else {
    fwrite((char *)&x, sizeof(double), 1, fptr);
    fwrite((char *)&y, sizeof(double), 1, fptr);
    fwrite((char *)&z, sizeof(double), 1, fptr);
  }
}


/*-----------------------------------------------
  Loads the object from the contents in a file.
-----------------------------------------------*/
void XYZ::get(FILE *fptr) {
  char buffer[128];
  if(fptr == stdin)
  {
    printf("%s (x, y, z): ", desc);
    fgets(buffer, sizeof(buffer), fptr);
    buffer[strlen(buffer) - 1] = '\0';
    XYZ::set(buffer);
  } else {
    fread((char *)&x, sizeof(double), 1, fptr);
    fread((char *)&y, sizeof(double), 1, fptr);
    fread((char *)&z, sizeof(double), 1, fptr);
  }
}


#endif _XYZ_
```

The final class, DATE_TIME, is a class that can be derived from another existing class, the DATE class. Listing 15.5 (datetime.cpp) contains the source for the DATE_TIME class. The most important thing to keep in mind when deriving classes from others is that the new class inherits all the properties of the parent class. This can be used to our advantage here just as it is when we derive new objects from the OODDS class. All that DATE_TIME does is add the values of hours and minutes to the base provided by the DATE class.

In C++, when you create a derived class, you also gain access to the member functions in the base class, so the get( ) and put( ) methods in the DATE class are used within the get( ) and put( ) methods in the DATE_TIME class. All that the DATE_TIME get( ) and put( ) methods deal with are the time extensions to the DATE class. The DATE get( ) and put( ) methods deal with the date portions.

You've probably noticed that in all the get( ) and put( ) methods in the DATE, XYZ, and DATE_TIME classes there is an **if**( ) block. This block checks whether the file to act on is a standard I/O file. If it is, then the method behaves a little differently

Listing 15.5 Source for the class DATE_TIME.

```
/*----------------------------------------------------
   Definitions for the DATE_TIME class.
--------------------------------------------------------*/
#ifndef _DATE_TIME_
#define _DATE_TIME_ 1

#include "oodds.cpp"
#include <time.h>
#include <stdlib.h>

class DATE_TIME : public DATE {
   int hour;
   int minute;
public:
   DATE_TIME();
   int set();
   int set(char * string);
   int time_set();
   int time_set(char * string);
   void put(FILE *fptr);
   void get(FILE *fptr);
};


/*--------------------------------------------------
   Constructor for DATE_TIME object. Initializes.
------------------------------------------------*/
DATE_TIME::DATE_TIME() {
   DATE::set_type("DATE_TIME");
}


/*--------------------------------------------------
   Sets both the time and date based on the
   system clock.
------------------------------------------------*/
DATE_TIME::set() {
   DATE_TIME::time_set();
   DATE::set();
   return(1);
}


/*--------------------------------------------------
   Sets both the time and date based on the time
   and date defined in the passed string.
------------------------------------------------*/
```

(continued)

Listing 15.5 *(continued)*

```
DATE_TIME::set(char * string) {
  int skip;

  if(strlen(string) == 0) {
    DATE_TIME::set();
  } else {
    skip = DATE::set(string);

    if(skip >= strlen(string)) {
      DATE_TIME::time_set();
    } else {
      DATE_TIME::time_set(&string[skip]);
    }
  }
  return(strlen(string));
}


/*----------------------------------------------
  Sets both the time portion of the object based
  on the system clock.
------------------------------------------------*/
DATE_TIME::time_set() {
  struct tm *t;
  time_t ltime;

  time(&ltime);
  t = localtime(&ltime);
  hour = t->tm_hour;
  minute = t->tm_min;
  return(1);
}


/*----------------------------------------------
  Sets both the time portion of the object based
  on the time defined in a string.
------------------------------------------------*/
DATE_TIME::time_set(char *string) {
   char *dt = string;

  if(strlen(dt) == 0) {
    DATE_TIME::time_set();
  } else {
```

```
    hour = atoi(dt);
    while(*dt != ':') dt++;
    dt++;
    minute = atoi(dt);
  }
  return(1);
}


/*-----------------------------------------------
  Puts the contents of the object to a file.
-------------------------------------------------*/
void DATE_TIME::put(FILE *fptr) {
  DATE::put(fptr);

  if(fptr == stdout)
  {
    fprintf(fptr, " %02d:%02d", hour, minute);
  } else {
    fwrite((char *)&hour, sizeof(int), 1, fptr);
    fwrite((char *)&minute, sizeof(int), 1, fptr);
  }
}


/*-----------------------------------------------
  Loads the object from the contents in a file.
-------------------------------------------------*/
void DATE_TIME::get(FILE *fptr) {
  char buffer[128];

  DATE::get(fptr);
  if(fptr == stdin)
  {
    printf("  Time (hour:minute): ");
    fgets(buffer, sizeof(buffer), fptr);
    buffer[strlen(buffer) - 1] = '\0';
    DATE_TIME::time_set(buffer);
  } else {
    fread((char *)&hour, sizeof(int), 1, fptr);
    fread((char *)&minute, sizeof(int), 1, fptr);
  }
}


#endif _DATE_TIME_
```

then if the pointer were to a disk file. For get( ), if the file is stdin, the function
prompts the user and accepts input. For put( ), the current state of the data is formatted
for output.

15.4 AN EXAMPLE APPLICATION

Now let's take all that's been developed so far and create an example application that
uses it. For our example let's develop an application that will copy an object-oriented
database file from one place to another. The allowed destinations are anything that
can be referred to by a file pointer. At a minimum, this is disk files and screen, but
could also include network connections and other devices. Listing 15.6 contains a
source for such an application, let's call it dbcopy, which uses all the classes presented in this chapter. A noteworthy aspect of dbcopy is that the class variables are
shared by both the input and output data streams. This is possible because the link
list that makes up the data record consists of pointers. This also makes the update of
input and output records symmetrical and automatic. A limitation to dbcopy is that

Listing 15.6   Source for the example application dbcopy.

```
/*---------------------------------------------------
   Example application dbcopy.
   ---------------------------------------------------*/
#include "const.h"
#include "oodds.cpp"
#include "date.cpp"
#include "datetime.cpp"
#include "xyz.cpp"
#include "oodb.cpp"

char *Usage[] = {
   "Creates or displays a database.",
   "",
   "Proper usage: dbcopy <infile> <outfile>",
   "",
   "If either <infile> or <outfile> is '-' then the",
   "standard I/O file is used.",
   NULL
};

main(int argc, char *argv[]) {  DATE date;
  DATE_TIME date_time;
  XYZ xyz;
  OODB in_dbase;
```

```
  OODB out_dbase;
  int i;

  char **cptr;

  if(argc < 3)
  {
     cptr = Usage;
     while (*cptr != NULL) {
        puts(*cptr);
        *cptr++;
     }
     exit(1);
  }

  if(in_dbase.open(argv[1]) == FAILURE)
  {
    perror(argv[1]);
    exit(1);
  }

  if(out_dbase.create(argv[2]) == FAILURE)
  {
    perror(argv[1]);
    exit(1);
  }

  in_dbase.field(&date, "date", "date object");
  in_dbase.field(&date_time, "date_time", "date_time object");
  in_dbase.field(&xyz, "xyz", "xyz object");

  out_dbase.field(&date, "date", "date object");
  out_dbase.field(&date_time, "date_time", "date_time object");
  out_dbase.field(&xyz, "xyz", "xyz object");

  in_dbase.message();
  for(i = 0; i < DB_NRECS; i ++)
  {
    in_dbase.get();
    out_dbase.put();
  }
  in_dbase.close();
  out_dbase.close();
  exit(0);
}
```

the record structure is specified by code within the application, but this is a self-imposed limitation. Changes could be made to the code to provide some external means to define the record structure. An approach like that taken in the function dds_compile_C( ) in Chapter 9 might be reasonable.

Even though dbcopy is a simple application, a brief discussion of its use is in order. First, dbcopy is a command-line application with the following syntax:

dbcopy input file output file

If *input file* is a dash (−) then the input file is stdin; if the *output file* is a dash, then the output file is stdout. You can use this command to create database files as well as display them. An example command is

dbcopy - example.db

which prompts you for DB_NRECS records and places the results in the file "example.db." The constant DB_NRECS and others used in dbcopy are expected to be in the include file "const.h" and are given in Listing 15.7 To display the contents of a database file you should enter a command such as

dbcopy example.db -

which will display the contents of the database file "example.db" on the screen in a crude tabular form.

15.5 SUMMARY

Even though dbcopy is a very primitive application with just demonstration value, the underlying classes and methods it uses can serve as an engine for a more powerful DBMS. Also, by using a base class for all database objects, the system as a whole is

---

Listing 15.7   Source for the include file const.h, which contains constants required for the application dbcopy.

```
/*--------------------------------------------------------
 Constants used in various methods and the application.
 --------------------------------------------------------*/
#ifndef _CONST_
#define _CONST_ 1

#define FAILURE 1
#define SUCCESS 0

#define DB_NRECS        3

#endif _CONST_
```

easily extensible. With a system like this, a developer can add new classes to the DBMS without having the source for the DBMS (source for the base class definition is required).

Not implemented in this chapter is a compiler to parse a C-style description of a data structure into an object-oriented dynamic data structure. This presents new challenges over how the compiler in Chapter 9 was implemented. The crux of this challenge lies with allowing the creation of new object classes at the discretion of the developer. This feature requires that there be some means to register new classes so that the compiler can recognize references to each class in the structure definition and then some means to create new instances of an object on demand. The actual implementation of this is left as a point to ponder.

Additional information on object-oriented databases can be found in [LYS88] and [TN88].

POINTS TO PONDER

15.1   What features of C++ make it possible to implement an extensible object-oriented dynamic data structure manager like that presented in Listing 15.2?

15.2   Describe how you would implement a compiler to parse a C-style description of an object-oriented dynamic data structure into a link list of objects.

15.3   Write a function that will create a new object of a specified type. A type is specified by a textual type name, and the function returns a pointer to an object of the desired type. This pointer should be readily usable by oodb( ). *Hint:* This means that the pointer is of type OODDS. It should be possible to add new types, at run-time, within an application.

15.4   Describe how a procedural object could be implemented. A procedural object is one that performs an action based on the contents of other objects in an object record.

Appendix A
Answers to Points to Ponder

CHAPTER 2
Dynamic Data Structures

2.1 An element is a particular item in a collection of data items. A key is some distinguishing characteristic of an element.

2.2 A schema is a list of operations, in the order that they are applied, without any key values considered. A history is a schema when key values are considered.

2.3 They are a schema and a valuation.

2.4 The schema is *IIID*, the valuation is {2 3 1 2}, the size is 2.

2.5 4! = 24.

2.6 It's a flat line at 1/4. All elements are equally likely.

CHAPTER 3
Designing Dynamic Data Structures

3.1 The three kinds of rebuilding are local, partial, and global. Global rebuilding involves the rebuilding of the entire data structure. Partial rebuilding involves rebuilding some significant portion of the data structure, and local rebuilding involves rebuilding only a small portion of the data structure.

3.2 Functional boundaries of how a data structure is used.

3.3 The two subjects are order-decomposable set problems and decomposable searching problems. Order-decomposable set problems involve operations on order sets of keys that have associated elements in a dynamic data structure. Decomposable searching problems involve extracting information from dynamic data structures. Every order-decomposable set problem is also be a decomposable searching problem. The reverse cannot be said.

3.4 A binary operator is a function or operation that can combine the results from a query applied to two data structures in such a way that it is equivalent to applying the query to a data structure that is the union of the two data structures.

3.5 There will be three distinct static data structures. The number of elements in each static data structure for $1 \leq N \leq 10$ is given in Table A.1.

3.6 A binary transform is a radix-2 transform.

Table A.1. The Number of Elements in Each of the Three Static Data Structures for a 3-Binomial Transform

N	(3)	(2)	(1)
1	1	0	0
2	1	1	0
3	1	1	1
4	4	0	0
5	4	1	0
6	4	1	1
7	4	3	0
8	4	3	1
9	4	3	2
10	10	0	0

CHAPTER 4
Dynamic Data Structure Analysis

4.1   They are the insertion costs $I(N)$, which characterize the costs associated with inserting an element into a dynamic data structure. Deletion costs $D(N)$, which characterize the costs associated with deleting an element from a dynamic data structure. Query costs $Q(N)$, which characterize the costs associated with extracting element or information from the dynamic data structure. Storage costs $S(N)$, which characterize the amount of storage require by the dynamic data structure.

4.2   The insertion $I(N)$ and preprocessing costs $P(N)$ are related by the formulas

$$P(N) = \sum I(i)$$
$$1 \le i \le N$$

$$I(N) = \frac{P(N)}{N}$$

and are valid only when the schema for a specific state is used.

4.3   The query penalty function is influenced by the number of static data structures that exist in a dynamic data structure at the time the query is performed. The processing penalty function is influenced by the number of static data structures into which any element has been built over the total history of the dynamic data structure.

4.4   The processing penalty functions.

4.5   One is marking elements as deleted even though they are still maintained in the dynamic data structure. A second approach is to use transforms that localize any rebuilds, for example, a linear linked list that requires only local rebuilds. A third approach is to maintain a ghost structure into which deleted elements are inserted. In this case the results of any query are the matches found in the real structure less the matches found in the ghost structure.

4.6   A k-binomial number is represented by the formula

$$N = (n_k) + (n_{k-1}) + \ldots + (n_1)$$

where n_i is the number of elements in the static data structure with binomial coefficient i and $n_i > n_{i-1}$. Given that

$$(n_k) \cdot (n_k)$$

for $1 \le i \le k$. and $n_k - (k + 1) > n_k - i$, we can state that

$$G(N) = (k!N)^{1/k}$$

CHAPTER 5
Configuration Control

5.1   Size, location, and type
5.2.   (a) Encapsulation and free access. (b) Type databases and indirect access.
5.3   Where the configuration information is maintained. This is quantified by the degree of dispersion between the configuration information and the data. Type databases have the highest degree of dispersion.
5.4   Type databases.

CHAPTER 6
Dynamic Adaptation

6.1   The transformation of all or part of a dynamic data structure into a usable data type.
6.2   To perform the transformation of elements in a dynamic data structure into a usable form.
6.3   A method is the application construct that provides the value realization in a data interpreter.
6.4   There are two methods. The first is implemented by using referential variables and the second, with the use of update lists.
6.5   Expression evaluation is value realization by assignment of the return value of functions, type casting, or argument evaluation. Binding is value realization by automatic assignment to application variables anytime all or part of a dynamic data structure is altered.
6.6   The value assigned to both a carrier variable and a pointer is an address of memory. With a carrier variable this value cannot be used to access the addressed area memory in the native language. Addressing must be performed through a call to a routine or function written in a different language. With a pointer, the addressed memory can be accessed through constructs in the native language.

6.7   The epoches are late and early. Any binding that results from a run-time action belongs to the late epoch, whereas any binding that is resolved at the time of compilation belongs to the early epoch.

6.8   Expression evaluation has a coaxed realization time. Referential variables have an instantaneous realization time. Update lists have delayed realization times.

6.9   The value output by a write operation will be the value of the last bound application variable to the element. Each application variable will assume the same value during a read operation.

CHAPTER 7
Data Description

7.1   It serves the function of communicating the structure of data to the application.

7.2   C structure definitions are concise, easy to read, and familiar to almost all developers who work in C. Flattened-format descriptors are two-dimensional, fixed-field tables and are simplistic in design and merge well with relational database management systems. The object definition language is a rich, generalized descriptive language that uses keyword–value pairs for describing data. The SFDU is a data encapsulation approach that provides a high-level method of describing data. It employs ID codes for specific data formats. It also uses the notion of control authorities for managing ID codes. ANSI X12.6 is a data encapsulation approach that provides a high-level method of describing data. It employs ID codes and specific arrangement of data elements to defining data structures. Most ID codes and the specification of arrangement can be found in companion standards (X12.3 and X12.22, respectively).

7.3   The flattened-format descriptor is best for two-dimensional data. The object definition language approach is best when the structure of the data is diverse, especially if it is multidimensional. The ANSI X12.3 approach is best when the data is in small discrete samples.

7.4   The C structure, flattened-format descriptors and the object definition language are self-contained. The SFDU and ANSI X12.6 approaches require external documentation to fully resolve.

7.5   The C structure, flattened-format descriptors, and the object definition language allow you to maintain the data separately, The SFDU and ANSI X12.6 require that the data be intermingled with the descriptions.

CHAPTER 8
A Software Engineering Perspective

8.1   In data-oriented approaches. Dynamic data structures also can play significant roles in other approaches to software engineering, but this is greatest with data-oriented approaches to software engineering.

8.2   In most situations the use of dynamic data structures reduces the project's size, reduces the complexity of the project, and reduces the degree of structure in the application. The reduction in the degree of structure is in both the functional and data domains of the application.

8.3   Each of the following: the representation of the dynamic data structures, the realization methods, and the data types that will be supported in the dynamic data structures.

8.4   It allows baselining of data structures to be delayed until later in the implementation phase than ordinarily would occur. It is highly flexible and very conducive to prototyping, and it allows for rapid adaptation to changing requirements.

8.5   It increases the reliability, efficiency, flexibility, and reusability of all aspects of the application that are dependent on or use dynamic data structures. This is because dynamic data structures provide a higher level of abstraction for data, and the support functions are "low-level" and hence slowly varying and relatively stable components.

8.6   By using dynamic data structures you can increase the information content in the code itself by requiring in-line data documentation. This makes it easier for maintenance personnel to understand the data structures used in the application. The use of dynamic data structures also minimizes change-related side effects. The main reason is because the support functions and the dynamic data structures themselves are very adaptive. Maintenance is also easier because of the reduction of size, complexity, and degree of structure inherent when dynamic data structures are used.

CHAPTER 9
Basic Toolkit

9.1   By direct access to the data values. This was detailed in Chapter 3.

9.2   With the following function call:

```
dds_get_element_value(
    dds_get_element(dds, "name",
    &dvalue, DDST_DOUBLE);
```

assuming that the element is a member of the dynamic data structure referred to by the variable "dds" and that the name of the element is "name." The value is returned in a double variable called "dvalue."

9.3   One approach is to implement the conversion matrix as a two-dimensional matrix of function pointers. The index of the matrix could be the values of the enumerated type DDS_TYPE. An application could then override the default conversion function, which converts between two specific types by replacing the proper function pointer in the conversion matrix. Presumably this would be done by use of a function call with the arguments of the "from" type, the "to" type, and the function pointer.

CHAPTER 10
Dynamically Linked Applications

10.1   Simply remove the portion of the code that checks to see if the passed dynamic
data structure that contains the arguments for the function matches that expected by the function.

10.2   It's already been done. Variables could be instantiated with the function
dds_add_element( ), which was presented in Chapter 9. All that is required of
the interpreter is that it determine the variable name, type, and desired value.
The type could be determined by the characteristics of the value being assigned to it. The value of the variable could be defined with the combination
of the functions dds_set_element_value( ) and dds_get_element( ), also presented in Chapter 9.

10.3   One possible modification of the parser would be to combine variable declaration with the assignment of a value to a variable. Such an assignment would
have the form of

```
variable name = value
```

where "variable name" would be the name of the variable and "value" would
be the value it is to have. The same rules for determining data types for
function arguments would be applied to variables. When a variable is first
used, it is added as a new element to a dynamic data structure. When a variable
is used in a function, it can be distinguished from literal values if variable
names consisting of any series of characters not enclosed in quotes and that
could not be considered a number.

CHAPTER 11
Nth-Generation Languages

11.1   One approach would be to maintain objects as a C structure where the data
portion was ordinary elements and the member functions were maintained as
a dynamic data structure that contained a list of registered functions.

11.2   One solution is as follows:

```
DDS_ELEMENT *lisp_eval(s)
char s{};
{
    int bogus;

    return(eval(s, &bogus));
}
```

11.3   One approach would be to maintain LISP variables as a dynamic data structure. When a variable is assigned a value, one of two things would occur. If

the variable does not already exist, then a new element of the proper type is created and added to the dynamic data structure. The name given to the element is the name of the variable. If the variable does exist, then the type of the element that corresponds to it is changed to match the type of the assigned value and the new value is then associated with the element. When a variable is reference, an element with the variable's name is searched for in order to extract its value.

CHAPTER 12
Database Applications

12.1

```
typedef
#include "ff.des"
RECORD;
```

12.2

```
#include "flatfile.h"

/*-------------------------------------------------
   Positions the data file pointer to the beginning
   of a specific record in a flatfile. Returns
   non-zero if it can not be done.
-------------------------------------------------*/
flatfile_set_rec(ffptr, recnum)
FLATFILE *ffptr;
int recnum;
{
   if(recnum <= 0) return(-1);

   return(fseek(ffptr->data, ffptr->reclen * (recnum - 1),
      SEEK_SET));
}
```

CHAPTER 13
Information Transfer

13.1   A remote procedure differs from an internal function in that it is external to the calling application. It differs from a shared library in that it can reside on any accessible host. Its most contrasted difference is the method in which it is called. All remote procedures are called using the same internal function

interface. The arguments to this function determine which remote procedure
is called.

13.2

```
#include "dds.h"
/*-------------------------------------------------
   Function to write the contents of a dynamic
   data structure to a network port.
-------------------------------------------------*/
rpc_dds_to_port(port, dds)
int port;
DDS *dds;
{
  char buffer[RPC_MAX_DDS_DESC];
  char *source;
  DDS_ELEMENT *dds_element;
  int size;

  if(dds == NULL) {      /* Nothing defined */
    return(0);
  }
  /* get textual description */
  if(dds_desc_dds(dds, buffer, RPC_MAX_DDS_DESC) == 0) { /* desc too
      big */
  return(0);
  }
  write(port, buffer, strlen(buffer) + 1);

  /* write data values */
  dds_element = dds->first_element;
  while(dds_element != NULL) {
    if(dds_element->data.type == DDST_STRING) {
      size = dds_element->data.value.s.len;
      source = dds_element->data.value.s.ptr;
    } else {
      size = dds_sizeof(dds_element->data.type);
      source = (char *)&dds_element->data.value;
    }
    write(port, source, size);
   dds_element = dds_element->right;
  }
  return(1);
}
```

CHAPTER 14
Distributed Information

14.1   The functions make_array( ), print_results( ), and portions of the decomp_query( ).

14.2   One possible approach is to modify the decomp_binop_add( ) function so that each element in the second DECOMP structure is compared to every element in the first DECOMP structure. The element in the second structure is added only if it does not match any element in the first structure.

14.3   The easiest solution is to always work from the last member of the linked list of ELEMENT arrays to the first, rather than from the first to the last as currently is the case. This would require changes to decomp_add_element( ), decomp_binop_add( ), and print_results( ). However, this only preserves the order in which elements are added to decomposable data structures and may not produce the proper results if you would like the combined results to be in a specific order. For example, suppose that you have two decomposable data structures, each with a field that goes from 0.0 to 4.0 in ascending order. After the two decomposable data structures are combined using decomp_binop_add( ), the resulting decomposable data structure has values in the field going from 0.0 to 4.0, then from 0.0 to 4.0. So you would have to reorder the resulting decomposable data structure to get the desired result.

CHAPTER 15
Object-Oriented Systems

15.1   There are three features of C++ that make object-oriented dynamic data structures possible: inheritance, heterogeneous link lists, and type-sensitive method calling.

15.2   One possible implementation is to start with the compiler that was implemented in Chapter 9. The changes to this would be as follows: (1) it would return a pointer to an object of the OODDS class and (2) each type declaration would be converted to a token, which in turn will be passed to a function that will return a pointer to an object of the desired type. All other features of the Chapter 9 compiler would remain the same.

15.3   By modifying the base class of OODDS to include a function to create an instance of an object, it would be possible to register new objects into an object template database and then create new objects of any class with a single function call. The new OODDS structure would look like the following:

```
#define OODDS_NAME_LEN 128
#define OODDS_DESC_LEN 254
#define OODDS_TYPE_LEN 64
```

```
struct OODDS {
  OODDS *next;
  char name[OODDS_NAME_LEN + 1];
  char desc[OODDS_DESC_LEN + 1];
  char type[OODDS_TYPE_LEN + 1];
  void set_desc(char * str = "");
  void set_name(char * str = "");
  void set_type(char * str = "");
  virtual int set(char * str = "");
  virtual void get(FILE * fptr = stdin);
  virtual void put(FILE * fptr = stdout);
  virtual OODDS *create();
};
```

An implementation of the function to register new types and one to create a new object on demand is as follows:

```
#include "oodds.cpp"
#include "oodb.cpp"


OODB Object_list;     /* Holds the registered objects */


/*-------------------------------------------------
   A function that will register an object into an
   internal database. This database is maintained as
   an object-oriented dynamic data structure.
   ----------------------------------------------*/
register_oodds(new_oodds)
OODDS *new_oodds;
{
  Object_list.field(new_oodds, "", "");
}


/*-------------------------------------------------
   Function that will search the internal database
   of registered objects and return a pointer to
   a new instance of the requested object. Returns
   NULL is no object when the textual type name given
   exists.
   NOTE: This function must be a friend of the OODB
         class.
   ----------------------------------------------*/
OODDS *make_object(type_name)
char type_name[];
{
```

```
extern OODB Object_list;
OODDS *ptr;

ptr = Object_list.first;
while(ptr != NULL) {
   if(strcmp(type_name, ptr->type) == 0) {
      return(ptr->create());
   }
   ptr = ptr->next;
}
return(NULL);
}
```

It's important to notice that the function make_object( ) must be a friend of the OODB class. An example of a create( ) method for the XYZ class is as follows:

```
/*--------------------------------------------------
  Example definition of a create() method for
  class XYZ.
  --------------------------------------------------*/
#include "oodds.cpp"
#include "xyz.cpp"

OODDS *XYZ::create() {
   return(new(XYZ));
}
```

Each class derived from the OODDS base class must define a create( ) method if it is to be registered. This is actually quite simple, as can be seen in the XYZ example just presented.

15.4   A procedural object could be implemented in one of two ways. One approach might be to embed the procedure in the get( ) and put( ) methods of the class. The other approach would be to include a pointer to a function in the data portion of the object. This function is in turn called by the get( ) or put( ) methods. This later approach is by far the most general.

Appendix B
Makefile

If you do use any or all of the source codes presented in this book, you might find Listing B.1 useful. It contains the source for a makefile that can be used with the application called "make," which is available on a variety of systems. Within this makefile the following naming convention is used for the source code presented in this book. Each listing presented in the book is given the basename of the chapter number and the sequence number by which it was referred to separated by an underscore. For example, the second listing in Chapter 9 would have a basename of "9_2." The extension applied to the basename is the appropriate language extensions, "c" for C and "cpp" for C++. Include files are given the name they are referred to in

Listing B.1 Makefile.

```
# When using Borland TurboC everything should be compiled
# with either the compact, large or huge model because of
# the way pointers to code and data are treated in the
# other models.
CFLAGS = -mc
LDFLAGS = $(CFLAGS)

# Implicit rule for use with C++ source code.
# Defingition specific to Borland C++, Version 2.0
CPP = bcc
.cpp.obj:
        $(CPP) -c $(CFLAGS) $<

#----------------------------------------------
# Everything
#----------------------------------------------
all : test_9.exe interp10.exe scpp.exe 12_8.exe 12_9.exe test_12.exe \
        test_13.exe test_14.exe 14_5.exe \
        rpc_disp.exe resource. exe fsglob.exe dbcopy.exe
```

(continued)

Listing B.1 *(continued)*

```
#-----------------------------------------------
# Chapter 9
#-----------------------------------------------


test_9.exe:     test_9.obj chap_9.lib
        $(LD) $(LDFLAGS) test_9.obj chap_9.lib


chap_9.lib: 9_2.obj 9_3.obj 9_4.obj 9_5.obj 9_6.obj \
            9_7.obj 9_8.obj 9_9.obj 9_11.obj 9_12.obj \
            9_13.obj 9_14.obj 9_15.obj fixlib.exe
        fixlib chap_9 $?


9_11.obj : 9_10.c 9_11.c


9_10.c : 9_10.1
        $(LEX) -o 9_10.c 9_10.1


9_11.c : 9_11.y
        $(YACC) -o 9_11.c 9_11.y


#-----------------------------------------------
# Chapter 10
#-----------------------------------------------


chap_10.lib: 10_1.obj 10_2.obj 10_3.obj 10_4.obj 10_5.obj fixlib.exe
        fixlib chap_10 $?


interp10.exe: 10-6.obj 10_7.obj chap_10.lib
        $(LD) $(LDFLAGS) -einterp10.exe 10_6.obj 10_7.obj chap_9.lib
  cha


#-----------------------------------------------
# Chapter 11
#-----------------------------------------------


scpp.exe:       11_1.obj 11_2.obj 11_3.obj 11_4.obj 11_5.obj 11_7.obj\
                chap_10.lib chap_9.lib
        $(LD) $(LDFLAGS) -escpp 11_5.obj 11_1.obj 11_2.obj 11_3.obj
            11_4.obj


lisp.exe:       11_8.obj 11_7.obj 11_5.obj chap_10.lib chap_9.lib
        K$(LD) $(LDFLAGS) -elisp 11_8.obj 11_7.obj 11_5.obj
  chap_10.lib chap_9.lib
```

```
#---------------------------------------------
# Chapter 12
#---------------------------------------------


12_8.exe:       12_8.obj chap_9.lib chap_12.lib
        $(LD) $(LDFLAGS) 12_8.obj chap_12.lib chap_9.lib

12_9.exe:       12_9.obj chap_9.lib chap_12.lib
        $(LD) $(LDFLAGS) 12_9.obj chap_12.lib chap_9.lib

test_12.exe:    test_12.obj chap_12.lib chap_9.lib
        $(LD) $(LDFLAGS) test_12.obj chap_12.lib chap_9.lib

chap_12.lib: 12_2.obj 12_3.obj 12_4.obj 12_5.obj 12_6.obj \
             12_7.obj fixlib.exe
        fixlib chap_12 $?

#---------------------------------------------
# Chapter 13
#---------------------------------------------


test_13.exe:    13_10.obj chap_13.lib chap_9.lib
        $(LD) $(LDFLAGS) -etest_13.exe 13_10.obj chap_13.lib
            chap_9.lib

rpc_disp.exe:   13_7.obj chap_13.lib chap_12.lib
        $(LD) $(LDFLAGS) -eresource,exe 13_9.obj chap_13.lib
            chap_9.lib

fsglob.exe:  13_8.obj chap_13.lib chap_9.lib
        $(LD) $(LDFLAGS) -efsglob.exe 13_8.obj chap_13.lib chap_9.lib

chap_13.lib:  13_2.obj 13_3.obj 13_4.obj 13_5.obj 13_6.obj fixlib.exe
        fixlib chap_13 $?

#---------------------------------------------
# Chapter 14 examples
#---------------------------------------------


14_11.exe: 14_11.obj chap_14.lib chap_12.lib chap_9.lib
        $(LD) $(LDFLAGS) 14_11.obj chap_14.lib chap_12.lib
            chap_9.lib

chap_14.lib: 14_3.obj 14_4.obj 14_5.obj 14_6.obj 14_7.obj 14_8.obj \
```

(continued)

Listing B.1 *(continued)*

```
                14_9.obj 14_10.obj fixlibe.exe
          fixlib chap_14 $?
#--------------------------------------------
# Chapter 15 examples
#--------------------------------------------


dbcopy.exe: dbcopy.obj
          $(LD) $(LDFLAGS) dbcopy.obj
```

listings. When you use Borland's TurboC, maintaining libraries can be rather cumbersome within a makefile. An application that can make maintaining libraries easier is in Listing B.2 and is called "fixlib." When compiled the listing in B.2 expects at least two command-line arguments. The first in the name of the library to add or replace object files in. The second and subsequent arguments are names of object files to use.

Listing B.2 Fixlib.

```
/*------------------------------------------------------
   Maintains TurboC libraries in a more concise fashion.
   Usually called from a makefile.

   Begun: 5/20/90 - Todd King
-------------------------------------------------------*/
main(argc, argv)
int argc;
char *argv[];
{
  int i;
  int init;
  char command[256];

  if(argc < 3) {
    printf("proper usage: fixlib libname module [module ...]\n");
    exit(0);
  }

  init = 1;
  for(i = 2; i < argc; i++) {
    if(init) {
      strcpy(command, "tlib ");
      strcat(command, argv[1]);
      init = 0;
```

```
      }
    strcat(command, " ");
    strcat(command, "-+");
    strcat(command, argv[i]);
    if( (i % 5) == 0) {        /* Do five at a time */
      system(command);
      strcpy(command, "");
      init = 1;
    }
  }
  if( strlen(command) > 0) { /* Some left to do. */
    system(command);
  }
  exit(0);
}
```

Selected Bibliography

Books

[AHU83] Aho, A. V.; Hopcroft, J. E.; and Ullman, J. D. (1983). *Data Structures and Algorithms.* Addison-Wesley, Reading, Mass.

[Ber85] Berk, A. A. (1985). *LISP: The Language of Artificial Intelligence.* Van Nostrand Reinhold, Princeton, N.J.

[Bra87] Bracket, M. H. (1987). *Developing Data Structured Databases.* Prentice-Hall, Englewood Cliffs, N.J.

[Cal79] Calingaert, P. (1979). *Assemblers, Compilers and Program Translation.* Computer Science Press, Rockville, Md.

[Cle86] Cleaveland, J. C. (1986). *An Introduction to Data Types.* Addison-Wesley, Reading, Mass.

[Dat75] Date, C. J. (1975). *An Introduction to Database Systems.* Addison-Wesley, Reading, Mass.

[Els73] Elson, M. (1973). *Concepts of Programming Languages.* Science Research Associates, Chicago, Ill.

[Geh83] Gehani, N. (1983). *Ada: An Advanced Introduction.* Prentice-Hall, Englewood CLiffs, N.J.

[KBR78] Kernighan, B. W.; and Ritchie, D. M. (1978). *The C Programming Language.* Prentice-Hall, Englewood Cliffs, N.J.

[GH80] Goos, G.; and Hartmanis, J. (1980). *The Programming Language ADA Reference Manual.* Springer-Verlag, Berlin.

[Knu68] Knuth, D. E. (1968). *The Art of Computer Programming,* Vol. 1: *Fundamental Algorithms.* Addison-Wesley, Reading, Mass.

[Knu73] Knuth, D. E. (1973). *The Art of Computer Programming,* Vol. 3: *Sorting and Searching.* Addison-Wesley, Reading, Mass.

[Lin86] Lings, B. J. (1986). *Information Structures: A Uniform Approach Using Pascal.* Chapman and Hall, New York.

[Ove83] Overmars, M. H. (1983). *The Design of Dynamic Data Structures.* Springer-Velag, New York.

[Pre82] Pressman, R. S. (1982). *Software Engineering: A Practitioner's Approach.* McGraw-Hill, New York.

[STR87] Stroustrup, B. (1987). *The C++ Programming Language.* Addison-Wesley, Reading, Mass.

[SW87] Stubbs, D. F.; and Webre, N. W. (1987). *Data Structures with Abstract Data Types and Modula-2.* Brooks/Cole Publishing Co., Monterey, Calif.

[Tre84] Tremblay, J-P. (1984). *An Introduction to Data Structures with Applications.* McGraw-Hill, New York.

[Wil84] Wilensky, R. (1984). *LISPcraft.* Norton, New York.

Academic Papers

[BS80] Bentley, J. L.; and Saxe, J. B. (1980). Decomposable searching problems. 1. Static-to-dynamic transformations. *Journal of Algorithms* **1**(4), 301–358.

[EO85] Edelsbrunner, H.; and Overmars, M. H. (1985). Batched dynamic solutions to decomposable searching problems. *Journal of Algorithms* **6**, 515–542.

[FFV80] Flajolet, P.; Francon, J.; and Vuillemin J. (1980). Sequence of operations analysis for dynamic data structures, *Journal of Algorithms* **1**(2), 111–141.

[FRS88] Francon, J.; Randrianarimanana, B.; and Schott, R. (1988). Analysis of dynamic algorithms in D. E. Knuth's model. In *Lecture Notes in Computer Science—CAAP '88* (p. 72–87), Spinger-Velag, Berlin.

[Knu77] Knuth, D. E. (1977). Deletions that preserve randomness. *IEEE Transactions on Software Engineering* **SE-3**(5), 351–359.

[LYS88] Lindsjorn, Y.; and Sjoberg, D. (1988). Database concepts discussed in an object-oriented perspective. In *Proceedings of the European Conference on Object-Oriented Programming*. Springer-Verlag, Berlin.

[Ove81] Overmars, M. H. (1981) Dynamization of order decomposable set problems. *Journal of Algorithms* **2**, 245–260.

[TN88] Tsichritzis, D. C.; and Nierstrasz, O. M. (1988). Fitting round objects into square databases. In *Proceedings of the European Conference on Object-Oriented Programming*, Springer-Verlag, Berlin.

[X12.22] *American National Standard for Electronic Business Data Interchange—Data Segment Dictionary*. ANSI X12.22-1986, American National Standards Institute, Inc.

[X12.3] *American National Standard for Electronic Business Data Interchange—Data Element Dictionary*. ANSI X12.3-1986, American National Standards Institute, Inc.

[X12.6] *American National Standard for Electronic Business Data Interchange—Application Control Structure*. ANSI X12.6-1986, American National Standards Institute, Inc.

Other Publications

[Gin89] Gingell, R. (1989). Shared libraries. *Unix Review*, **7**(8), 56–66.

[CCS87] Consultive Committee for Space Data Systems. (1987). *Recommendation for space data systems standards: Standard formatted data units—Structure and construction rule. CCSDS 620.0-R-2, Red Book*, Issue 2.0.

[Kin88] King, T. (1988). *Dynamic run-time structures. Dr. Dobb's Journal*, **145**, November.

Index